Sustainable Tourism and Natural Resource Conservation in the Polar Regions

Sustainable Tourism and Natural Resource Conservation in the Polar Regions

Special Issue Editors

Machiel Lamers
Edward Huijbens

MDPI • Basel • Beijing • Wuhan • Barcelona • Belgrade

MDPI

Special Issue Editors

Machiel Lamers
Wageningen University
The Netherlands

Edward Huijbens
University of Akureyri
Iceland

Editorial Office
MDPI
St. Alban-Anlage 66
Basel, Switzerland

This is a reprint of articles from the Special Issue published online in the open access journal *Resources* (ISSN 2079-9276) in 2017 (available at: http://www.mdpi.com/journal/resources/special_issues/polar_tourism)

For citation purposes, cite each article independently as indicated on the article page online and as indicated below:

LastName, A.A.; LastName, B.B.; LastName, C.C. Article Title. *Journal Name* **Year**, *Article Number*, Page Range.

ISBN 978-3-03897-011-8 (Pbk)
ISBN 978-3-03897-012-5 (PDF)

Contents

About the Special Issue Editors

Machiel Lamers, Associate Professor, works at the Environmental Policy Group at Wageningen University, the Netherlands. His main research interests are in new modes of governance in sustainable tourism and conservation tourism across the world, including the Polar Regions.

Edward Huijbens, geographer and scholar of tourism, and professor at the school of social sciences and humanities at the University of Akureyri, where he is also department head for the faculty of social sciences and law. Edward works on tourism theory, issues of regional development, landscape perceptions, the role of transport in tourism and polar tourism. He is the author of over 30 articles in several scholarly journals such as Annals of Tourism Research, Journal of Sustainable Tourism, Tourism Geographies and has published three monographs both in Iceland and internationally and co-edited four books.

Preface to "Sustainable Tourism and Natural Resource Conservation in the Polar Regions"

This Special Issue stems from the fifth IPTRN conference which was held in NE Iceland at the end of August 2016. Membership of the IPTRN network includes university academics, consultants, tourism operators, representatives of government organizations and graduate students dedicated to researching tourism in Arctic and Antarctic settings. The IPTRN strives to generate, share and disseminate knowledge, resources and perspectives on polar tourism; and strongly supports the development of international collaboration between members. Biennial conferences and community workshops are meant to solidify this focus on international collaboration between members. Community workshops were included in these events and brought participants' insights to bear on local tourism issues. The first IPTRN conference was held in 2008 in Kangiqsujuaq, Arctic Canada, followed by a second IPTRN conference in 2010 in Scandinavia, a third IPTRN conference in 2012 was held in Nain, Labrador, Canada, and a fourth conference in Australasia in 2014 (Christchurch/Akaroa, New Zealand). The sixth IPTRN will be held in 2018 in the Yukon, Canada, and the seventh in 2020 in Ushuaia, Argentina.

Machiel Lamers, Edward Huijbens

Special Issue Editors

resources

MDPI

Editorial

Sustainable Tourism and Natural Resource Conservation in the Polar Regions: An Editorial

Edward Huijbens [1],* and Machiel Lamers [2]

[1]   Icelandic Tourism Research Centre, University of Akureyri, 600 Akureyri, Iceland
[2]   Environmental Policy Group, Wageningen University, PO Box 8130, 6700EW Wageningen, The Netherlands;
      machiel.lamers@wur.nl
*   Correspondence: edward@unak.is; Tel.: +354-460-8619

Received: 28 August 2017; Accepted: 31 August 2017; Published: 2 September 2017

Abstract: This editorial provides an introduction to the special issue of Resources on Sustainable Tourism and Natural Resource Conservation in the Polar Regions, which proceeds the fifth bi-annual conference of the International Polar Tourism Research Network (IPTRN). The conference and coinciding community workshop on tourism development were organized at the edge of the Arctic in the community of Raufarhöfn (pop. 160) in Northeast Iceland from 29 August to 2 September 2016.

Keywords: tourism; Arctic; Antarctic; polar; research

1. Introduction

This special issue proceeds the fifth bi-annual conference of the International Polar Tourism Research Network (IPTRN). The conference and coinciding community workshop on tourism development were organized at the edge of the Arctic in the community of Raufarhöfn (pop. 160) in Northeast Iceland from 29 August–2 September 2016, and hosted by the Icelandic Tourism Research Centre in collaboration with Norðurþing municipality, the Canadian Embassy in Iceland, The University of Akureyri, Norðurhjari—Tourism Partnership, Rif Field Station and the Northeast Iceland Development Agency.

The title of the conference in Raufarhöfn was Tourism, People and Protected Areas in Polar Wilderness, following an earlier event of the IPTRN in 2010 with the same title [1]. In total, 40 papers were presented in seven sessions that ran individually through the five days of the conference. In between sessions were field excursions and meetings with tourism entrepreneurs and service providers in the region. In addition a community workshop was hosted at the conference venue on the fourth day. The community workshop focused on tourism development in collaboration with local stakeholders, with input from conference participants identifying issues of tourism development in the Polar Regions, and how these can be addressed in situ using participatory frameworks.

The impetus for this conference and the preceding IPTRN events was the rapid, albeit sporadic, growth of tourism in the Arctic and Antarctic. Through the democratization of travel, transport technology developments and increasing accessibility, some parts of the Polar Regions are witnessing increasing inbound tourism. Tourism operations in the Polar Regions capitalize on the regions' natural assets, landscapes and remoteness. Despite significant differences, for instance, with regard to sovereignty questions or the history of human habitation, parallels can be drawn between the Arctic and Antarctic regions. In addition to both being remote, these parallels are primarily based on the Polar Regions' biogeographic characteristics, extreme climatic conditions, widespread perceptions of being a relatively inhospitable environment (for humans), and a high marine biodiversity and productivity. Tourists from across the world are attracted by the pristine character of the Polar Regions, their sparsely- or non-populated wilderness, and their unique historical and cultural assets [2]. At the same time, the Polar Regions are more and more embroiled in the geopolitics surrounding the region's energy resources and minerals. This is oftentimes at odds with global conservation ambitions, and the

Polar Regions' key qualities when it comes to tourism, i.e., that they remain relatively untouched by human activity, and for the most part can be regarded as wilderness areas. Additionally, the Arctic and the Antarctic are among the regions in the world where climatic changes are most rapid and profound, turning them into a focal point of the global environmental debate. Tourism development can be seen as both a contributor and a victim of these developments, with potential implications for natural resource use, ecosystems and peripheral communities [3].

Tourism development in the Polar Regions may increase awareness about these issues, while at the same time potentially negatively affecting the regions' wilderness character and the cultural integrity of local communities. This special issue explores how tourism development in the Polar Regions is, or can be, managed to enhance the conservation of natural resources, the protection of the environment the wellbeing of peripheral communities and the experiences of visitors.

2. Tourism in the Polar Regions

Reliable and regionally comparable statistics on tourism development across the Polar Regions are hard to come by, and even more difficult to compile [4]. In a recent publication by several IPTRN steering committee members, three examples are provided of the size and value of tourism in the Arctic [5]. We use the same examples here, but update the figures to give an indication of the scope and pace of tourism growth. In the autumn and winter of 2013–2014, 273,100 out-of-state visitors visited Alaska, followed by almost 1.6 million out-of-state visitors in the summer of 2014. A considerable proportion of these visitors are arriving on large cruise ships. This inbound tourism is estimated to have sustained 38,700 full- and part-time jobs, including all direct, indirect, and induced impacts, and generated USD $173,6 million in taxes and revenues, USD $1.83 billion in visitor spending and an overall economic impact of USD $3.92 billion [6]. Iceland has seen inbound tourism grow eightfold since 2002. That year the Icelandic Tourist Board (ITB) counted 246,580 international passengers departing through Keflavík international airport, which is used as a proxy for all inbound tourism, as all come and go through this one gateway. In the year 2016 this figure stood at almost 1.8 million. In 2016 all tourism services (domestic and international) accounted for 39.2% of Iceland's export revenue (ISK 466 billion) [7]. Similarly, on mainland Europe, visitor nights in Finnish Lapland, the most Arctic region of the European Union, grew from 1.7 million in 2001 to 3.2 million in 2016, remaining fairly constant at 10–12% of the market share for all of Finland [8]. These are astounding figures indeed from three Arctic mass tourism destinations. Of course, considerable geographical variation in inbound tourism numbers and growth exists, and in addition to mass tourism sites, numerous ecotourism niches are present in both the Arctic and the Antarctic, for example expedition cruising [9]. Nevertheless, where inbound tourism grows, so does the economic value of tourism (at local, regional and national levels), including the hard-to-measure socio-cultural and environmental effects the sector has.

The benefits of polar tourism might be daunting to realize, as challenges particular to their operation include pronounced seasonality and difficult access to tourist markets. When it comes to the local communities, they are generally small and remote, yet different in the two polar realms. In the Antarctic, there is no indigenous population; social interaction and contention mainly exists between the existing scientific community and tourism development needs. While access to tourism sites is difficult (geographically and financially) in both Polar Regions; the Arctic is also faced with human development needs of indigenous communities and human capital issues (e.g., need for human resources and service training). In addition, while winter and northern lights tourism appears to be a growing phenomenon, extensive glaciation and sea ice coverage, as well as prolonged periods lacking daylight hours, has up until now resulted in stronger seasonality of tourism in the Polar Regions than elsewhere in the world.

The Polar Regions are often touted as the 'canary in the coalmine' when it comes to climate change. However, with their delicately balanced ecosystems in risk of collapse or transformation with global climate change, these changes also open up and facilitate access to the area and its hitherto largely unexplored tourism potential [3]. Newly accessible destinations and tourism experiences can be developed with the operational premise that tourism can help preserve communities' natural and cultural resources, and facilitate some sense of historical continuity and contribute to their future viability within a rapidly globalizing world. At the same time, using carbon-fueled travel to get to the Polar Regions in turn contributes to and enhances the effects of climate change [10]. Some claim that, since the Polar Regions most pronouncedly demonstrate the effects of climate change, travel to its destinations may contribute to a growing awareness of the issues of climate change [11]. Others have explored different tourism futures of the Anthropocene, whereby tourism's entanglements with the global ecosystem are analyzed [12].

3. Polar Tourism Research

Polar tourism is an evolving and maturing field of academic interest, as Stewart et al. clearly demonstrate in their recent comprehensive overview [13]. In their paper, they provide a thematic outline of published research on polar tourism based on eight themes. The two predominant themes deal with development and management of polar tourism, most often with a particular geographical focus. Tourist experiences feature thereafter as a focal area of research, followed by global change, governance and impacts of polar tourism. The last two, and least studied, areas of research deal with communities and their varied relations to polar tourism and reviews of polar tourism research.

Polar tourism research reviews, like the recent Stewart et al. paper, focus on understanding which scholars play a role in this emerging field, and how their publications are spreading through the academic community and further afield. Stewart et al. demonstrate in their paper that "the groups creating and expanding our understanding of polar tourism phenomena are still relatively small and are brought together by a handful of key tourism researchers. However, the scholars driving polar tourism research have begun to institutionalize their interactions and capacity building through IPTRN" [13] (pp. 77–78).

3.1. The IPTRN and Its Conferences

The IPTRN was created in 2006 by a group of academics as a means of providing a forum for researchers working on tourism and its intersection with environmental, cultural, and economic issues in Polar Regions. The IPTRN strives to generate, share and disseminate knowledge, resources and perspectives on polar tourism, and strongly supports the development of international collaboration and cooperative relationships between members. Membership in the network includes university researchers, consultants, tourism operators, government organizations, community members, and graduate students dedicated to analyzing tourism in Arctic and Antarctic settings. The network has held five community-embedded workshop conferences, starting in 2008 in Montreal/Kangiqsujuaq, Canada, the second in 2010 in Abisko, Sweden, the third in 2012 in Nain, Canada and the fourth in 2014 in Christchurch/Akaroa, New Zealand. Each has led to publications identifying issues surrounding the field of polar tourism [1,14–16]. The biannual conferences play a key role in institutionalizing research efforts through the IPTRN and provides a prime venue to review topical and innovative research in the field. In this sense, the IPTRN events can be considered nodal points of dissemination.

The fifth conference held in Raufarhöfn, North-East Iceland, in September 2016, explored how expectations towards tourism development in peripheral places can be managed to contribute to the cultural wellbeing of peripheral communities and/or enhance the protection of the environment. Presentations at the conference gave insights into how tourism operations in the polar-regions capitalize on the regions' assets, including their landscapes, wildlife and remoteness, with examples from the Antarctic and Arctic realm. In retrospect, five strands of research emerged as on-going when it comes to tourism studies within the Polar Regions, judging from the papers presented at the last IPTRN conference in 2016.

Firstly, and most prominently, were efforts towards understanding the polar landscape and coming to terms with its wilderness quality and the management implications thereof, be it through comparison between different regions of the Arctic and the Antarctic, or through a comparison of different viewers, the construction of the polar landscape, its aesthetic and scientific value. Gauging this wilderness quality becomes paramount for understanding a region's tourism potential, when, where and for whom. Under this first strand of research, the educational aspect of polar travel was also explored, examining the way in which visits to the Polar Regions in one way or another involve study or learning by those undertaking such journeys.

The second strand dealt with issues of environmental management and environmental degradation due to visitation. The environmental impact of tourism is visible, for example, in the trampling of delicate flora in the Polar Regions and damage to biota that will take decades—if not centuries—to naturally regain its former status. The conference also addressed how to manage the threat of degradation by, for example, temporary closures, developing infrastructure and tourism guidelines to direct people and their activities.

The third strand dealt with cruise tourism in the Arctic and Antarctic, which in many polar destinations is the predominant means of access. This ever-growing segment of tourism in the Polar Regions is cause for concern, as it is difficult to manage and regulate. Cruise tourism in the Polar Regions holds implications for safety, rescue capacity and marine and coastal cultural and natural heritage preservation. How the polar cruising industry is organized, and what drives its growth and organization, was gauged, including the use of ICT, vessel tracking, and weather and sea ice information.

The fourth strand explored during the conference dealt with some of the key experiences and attractions of the Polar Regions, including the northern lights, its glaciers and the wildlife inhabiting the region. How darkness and light have a role in the experience of the polar realm and how this is mediated through social media was explored, as was the role of polar bears and how tourism is developed around these iconic figures of the North.

Lastly, culture and climate change were discussed in terms of societal resilience, tourism land-use struggles with extractive industries, the construction of place-meanings at current and historically, and how to manage tourism to attain sustainable community development. The complementarity of reindeer herding, or other cultural practices, and tourism were also the focus of analysis.

As can be seen from these five strands, the field of polar tourism studies is a wide-ranging one, as the field of tourism studies more generally is. The current special issue resulting from the conference will, to some extent, capture this diversity and range of scholarship.

3.2. This Special Issue

A total of 12 papers were submitted in response to a call for this special issue circulated in the wake of the conference in Raufarhöfn. We, the editors, were in charge of the peer-review process and once completed, seven papers were finalized for publication in the special issue in late summer 2017. Although the seven papers deal with a range of topics, underpinning them all is the need to come to terms with the rapid and dramatic changes occurring in the Polar Regions, be they biophysical, economic or political. All share the aspiration of making tourism in the Polar Regions sustainable. Whether tourism will be a pillar of, or impediment to, sustainability depends largely on the actors participating in tourism management and public administration, and the actions they take. Actors in polar tourism are many and varied, including destination and natural resource managers, governmental and non-governmental administrators, community residents, tourism operators, emergency responders, scientists, and tourists themselves. Each of these actors have different, and potentially conflicting, perspectives on and interests in tourism. For each of these interests, tourism can provide many direct benefits and many indirect benefits for natural resource protection, cultural sustainability and global society. However, tourism can also damage the quality of natural resources, jeopardize the integrity of cultures, and endanger tourists and community members.

The seven papers can roughly be grouped into two categories. The first set of four papers deals with methods and key assets for developing sustainable tourism operations in the Polar Regions. The second set of three papers deals more with the implications of different means of access to the more remote parts of the Polar Regions. In the following paragraphs, we will introduce the papers of these two sets.

3.2.1. Methods and Assets for Sustainable Polar Tourism

Barr focuses on the Polar Regions' maritime heritage, claiming that considerable attention is being paid to better understanding and more effectively protecting natural resources in the Polar Regions, while far less is being done to identify and preserve the regions' significant maritime heritage resources. He claims that the uses of historical records detailing the long-standing human inhabitations of the Arctic can help in identifying significant marine cultural heritage landscapes. Their identification will not only assist in establishing regional priorities for targeted archaeological surveys and investigations, but will also likely minimize what will be lost forever as the inevitable "ice-free Arctic", as well as its expanded human footprint, approaches.

Bickford et al. in their paper see tourism as a business opportunity in Arctic countries. However, to ensure the sustainable use of potential tourism resources, they argue that business practices should be dominated by the ethos of ecotourism based on government and social permission to carry out their operations. They argue that government and community acceptance can be facilitated through a social license to operate (SLO). A social license to operate is not a formal agreement or document, but ongoing negotiation, practices and acts of corporate social responsibility (CSR). They claim that sustaining local and traditional resources and lands, especially in the Arctic, becomes a key factor in decisions regarding tourism development. The way to achieve this is through responsible businesses practices of CSR and SLO in ecotourism.

Bystrowska et al. in their paper detail how information and communication technology (ICT) is increasingly used to support the sustainable management of nature-based tourism sites. Key challenges to successful management are the remoteness and risks associated with Arctic tourism. Their argument is developed from a case study of an expedition cruise operators' network in Svalbard and how the use of ICT affects collective action and sustainable management of tourism sites. Through increased noticeability, the creation of artificial proximity and the development of new management practices, ICT can help overcome the challenges of collective action that are posed by the Arctic environment. They emphasize that the successful application of ICT depends on a high level of social capital; in particular, norms to guide interactions between actors in the network.

Stewart et al. start off their paper with the claim that the absence of basic statistics and research hampers the development of management plans or visions for tourism in the Polar Regions. They demonstrate this through their focus on the New Zealand Sub-Antarctic Islands, which are among the most remote and hostile within New Zealand waters. With their remoteness and their recent World Heritage Area status, the Islands have long appealed to visitors wishing to explore and understand the Islands' rich natural and cultural environments. The need for developing and implementing a visitor monitoring program has been identified to determine the effects of visitors on natural and cultural assets, as well as on the visitor experience itself. However, there is only piecemeal data published on visitor numbers upon which to base visitor monitoring, and there is only limited evidence regarding the range of possible impacts visitors may have, including their direct and indirect impact on wildlife, soils, and vegetation. The authors try to remedy this lack of primary data through secondary data, but the point remains that the best of intentions for tourism development in the Polar Regions can be thwarted as there is limited (or no) data and a lack of capacity to provide these.

3.2.2. Issues and Implications of Tourism Operations in Polar Marine Areas

The paper listed under the second theme deal with various implications of accessing remote marine parts in the Polar Regions. Johnston et al. in their paper focus on marine tourism in Arctic Canada. They identify how climate change and a range of environmental risks and other problems present significant management challenges. In their paper, they describe the growth in cruise tourism and pleasure craft travel in Canada's Nunavut Territory and outline issues and concerns related to existing management of both cruise and pleasure craft tourism. More specifically, three key strategic issues are discussed: the need to streamline the regulatory framework, the need improve marine tourism data collection and analysis for decision-making, and the need to develop site guidelines and visitor behavior guidelines.

Manley et al. in their paper approach polar expedition cruising from the tourist perspective. They investigate the motivations for, and the educational dimensions of, expedition cruising, using entrance surveys prior to embarking on four separate itineraries in the Arctic. Analysis of the survey, semi-structured interviews, participant observations and a post-trip follow-up survey to assess attitudinal changes highlighted that, unlike mainstream cruisers, expedition cruisers are motivated by opportunities for novel experiences and learning. Subsequently, the educational programs offered by expedition cruise companies are an important component of the cruise experience.

Finally, a key issue when it comes to marine tourism development in the Polar Regions is risk. Aase explores the use of Automatic Identification System (AIS) data collected from satellites for supporting search and rescue (SAR) operations in remote waters. A case study is presented discussing the Ortelius incident in Svalbard in early June 2016, using data recorded by the Norwegian polar orbiting satellite AISSat-1. The Ortelius is a tourist vessel that experienced engine failure whilst no Norwegian Coast Guard vessels were in the vicinity. The Governor of Svalbard had to deploy her vessel Polarsyssel to assist the Ortelius. The paper shows that satellite-based AIS enables SAR coordination centers to swiftly determine the identity and precise location of vessels in the vicinity of the troubled ship. This makes it easier to coordinate SAR operations.

4. Concluding Remarks

All in all, the seven papers show that polar tourism research is a wide-ranging field, and is rapidly growing, as tourism operations swell in the Polar Regions. What we see emerging in particular from this special issue is a more detailed analytical focus on a range of issues identified as central to polar tourism research. As a sign of a maturing field, the research presented at the conference and detailed in this special issue adds empirical and analytical scope to the field, and moves away from the charting of general contours or description of issues in polar tourism. What can also be seen are the ways in which general topics of interest in the wider academic community are being brought to bear on the particularities of polar tourism development. It is our expectation and hope that with the growth of polar tourism, scholarship on the topic will grow alongside it. The IPTRN conferences and publications keep track of these developments and provide fertile ground for this maturing field of study. You are welcome to join us for the next IPTRN conference in the Yukon territory of Arctic Canada in June 2018.

Conflicts of Interest: The authors declare no conflict of interest.

References

1. *New Issues in Polar Tourism. Communities, Environments, Politics*; Müller, D.K.; Lundmark, L.; Lemelin, R.H., Eds.; Springer: Dordrecht, The Netherlands, 2013.
2. *Tourism and Change in Polar Regions: Climate, Environments and Experiences*; Hall, C.M.; Saarinen, J., Eds.; Routledge: New York, NY, USA, 2010.
3. Lamers, M.; Amelung, B. Climate change and its implications for cruise tourism in the polar regions. In *Cruise Tourism in Polar Regions: Promoting Environmental and Social Sustainability*; Luck, M., Maher, P.T., Stewart, E., Eds.; Earthscan: London, UK, 2010; pp. 147–163.
4. Fay, G.; Karlsdóttir, A. Social indicators for arctic tourism: Observing trends and assessing data. *Polar Geogr.* **2011**, *34*, 63–86. [CrossRef]
5. De la Barre, S.; Maher, P.; Dawson, J.; Hillmer-Pegram, K.; Huijbens, E.; Lamers, M.; Liggett, D.; Müller, D.; Pashkevich, A.; Stewart, E. Tourism and Arctic Observation Systems: Exploring the relationships. *Polar Res.* **2016**, *35*. [CrossRef]

6. McDowell Group. Economic Impact of Alaska's Visitor Industry. 2013–2014 Update. Prepared for State of Alaska Department of Commerce, & Economic Development, Division of Economic Development. Available online: http://www.akrdc.org/assets/docs/vis%20industry%20impacts%202013_14%203_24.pdf (accessed on 24 August 2017).

7. Icelandic Tourist Board. Tourism in Iceland in Figures. June 2017. Available online: https://www.ferdamalastofa.is/static/files/ferdamalastofa/Frettamyndir/2017/juli/tourism-in-iceland-2017.pdf (accessed on 24 August 2017).

8. Visit Finland—Travel Trade. Annual Trend. Available online: http://www.visitfinland.com/travel-trade/graph/vuositason-kehitystrendi/ (accessed on 24 August 2017).

9. Van Bets, L.; Lamers, M.; Van Tatenhove, J. Collective self-governance in a marine community: Expedition cruise tourism at Svalbard. *J. Sustain. Tour.* **2017**, 1–17. [CrossRef]

10. Farreny, R.; Oliver-Solà, J.; Lamers, M.; Amelung, B.; Gabarrell, X.; Rieradevall, J.; Boada, M.; Benayas, J. Carbon dioxide emissions of Antarctic tourism. *Antarct. Sci.* **2011**, *23*, 556–566. [CrossRef]

11. Eijgelaar, E.; Thaper, C.; Peeters, P. Antarctic cruise tourism: The paradoxes of ambassadorship, "last chance tourism" and greenhouse gas emissions. *J. Sustain. Tour.* **2010**, *18*, 337–354. [CrossRef]

12. *Tourism and the Anthropocene*; Gren, M.; Huijbens, E. (Eds.) Routledge: London, UK, 2016.

13. Stewart, E.J.; Liggett, D.; Dawson, J. The evolution of polar tourism scholarship: Research themes, networks and agendas. *Polar Geogr.* **2017**, *40*, 59–84. [CrossRef]

14. *Polar Tourism: A Tool for Regional Development*; Grenier, A.A.; Müller, D.K., Eds.; Presses de l'Université du Québec: Québec City, QC, Canada, 2011.

15. Lemelin, R.H.; Maher, P.; Liggett, D. (Eds.) From talk to action: How tourism is changing the Polar Regions. In Proceedings of the 3rd International Polar Tourism Research Network (IPTRN) Conference, Nain, Nunatsiavut, NL, Canada, 6–21 April 2012; Centre for Northern Studies Press, Lakehead University: Thunder Bay, ON, Canada, 2013.

16. Liggett, D.; Stewart, E. (Eds.) Polar tourism (research) is not what it used to be: The maturing of a field of study alongside an activity. *Polar J.* **2015**, *5*, 247–256. [CrossRef]

resources

MDPI

Article

"An ounce of Prevention is Worth a Pound of Cure": Adopting Landscape-Level Precautionary Approaches to Preserve Arctic Coastal Heritage Resources

Bradley W. Barr

Visiting Faculty, Master's Program in Coastal and Marine Management,
Háskólasetur Vestfjarða/University Centre of the Westfjords, Suðurgötu 12, 400 Ísafjörður, Iceland

Academic Editors: Edward H. Huijbens and Machiel Lamers
Received: 24 February 2017; Accepted: 19 April 2017; Published: 26 April 2017

Abstract: The Arctic region is changing rapidly and dramatically as a result of climate change, perhaps two to three times faster than other areas of the world. Its inaccessibility, remoteness, and low population density no longer offers sufficient protection from expanding human use and development for its rich and diverse natural and cultural heritage. While considerable attention is being focused on better understanding and more effectively protecting its natural resources, far less is being done to identify and preserve this region's significant maritime heritage resources. This remoteness and inaccessibility that has protected Arctic resources for so long has also constrained our capacity to conduct sufficient archaeological studies to inform and guide the place-specific identification and preservation of what remains of this compelling history and heritage. The wilderness landscape of the Arctic has a rich and relatively well-documented historical record, spanning more than 2000 years of exploration and commerce, and of Indigenous cultures stretching further back over 4000–6000 years. More effectively using this historical record to identify significant maritime cultural landscapes in the Arctic and expanding the use of precautionary approaches to the preservation of these landscapes will not only assist in establishing regional priorities for targeted archaeological surveys and investigations, but will also likely minimize what will be lost forever as the inevitable "ice-free Arctic", as well as its expanded human footprint, approaches.

Keywords: Arctic; maritime heritage resources; precautionary approaches; maritime cultural landscapes

1. Introduction

Many words have been used to attempt to appropriately describe the Arctic, including "vast", "remote", "unforgiving", "harsh", and "wilderness". It has also been described as a place attracting privileged white men engaging in the "masculinist fantasy" of exploration [1], which apparently has potential and profound geopolitical repercussions that shape the way that it is perceived, governed, and exploited [2]. It is a place that has always attracted the interest of people in more southerly latitudes, either for inspiration or for the many and diverse resources it might provide. Unlike the other pole, it is inhabited, albeit sparsely, and has been for thousands of years. In recent times, it has also been the subject of much debate, stirring deep scientific and geopolitical controversy and concern as a result of the rapidly changing climate, its effect on the socio-ecological systems operating there, and the interplay of countries with various interests in this region [3]. Every year has brought reports of changes like the unprecedented retreat of multi-year sea-ice extent and thinning [4], and a greater frequency and severity of storms and unprecedented coastal erosion that is threatening some coastal villages, critical infrastructure, and, increasingly, culturally-significant sites [5].

As the sea-ice retreats, what was once a region where only intrepid mariners and explorers dared to navigate and Indigenous communities subsisted in relative isolation, is now becoming more accessible. With this greater access, more people are coming to the Arctic, not only to find and exploit the resources that have so long been protected by the ice and harsh conditions, but to experience an iconic wilderness that is likely to be, in the not so distant future, melting away, forever changed as the climate warms. This expanding human access and use is accompanied by increasing threats to Arctic resources, compounding what is happening as a direct result of climate change. While addressing and mitigating the underlying drivers of climate change may, at this point, present greater challenges than the global community is able or willing to confront, the active management and preservation of both natural and cultural resources of the Arctic will be required to sustain at least some of what will be lost. Therefore, the underlying purpose of this paper is to discuss, and perhaps begin a dialogue about, how this more effective stewardship might be accomplished.

1.1. Expanded Human Uses in the Arctic May Be Slower than Expected

Recently, as reflected in some presentations at November 2016's Arctic Circle Conference in Iceland, expert opinion has begun to partially back away from the crisis narrative surrounding climate change in the Arctic that has been offered in the past few years. It now suggests that some of the expanded human uses on the horizon for the Arctic, including commercial shipping and oil and gas exploration and development, still constitute "opportunities" or "threats" (depending on one's point of view), but it may take a little more time before we see a sufficiently "ice-free" Arctic which is economically favorable to these activities. Such a recalibration of expectations may offer some "breathing room" for thinking about, and actually beginning the process of, preserving significant natural and historical resources before the ships are able to more routinely navigate through what remains of the ice, the needed deep-water ports are developed, and rigs and pipelines are constructed and operational.

The term "historical resource" is defined here as encompassing prehistoric/historical archaeological sites and/or the built environment which includes historic sites, structures, objects, districts, and landscapes [6]. It is used interchangeably with "maritime heritage resource" throughout this discussion.

1.2. Tourism May Be the Exception

This anticipated delay in the growth and expansion of commercial shipping and petroleum exploration and development in the waters of the Arctic may not, however, be the case with regard to Arctic tourism. Illustrative of this continuing expansion, the Northwest Passage, identified as "the most popular expedition cruise area in the Canadian Arctic" [7] (p. 142) was projected to experience "an increase in planned cruises by 70% over the period 2006–2010" [8]. Hall and Saarinen [9] (p. 8) report that, as of 2010, "well over five million tourist trips" were taken to the Arctic each year, and also offered, for context, the following observation:

> ... the number of tourists is continuing to grow and represents a significant figure in relation to permanent populations and concentration in a relatively small number of accessible areas in space and time. For example, the number of fly-in tourists per year now exceeds the population of Greenland, with the number of cruise guests already being over half. A similar situation with respect to number of visitors per year in relation to permanent population also exists in Iceland, Svalbard, and northern Norway, Sweden and Finland above the Arctic Circle. (p. 417)

This "more visitors than residents" situation is further supported by the reported estimate [9], as of 2010, that five million tourists visit the Arctic each year, while the population of the Arctic has been contemporaneously estimated [10] (p. 121) at around four million residents. Currently, the number of tourists visiting Iceland has been estimated at four times the resident population [11]. This all suggests that the enthusiasm for Arctic tourism continues to grow and expand.

Cruise ships carried 1.3 million passengers to the Arctic in 2014 [12], which represents more than a quarter of all visitors to the region. In just a single year—2016—a somewhat surprising number of ice-capable expedition ships—a total of nine—were ordered and under construction, to be available for maiden voyages between 2018 and 2020 [13–15], adding around 1600 passenger berths to the existing fleet. Further encouraged by the successful transit of the Northwest Passage in 2016 by the *Crystal Serenity* [16], other non-Polar Class cruise ships are being repurposed for Arctic routes [17,18], and it is likely that more will follow. There has even been a somewhat speculative proposal for an "all-terrain" amphibious Polar cruise ship that could access coastal areas on tracks or wheels [19]. This rapid expansion, in 2016, of the expedition cruise ship fleet offers something more than simply speculation that a potentially significant increase in cruise ship tourism targeted for the Arctic is on the near horizon. Coastal infrastructure development to support this coming increased activity and presence will also be required, and will not be far behind.

Of course, the Arctic is a big place, and tourism activity is not evenly distributed across the region. Tourism activities are being conducted on both land and sea, are concentrated in particular areas of the Arctic that are attractive both in terms of the natural and historical resources that are present, and where the infrastructure and relative ease of access is favorable [20]. As summarized by Bystrowska and Dolnicki [20], "there is much regional variability in organization of tourism, its structure and trends, depending on endogenous features of a given area that influence type of tourists and tourism" (p. 38). In terms of what may be driving this growing interest in visiting the Arctic, for the most part, people are attracted to the Arctic to experience its wildness and iconic natural resources (e.g., polar bears, whales, scenic wilderness vistas, and ice) [20,21], but many are also interested in visiting places with historical and cultural value [20]. One other additional important element of this attraction seems to be "last chance tourism" [11,22,23], where potential visitors are aware of the unprecedented changes occurring in the Arctic, believe the iconic resources that attract them to the North will be lost as a result of these changes, and therefore want to visit before the opportunity is lost. Clearly, the potential impacts on the natural and historical resources in the Arctic from tourism should be addressed cumulatively with regard to the potential adverse effects from other expanding human activities, but it appears that tourism is perhaps the more immediate concern.

1.3. Climate Impacts on Historical Resources

Impacts from the changing climate of the Arctic are no less potentially damaging to historical resources than they are to natural resources. Murphy et al. [24] categorize these climate change-related impacts on coastal and maritime heritage environments as:

- direct physical impacts causing accelerated erosion or increased flooding
- indirect impacts that are a consequence of decisions taken now by coastal managers anticipating future climate change (such as "non-intervention" approaches to coastal defense)
- indirect impacts related to attempts at climate change mitigation (including the expansion of the renewable energy sector)
- northward expansion of alien fauna.

Regarding this last category of impacts, there has been a recent report [25] of the presence of shipworms in the wood of an historic shipwreck near Spitsbergen. This is the first reported occurrence of these wood-boring organisms in the Arctic, raising concerns within the maritime archaeological community about the fate of wooden shipwrecks that heretofore were not exposed to this threat.

As summarized by Barr et al. [26] (p. 162), with regard to the physical alteration of historical resources at submerged and coastal sites diminishing their archaeological integrity, direct impacts that could be relevant to Arctic historical resources include: fill, excavation, or dredging attendant to coastal infrastructure development; artifact collecting or salvage; prop-wash; groundings of ships; and discharges and spills from vessel accidents and cleanup operations. Indirect impacts to archaeological sites may include increased erosion and sedimentation affecting coastal landforms and nearshore sediments resulting from longer ice-free periods combined with more intense and frequent storms, expanded tourist visitation that potentially increases opportunities for disturbing coastal archaeological sites, and the loss of permafrost (combined with increased erosion) that exposes sensitive coastal archaeological sites to further disturbance and degradation of organic materials and artifacts [27]. Further, with specific reference to expanding cruise ship operation in the Arctic, cruise tourism without appropriate management can overwhelm coastal communities' infrastructure, raise local concerns about vessel discharges (e.g., food, garbage fuel, and sewage) and interference with cultural subsistence (e.g., hunting and fishing), and heighten community and government agency concerns about the capacity (and cost) to respond to the catastrophic sinking of ships in remote areas and ensuing the search and rescue of survivors [7]. Like other maritime transportation operations, such issues of ship collisions with whales, and wildlife disturbance more generally, as well as noise impacts on marine mammals from vessels and infrastructure development activities, are also management concerns that will likely need to be addressed in this region.

1.4. Purpose, Objectives, and Rationale

The call for papers for this special volume of *Resources,* targeted at papers presented at the recent International Polar Tourism Research Conference, held in Iceland in September 2016, sought to include contributions that "explore how expectations towards tourism development in the polar regions can be managed to enhance the conservation of natural resources, the protection of the environment, and the wellbeing of peripheral communities". While I attended this conference, and presented a paper on another topic, I have contributed this paper identifying the pressing need for the awareness of and action addressing the identification and preservation of coastal and maritime heritage resources in the Arctic precisely because it is a topic not explicitly included in the call for papers. This is an issue that is often overlooked, and deserves some much-needed attention.

Given that what draws tourists to the Arctic is principally its iconic natural resources, the effective preservation of an intact and functioning Arctic ecosystem should be something of a compelling interest to those who have a stake in this potentially important element of the economic sustainability of the region. The identification and preservation of places of high biodiversity and productivity throughout the Arctic would therefore be justified as a priority, ensuring that these places will be sustained intact for not only their intrinsic ecological integrity, but also as venues where tourists will continue to find the iconic natural resources and attributes that are an expected part of the experience of visiting the Arctic. Consistent with this intuitively important focus on natural resource protection and management, the Arctic Council, its constituent Arctic states, and other participants in this deliberative body, as well as a number of environmental non-governmental organizations have adopted the protection of the Arctic environment as a primary focus—and some have a mandate [28]—to address issues of sustainable development and environmental protection. There are many academic and agency scientists conducting important research relevant to acquiring a deeper knowledge of the Arctic environment, its diverse natural resources, and the impacts of the changing climate and its attendant increases in human activity as the sea ice retreats.

The greater emphasis on protecting natural resources and preserving the integrity of the Arctic ecosystem is likely to have some indirect benefits to identifying and preserving maritime heritage resources. The increased seabed mapping of habitats and features, for example, is likely to produce data that can be used to locate shipwrecks and potential submerged archaeological sites. Protected areas established to preserve natural resources may also offer some protection and an oversight of historic resources located within the boundaries of that site. It is reasonable to suspect that sites possessing high biodiversity, including iconic species which were once commercially hunted, would be sites where human activity might also have been concentrated at some point in the past. While these indirect benefits may be helpful, effective preservation of maritime heritage resources requires supporting research be conducted by knowledgeable and qualified maritime archaeologists to address somewhat different management and preservation actions than ecosystem protection. Additionally, the management strategies that may be adopted to accomplish place-based historical resource preservation are different, involving those such as managing the impacts related to the disturbance from expanded access and directed archaeological surveys to identify significant historical resources. These two different management goals can be accomplished together [29], but both need to be explicitly included in the goals and scope of the authority for that protected area.

As a general observation, far fewer of the many academic, agency, and policy researchers who have an interest in the Arctic are engaged in conducting the much-needed research and policy analysis directed specifically at identifying and preserving historical resources. Nor are there, relative to research on natural resources, nearly as many research programs (or available funding sources) targeted at better understanding, mitigating, or adapting to potential climate change impacts on historical resources. There also seems to be a somewhat greater, and justified, emphasis in the Arctic Council and other intergovernmental and advocacy organizations for understanding and incorporating Indigenous cultural interests in their deliberations, as well as in the science that they encourage and support to inform their actions and recommendations. In this emphasis, at least one element of "cultural heritage" is being addressed to some degree, but arguably, the broader scope of historical resource identification and preservation has attracted far less attention.

It is the purpose of this paper, therefore, to attempt to raise the profile and to increase awareness of the pressing need of place-based historical resource identification and preservation in the Arctic. In addition, ideas and recommendations are offered regarding how key places could be identified, and might be effectively preserved utilizing the existing management tools available, when our knowledge of the spatial distribution of these resources is limited. This constitutes the foundation for the central question posed by this paper:

> *Is there an effective and efficient way to identify the most potentially significant Arctic heritage areas, recognizing that the terrestrial and maritime archaeological information available may be insufficient in many places throughout the region to accomplish this task, and acknowledging the rapid pace of climate change in the Arctic and the attendant threats posed to historical resources?*

Realistically, not every historical resource in the Arctic is worthy of protection, nor could they all be preserved even if they were. As a purely practical matter, if significant historical resources are lost due to climate change and inadequate management, there will be fewer interesting places in the Arctic for tourists to visit. If these places are not identified and preserved, as well as effectively managed and interpreted appropriately so that visitors are aware of what they are experiencing and can learn the important lessons these places can teach us, something important will be lost.

As the Arctic Council's Conservation of Arctic Flora and Fauna (CAFF) committee has observed [30], there are important cultural and societal reasons for establishing protected areas:

- *Cultural and Heritage values can include the importance of protected areas in representing the characteristics that formed a society's distinct character and the historical importance of a site in shaping a society or people; spiritual values attributed to a site are also included.*
- *Recreation values can include the worth of a site for consumptive (i.e., sport hunting) or non-consumptive (hiking, camping, photography, etc.) activities.*
- *Societal values can include the importance of a protected area to a society at large often reflected in the funding or political priority attached to the site.*
- *Landscape values can include the visual characteristics and their relative importance to local communities, nations or internationally.*
- *Educational values can include the use of a site to train or teach people and make them aware of their physical and natural surroundings and its biodiversity.*
- *Scientific and research values can include the importance of a site in contributing to an overall understanding of the natural environment and the consequences of natural vs. human-caused, or anthropogenic, changes.* (p. 110)

Rey [31] has eloquently offered that "the Arctic is a unique feature which is part of the common heritage of mankind and, as such, deserves reverence and protection". The UNESCO World Heritage Program [32] (p. 8) has made a similar statement about the need to preserve Arctic resources:

> ... *the Arctic region is important for global processes and is to be considered as precious heritage for humankind. The region includes a number of unique and outstanding natural and cultural heritage places which require protection, improved management and international recognition due to their vulnerability.* (p. 8)

All of the Arctic states have formally adopted laws, regulations, and policies—as statements of the collective will of their citizens—to identify and preserve terrestrial and submerged heritage. These heritage protection laws are implemented both through governmental agencies responsible for the stewardship of historical resources throughout that country and its sovereign waters, as well as through national protected areas programs charged with the place-based preservation of natural and historical resources. Therefore, the question should be not whether we act affirmatively to meet these legal mandates, but how to best accomplish the task.

2. Background—The Importance of Arctic History to Inform Preservation Priorities

Frontiers have always been important in our collective history, but particularly to North Americans. Exploring and, ultimately, "taming" the wilderness frontier is a central element in shaping this continent and its people. Certainly, the collected essays of Fredrick Jackson Turner [33] provide ample evidence of this importance in the United States, and no less so in Canada [34]. No frontier has seemingly been more alluring to North Americans than the Arctic. While Canadians have, arguably, more of an "Arctic identity" than Americans, including reference to the "True North Strong and Free" in their national anthem, every license plate in Alaska includes the words, "The Last Frontier". While the geographic focus of this discussion is the North American Arctic and Greenland, north of the Arctic Circle, it is also relevant to the entire Arctic region more generally.

2.1. Indigenous Migration and Habitation

As early as 6000 years ago, representatives of the Birnirk culture migrated across the Bering Strait from Siberia, based on the most recent, extensive genetic analyses of Raghaven et al. [35]. This research further suggested that a number of "Paleo-Eskimo" cultures arose from this initial pulse of migration, including the Saqqaq, Denbigh, and Dorset, became established during an Eastward expansion through the North American Arctic, and persisted for around 4000 years. There was a separate migration of what were call "Neo-Eskimo" Thule cultures that were the predecessors to the contemporary Inuit, replacing the "Paleo-Eskimo" cultures around 1000–700 BCE. The Paleo-Eskimo and Neo-Eskimo people were thought to have distinct cultural traditions and lifeways, and left a complex, if somewhat elusive and unsurprisingly limited, archaeological record.

Over these thousands of years, many habitation sites have been occupied and abandoned, and culturally and spiritually meaningful places have been constructed and reclaimed over time by the land and the sea. These Paleo-Eskimo and Neo-Eskimo cultures were, to one degree or another, maritime peoples, living on the coasts and relying on sea mammals and other marine species for sustenance, and there are remnants of their lives scattered throughout the North American Arctic. There is little doubt that only a small fraction of this valuable archaeological record has been located and studied. These cultures experienced and adapted to past documented climate change events, which makes the potential to learn from their experiences, through archaeological investigations, even more important.

2.2. History of Commerce and Exploration

Likewise, this is a region of the Arctic with a storied history of exploration and commerce. Explorers, over the last few centuries, have chased the enticing yet elusive "holy grails" of successfully navigating the Northwest Passage and reaching the North Pole. Along the way, the failed attempts to attain these goals have left, in their wake, many ships of exploration lost, as well as the remains of encampment sites of the surviving crews. These events offer compelling stories of survival—and more often of not surviving these tragic circumstances—that not only captured the imagination of the public, but were extensively reported in contemporary newspaper accounts and later studied by historians seeking to better understand and interpret these events.

Similarly, the whaling and the fur trade enterprises represented significant and economically important activities in the Arctic at various times from the 16th Century until the beginning of the 20th Century. The highly lucrative fur trade drove European, and later North American, exploration of the Arctic, often involving first contact with, and in many cases the exploitation of, Arctic Indigenous populations. First in the Eastern regions, and later in the Western Arctic, the fur trade filled in the many blank places on the maps, as the competition among the various companies that conducted this enterprise rose and fell with the economic vagaries of supply and demand, and as the sovereign interests in colonial expansion in this new world were pursued [36]. Whaling was another important agent of change, helping to shape the future of the North American Arctic. Like the fur trade, whalers expanded the limits of the "known world", pushing ever further into the maritime landscape of the Arctic frontier wilderness seeking out new and productive whaling grounds. Whaling was an industry that had a global reach and influence, one that left a profound effect on the places where whales were hunted, and the ports that serviced the industry. Clearly, this was the case in Hawaii [37], where commercial whaling in the 19th Century had a profound effect on the economy, culture, environment, and politics of this island nation. The Eastern Arctic region of North America possessed some of the earliest and most productive of these whaling grounds, which were, at various times, exploited by European and American whalers who risked great peril to find and catch whales surrounded by the ever-present danger of ice. In the latter half of the 19th Century, the key geography was the Western Arctic. It was the previously unexploited populations of bowhead whales that these Yankee whaling fleets pursued until it became economically unsustainable from overexploitation, catastrophic events that resulted in the losses of many whaling ships to ice and storms, and the discovery of oil in Pennsylvania. The Arctic of North America was, without question, a fundamental part of the global landscape of whaling which left, in its wake, places much different than they were when they first arrived. Fortunately, as the whaling industry was of great economic interest to the countries that engaged in this enterprise, it also left a wealth of documentation including ship logs and journals, and extensive contemporary newspaper coverage—and a relatively large number of historians who have collected and interpreted this information—that tell this story in considerable detail. The Arctic whaling heritage landscape is, therefore, well defined and documented.

2.3. How This History Can Be Relevant in Guiding the Identification and Preservation of Arctic Historical Resources . . . and What More May Need to Be Done

While Arctic history may be reasonably well documented, the archaeological research required to provide site-specific information to effectively preserve historical resources is not as well developed. Those participating in the Arctic Council's efforts to identify "areas of heightened natural and cultural significance" [38] observed:

> Better documentation of areas of heightened cultural significance is also needed throughout the Arctic. Traditional use areas have been recorded in some areas, but in others they are missing or decades out of date. Assessing the ways in which use areas are changing due to climate change as well as technological advances is also necessary, to avoid limiting protection to areas that are not sufficient for current or future needs. Archeological and historical sites are known in many places, but often only superficially, and other regions simply have not been surveyed to determine what is there. (p. 113)

Such information will be critically important when the predicted expansion of human uses and development occurs as we approach an "ice-free Arctic". Particularly with regard to maritime archaeology, most of the effort has been devoted to intensive searches for relatively few significant historic shipwrecks, such as the recent discoveries in Canada of the Franklin ships, *Erebus* [39] and *Terror* [40].

What are notably lacking are maritime and coastal archaeological surveys at the landscape scale. For example, in 2014, the Alaska Region of the U.S. Bureau of Ocean Energy Management (BOEM) proposed a project, in their Environmental Studies Program proposal [41], to conduct baseline archaeological surveys in the Beaufort and Chukchi Seas. These baseline surveys would address "limited information available regarding potential submerged cultural resources in areas of potential future industry activity, even though there is high possibility that archeological sites exist in these locations" [41] (p. 156). This important proposed work was not funded in 2014, and subsequent yearly updates of this planning document have not continued to include this proposal. Such surveys can help to better identify regional priorities regarding where additional site-specific research is needed, and perhaps more importantly, to help raise awareness about the pressing need for expanded attention to, and funding of, Arctic heritage preservation efforts and the research needed to support this work. Without question, it will take time and considerable funding to acquire sufficient archaeological documentation to begin to preserve these Arctic maritime heritage landscapes and resources as development and human activities increase. In the interim, perhaps we might begin with a process that could lead to more effectively identifying and preserving these landscapes and resources by using this extensive historical record to, as systematically as possible, help identify the places in the Arctic that may be priorities for more detailed archaeological investigation, and offer some precautionary protection for these landscape areas until the essential archaeological investigations can be completed.

3. Discussion—Challenges and Opportunities

Only recently has the pace of discovery of important Arctic maritime heritage resources begun to increase as the sea-ice cover retreats, providing longer windows of opportunity to conduct field research and more open water to facilitate ship-based seabed surveys. However, the region remains insufficiently explored and documented to ensure that even the most significant historical resources are identified and preserved [38]. This slowly expanding knowledge is arriving at a time when increasing human use and development, and climate change itself, are posing significant threats to effective heritage preservation.

3.1. Existing Tools for Preservation of Historical Resources May Be Inadequate

There are requirements in many of the statutory authorities addressing the protection of historical resources, such as the National Historic Preservation Act (NHPA) in the US, as well as similar authorities in other Arctic states. There are also various impact assessment requirements when major development projects are proposed. While these can identify resources that could be adversely affected by the proposed activity, project-specific impact assessments are typically conducted as part of what is usually an environmental impact-focused process, like the National Environmental Policy Act (NEPA) and similar Environmental Impact Assessment (EIA) requirements in other jurisdictions. Usually, these are the responsibility of the oversight agency of the national, and sometimes sub-national, governments, and while the developer proposing the work is required to supply information relevant to identifying and assessing the condition of archaeological resources that might be damaged or adversely impacted by the development, these assessments are, for the most part, based on a review of existing, available information, and sometimes very limited field surveys. Comprehensive assessments are costly, complex, and challenging, particularly in the Arctic, and are often predicated more on minimizing delays to initiating the work than on actually finding and preserving what maritime heritage resources may be present at the site. The agencies responsible for conducting these project reviews are often understaffed and underfunded, and often lack specific expertise in the preservation of archaeological resources, making effective oversight challenging. This is particularly an issue when there are many proposals being evaluated at the same time as a result of some opportunity, like climate change in the Arctic, that creates conditions where development is not just possible, when it was previously more challenging, but economically favorable. There may be competing interests pursuing these opportunities, and political pressure to streamline review processes to ensure economic opportunities are not lost as a result of satisfying regulatory requirements. Clearly, this was the case in Canada when the government revised the Canadian Environmental Assessment Act in 2012. According to Gibson [42] (p. 179), this resulted in federal environmental assessments being "few, fragmentary, inconsistent and late". Considering that archaeological resource assessments are generally only a part of and largely ancillary to the environmental impact components of these reviews, such EIA processes are likely to be only cursory at best in terms of identifying and effectively preserving maritime heritage resources. Interestingly, most Indigenous people do not parse resources into "natural" and cultural", instead perceiving the environment as infused with culture value [43]. For the Arctic, where many Indigenous people live and, therefore, where their interests and perspectives are especially important, adopting this more expansive and integrated worldview may be particularly appropriate.

An example may help to demonstrate this challenge. In 2007, the US Minerals Management Service (now BOEM), published an Environmental Impact Statement and Environmental Assessment (EIS/EA) for the proposed oil and gas lease sale for the Chukchi Sea [44]. A document of more than 630 pages—constituting just the first volume of this assessment—addressed the potential impacts to prehistoric and maritime archaeological resources from the various activities being proposed, but provided only slightly more than two pages of background information regarding these resources. Throughout the document, the individual proposed activities were briefly evaluated as to their potential impact on archaeological resources, but more often than not, the conclusion was that there could be adverse effects, and site-specific surveys and assessments would be conducted before these activities were initiated. If resources were discovered, avoidable impacts would be minimized or mitigated. When, in 2012, Shell proposed to move forward with drilling operations in the Chukchi, a subsequent assessment was conducted by BOEM [45] and reported that, for the proposed drilling site, "historical properties will be affected" and that "no new information that would modify or change this finding" had been submitted subsequent to the original review [45] (p. 74). That section of the document concluded, perhaps over-broadly, that "no sites have been identified by the Alaska OCS region for the East Chukchi Sea", notwithstanding the earlier mention in this section of the identification of a small number of historic shipwrecks that could be present in this offshore area of the Chukchi, based on the extensive shipwreck database compiled by BOEM and published online in 2011 [46]. Interestingly, Shell's submission of "Revision 2" of their exploration plan [45] contains a number of maps showing the proposed drill site that identify multiple magnetic anomalies, which do not seem to be further discussed in the text of that submission. Magnetometry is routinely conducted by maritime archaeologists to identify potential shipwreck sites or parts of sunken ships, and these anomalies identified on the maps could represent potential shipwreck sites, but no further mapping was pursued to confirm or reject this potential. While all of this documentation may represent accurate statements of what was known at the time the assessment was prepared, it appears to be based largely on presumption and little actual site-specific field survey effort. Based on the more than 40 years of experience by the author in evaluating such assessments, however, it represents the rigor of current practice. As King [47] (p. 253) has suggested, "there is plenty of room in most EIA laws for bad work to be done—for serious impacts to be missed, ignored, or buried, for decisions to be made that do not give full consideration to cultural values, for the public to be excluded".

Another example of this challenge also relates to the proposed oil and gas development in the Chukchi Sea. Shell Oil identified a potential route for a pipeline from this oil field [44], which would come ashore near Wainwright, Alaska, "between Icy Cape and Point Belcher" (p. IV-10). Coincidentally, there is considerable documentation of an event of great historical significance along this stretch of the Chukchi coastline were the pipeline was proposed to make landfall. As reported by Barr et al. [26], in September of 1871, 32 whaling ships were caught in the ice, and 1219 people were left stranded with little hope of rescue. While 31 of the 32 ships were lost, striking a blow to the Yankee whaling industry, all the officers, crew, and captains' families aboard these ships found their way to safety. This was a profoundly important event in the history of whaling, and recommends this area as a potentially significant element of the global whaling heritage landscape. In 2015, maritime archaeologists from the U.S. National Oceanic and Atmospheric Administration's Maritime Heritage Program went to this place to conduct systematic seabed surveys to determine if any wreckage still remained and could be located [26]. In the nearly two weeks of field operations, it was not until the last day of the survey that six pieces of wreckage were discovered. While none of the ships were found intact, sections of whaling ships were identified that included a number of artifacts typical of whaling ships of that period (Figure 1). This research demonstrated that targeted and systematic field surveys are required, guided by the available historical documentation of that maritime landscape, to locate sites of maritime heritage resources at what is presumed to be an historically significant site, even after 144 years of increasingly severe and frequent storms, as well as the extraordinary erosion and deposition of coastal sediments and annual disturbance by ice movement at the site. Historical documentation can clearly be sufficient, lacking more detailed archaeological data, to identify places where historically-significant maritime heritage resources are likely to be located.

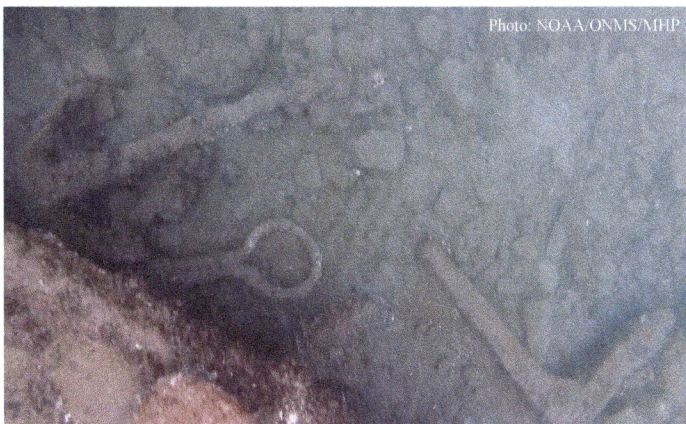

Figure 1. Artifacts from the whaling ship wreck site, off Wainwright, AK [26].

Therefore, as was done along the Chukchi Sea coast [26] for a significant event in the 19th Century history of Yankee whaling, other places might be identified and evaluated, based on the historical record, to begin to more effectively preserve significant maritime heritage landscapes in the Arctic. Clearly, no resource is evenly distributed throughout any area, but is concentrated in specific places for particular reasons. Just as many important species are distributed throughout an area because of their life history characteristics, seeking out habitat characteristics that are favorable to sustaining their population, historical resources, like shipwrecks, are distributed in specific places. Maritime cultural landscape elements "favor" specific locations, because, for example, they are traditional maritime transportation corridors. Ships that pass through such corridors are subject to frequent violent storms—or ice, in the Arctic—that often put these ships in peril. It is no coincidence that shipwrecks are concentrated in what are euphemistically called "graveyards". By understanding and identifying these landscape elements to find shipwrecks or important paleo-environments, the search for physical remains can be targeted more effectively.

3.2. Identification of Maritime Cultural Landscapes May Be Valuable but Not Sufficient

However necessary identifying important maritime cultural landscapes in the Arctic—and elsewhere—might be, this is not sufficient, in and of itself, to empower the preservation of these historically-significant places. Another critical element would be the broader adoption of precautionary approaches to the preservation of historical resources. Archaeological sites are extremely fragile and even what might appear to be minor disturbance or damage can destroy the integrity of the site and diminish what can be learned from careful study and documentation [48]. Understanding site formation processes helps to tell the story of what is there, how it came to be, and what we can learn from the site, not only about the artifacts present, but also the environmental forces and site conditions that created and modified what is observable today. Therefore, even a small and seemingly insignificant alteration of that site, such as tourist digging through a cairn looking for souvenirs or the wake of a passing ship disturbing a shallow shipwreck site, could have a profound impact on the historical and archaeological value of that site. Most of the statutes that protect maritime heritage resources recognize the need to avoid disturbing what has been discovered, but few actually state, a priori as a fundamental principle, that what has not been found but is likely to be present in that place deserves similar, or at least some *de minimus* protection. An analogous approach has been extensively used in managing natural resources. Habitat suitability analysis [49], conducted at the landscape level, is often applied to situations where incomplete spatial information is unavailable regarding the distribution and abundance of species and community types. If the preferred habitat characteristics of these resources are known, and if there is information on the geographical extent of places that possess these preferred physical, chemical, and biological characteristics, suitable habitat areas can be identified. While it may be uncertain whether those particular species or biological assemblages are present in a place, knowledge of the geographic extent of the suitable habitat for supporting that species or community can be used to protect that place from human alterations that might make it less suitable and thereby diminish its ecological value. In the case of historical resources, this analogous application of suitability analysis, where the historical information is used to identify significant maritime landscapes, could be thought of as defining and locating a "heritage habitat".

A number of authors [50–54] have suggested that, while potentially quite valuable as a resource management strategy, the "precautionary principle" is not particularly well defined. Its origin appears to be linked to controlling the discharges of contaminants into the environment [50,53]. In that context, it has been generally described as, where scientific uncertainty exists, actions that should be taken "in anticipation of environmental harm to ensure that this harm does not occur" [50] (p. 4), rather than waiting for the uncertainty to be resolved. This also shifts the burden of proof from the regulator to those proposing the project, that the action, whatever it might be, will not cause harm to the environment. In a world where development or other human activity involves sometimes substantial financial investment, often contingent on swiftly passing through the regulatory process, the precautionary principle presents challenges in its practical implementation.

Notwithstanding these challenges, applying the "a more flexible version" [53] (p. 578) of precaution to resource protection has been devised through adopting "precautionary approaches". Principle 15 of the UN's Rio Declaration on Environment and Development [55] offers something of a consensus definition for this "more flexible version" of precaution:

> In order to protect the environment, the precautionary approach shall be widely applied by States according to their capabilities. Where there are threats of serious or irreversible damage, lack of full scientific certainty shall not be used as a reason for postponing cost-effective measures to prevent environmental degradation.

Adopting precautionary approaches to the preservation of cultural heritage resources is not a particularly novel idea, either generally or for the Arctic. Hagen et al. [54], for example, discusses the implementation of precautionary approaches for protecting historical resources in Svalbard. However, such contemporary applications are not common. Most statutory protections afforded to cultural heritage resources, and the environment more generally, are intently focused on protecting identified and documented structures, artifacts, and other physical attributes of that place. Notwithstanding this potential limitation, especially as regards EIA laws and processes, "in theory" EIAs "require consideration of impacts on *all* aspects of the environment", including historical resources [47]. Therefore, a broader application of precautionary approaches to the preservation of maritime heritage resources is not necessarily an idea that should be rejected out of hand as too radical a notion. It may be a somewhat challenging to fully understand, as preventing harm is "a matter of causing the non-occurrence of an event" [56], but in the end, perhaps expanding the application of precautionary approaches to preserving cultural heritage will benefit from our thinking a bit more abstractly about the task at hand.

3.3. Proposed Approach Linking Maritime Cultural Landscapes and Precautionary Approach

Quite simply, what is being proposed here is to carefully and systematically read Arctic history, and from this extensive historical record, to identify the maritime cultural landscapes where significant things happened. Arctic states could then use existing administrative discretion, as stewards of these resources, to implement precautionary approaches for the preservation of these significant Arctic heritage landscape-scale "habitats". Perhaps it could begin with just a few particularly important and well-documented landscapes, such as the whaling landscape of the Western Arctic—from the Bering Strait to Hershel Island—or larger geographies like the Northwest Passage, as its storied history is both well-known and recognized as globally significant. The intent to apply a more precautionary approach to preservation might most effectively be embodied in national policy, permitting some greater flexibility in its implementation than the much more challenging task of attempting to modify laws and regulations. It would mean that those who want to propose development, or who wish to expand human activities that could have the potential to harm or diminish the Arctic's cultural legacy, would have to work a bit harder to ensure that the development or expanded use they are proposing will not result in harm to maritime heritage resources. Effective stewardship requires both transparency and predictability, and developing and implementing a national policy affecting these identified landscapes would satisfy these requirements.

3.4. Ongoing Initiatives into Which This Approach Might Be Integrated

There are a number of ongoing initiatives, the most promising and comprehensive under the leadership of the Arctic Council convened by the Protection of the Arctic Marine Environment (PAME), to establish additional marine protected areas (MPAs) in the Arctic [57]. While the outcome of the Arctic Council's efforts on Arctic MPA planning has not yet produced any progress in actually establishing any MPAs in this region, there seems to be some intent to ultimately move in this direction. In any case, MPAs represent another useful approach to adopting this strategy. MPAs provide place-based management and oversight of resources, and many programs include maritime heritage values within the scope of their protection. As new MPAs are being evaluated, and as existing sites' management plans are revised and adapted, maritime heritage landscapes, and the intent to preserve these landscapes through a precautionary approach, could be integrated as a management strategy, complementing ecological landscape approaches such as ecosystem-based management [29]. Implementing such a strategy within an MPA may be useful to help ensure that sufficient resources are provided to conduct an oversight of this implementation and an evaluation of its effectiveness. It might also assist, as national MPA systems are generally considered to be areas of significant resource value, in identifying these landscapes as priority areas for investment, attracting additional funding to conduct critical baseline systematic surveys of maritime heritage resources. As Hagen et al. [54] have observed with regard to the preservation of historical resources in Svalbard, it may be useful and appropriate to adopt a precautionary approach, but "a shift towards a more integrated and evidence-based management will contribute to more trusted and reliable, and thereby acceptable, decisions".

At the international level, another potential avenue for advancing this idea of identifying and preserving maritime heritage sites and landscapes in the Arctic is the identification of World Heritage Sites (WHS). As early as 1994 [32] (p. 8), the Arctic was singled out as a significant gap in the WHS System. The IUCN, in their more recent evaluation of the geographic representation of marine WHS [58], found that the Arctic has only one such site inscribed, representing less than 0.1% of the region. Currently, there are only two natural heritage sites inscribed, but no cultural heritage or "mixed" sites (i.e., recognizing both natural and cultural heritage values). As a program established to identify and help preserve places of "outstanding universal value", one might be intuitively justified in concluding that the Arctic is underrepresented. The IUCN [59] has evaluated the region to determine where "ecologically and biologically significant areas" (EBSA) are located and identified twelve areas that met or exceeded most or all of the EBSA criteria (areas they termed "Super EBSAs"). While the Super EBSAs identified were not evaluated for their heritage value, they include areas, like the coast of the Chukchi and Beaufort Seas, and areas of the Northwest Passage, that likely would encompass heritage areas of "outstanding universal value". Recently published findings of another UNESCO Expert Panel [60] identified only potential natural Arctic marine WHS, but such a process could serve as a model for similarly identifying Arctic cultural heritage sites of outstanding universal value. Finally, there are two mixed sites located above the Arctic Circle on the Canadian tentative list [61] and two cultural sites nominated for Greenland [62]. This may be an opportunity to begin to both fill the identified gap of Arctic site representation in the WHS List, and especially to expand the inscription of mixed and cultural heritage sites in this underrepresented region.

There may be a little more time before human use and resource exploitation expand into the places in the Arctic that contain both resources and qualities of economic value, and that are also part of the rich cultural legacy of this region. These are places that are no longer sufficiently protected by seasonal and multi-year sea ice and remoteness. However, there is little doubt that many more people will be coming to the Arctic, and development will occur as the economics become more favorable.

3.5. Need to Consider Bigger Picture of Expanding Human Uses

While the expansion of Arctic tourism may be happening more quickly than some of the other projected activities catalyzed by climate change, there is a need to consider response and adaptation in the larger context. The concern is one involving the consideration, cumulatively, of all human activities and infrastructure developments needed to support this expanded human use of the Arctic.

- As a non-renewable resource, oil and gas reserves will likely become more attractive for development when the price of oil begins to rise once again [63]. Clearly, there are a number of issues with regard to this activity, from the actual drilling and the attendant development of operational drilling sites, to the coastal infrastructure needed to move the product to market, house workers, and provide port facilities for vessels supporting the extraction operations.
- Commercially-important fish species are also headed North with warming Arctic seas. Visions for a coordinated fishery management system, and collaborative research, for the circumpolar Arctic states is still being debated [64]. Existing national efforts to preserve these stocks are under growing threat by fishing interests from around the world who want greater access, which will potentially contribute to both expanding human activity and the need for coastal facilities and infrastructure to support this industry.
- Maritime transportation, both vessels that transport cargo and increased traffic from other development activities (e.g., oil and gas exploration and development, commercial fishing vessels, cruise ships, for example) is also projected to greatly expand [38], but perhaps not as quickly as first thought. The Arctic is a challenging place to navigate. Ice, more frequent and intense storms than in the past, navigation charts that are sometimes based on hydrography from the 19th and early 20th centuries, vessels with limited capabilities to safely operate when unanticipated changes in ice conditions are encountered, and the relatively shallow waters of the narrow passages through the Arctic are all contributing to the threats to both natural and heritage resources and landscapes. Even private vessels are arriving in the Arctic in increasing numbers [65], adding to the challenges of the safe and effective management of navigation. Again, infrastructure to support expanded navigation will also be required. While the International Maritime Organization's adoption of the Polar Code in 2017 [66] is one step forward in addressing at least some of the most significant shipping safety concerns, how much it may contribute to providing protection from maritime transportation-related impacts to significant natural and historical resources in the Arctic remains to be demonstrated.

One other expanding human activity also results in some particular concern with regard to preserving both the natural and historical resources throughout the Arctic. From 2007, when the Russian Federation supported a scientific expedition [3] (p. 7) which included the planting of a Russian flag on the seabed near the North Pole—an act involving little if any real consequence but which spun-up a storm of controversy over issues of Arctic sovereignty [2]—there has been increasing activity in the Arctic related to an expanding military presence and operational capability. Beyond the potentially important geopolitical implications of this rapidly escalating activity, this expanded presence also contributes to the growing human footprint in the Arctic: more ships result in more coastal support facility development. Given that most of these military-related activities are not subject to many of the EIA requirements of the Arctic states, nor are many environmental and cultural resource preservation laws directly applicable, this element of expanding human activity and development represents a unique challenge.

As regards tourism, all indications are that cruise ship operations are expanding ahead of other potential human uses, and, as discussed above, many of these new passengers will want to visit interesting heritage sites, and operators will want to meet this expectation. One would suspect that tourism operators would be seeking new and different historical resource venues to explore, to better service returning passengers, and to optimize the passenger experience generally, which may add new sites and new challenges, but also might result in some "citizen science" contributions to the identification of potentially undiscovered sites. More guidance and oversight of this activity will be required so that this expanded visitation will not harm or diminish the heritage value of these sites. For example, many of the expedition cruise ships are now deploying remotely operated vehicles (ROV) [14], and will be operating very close to the historic shipwrecks that they are exploring with their passengers. Some sort of oversight and guidance (e.g., training requirements for operators, minimum approach distances for ROV to the wreck) will be required to help ensure that the potential for damage to the wreck is minimized. As most of these exploration cruise ships also carry and deploy zodiacs to land passengers on shore for exploring coastal sites, guidance and oversight will also be required here. Tour guides will need to be trained to identify and control passenger behaviors (such as collecting "souvenirs", particularly, but also perhaps simply treading carefully while ashore, as sites can be fragile and may lose archaeological integrity from even minor, unintentional, disturbance) that might result in some impact to the historic resources that are encountered ashore. Land-based tourism will also likely require similar oversight and guidance. Needed infrastructure development, supporting both land and cruise-based tourism, will require careful and informed assessment and planning to avoid the destruction of places where historical resources are likely to be present. While the fundamental goal of preserving maritime heritage resources is for their intrinsic value and the knowledge they can provide, as a practical matter, if the significant heritage sites are degraded, one would expect that the attractiveness of the Arctic as a tourism venue would also likely diminish.

3.6. Additional Recommendations for Targeted Collaboration

There are many key players with a stake in this enterprise of Arctic heritage preservation. Tourism operators, tourism organizations established to offer advice and often "best practices" guidance, the governmental agencies that oversee place-based management and preservation of protected areas, the local residents who have much to gain and lose with this expanded visitation and human use, archaeologists and historians who study the Arctic, and the visitors themselves. Greater collaboration and communication among and within these stakeholder groups is essential to find a workable and effective solution to help ensure that these resources will be preserved.

3.6.1. Development of a Research Coordination Network (RCN)

As regards the essential research needed to guide and inform this effort, it might fruitful to develop some sort of RCN potentially funded by the US National Science Foundation [67]. Such a network, focused on better coordinating and prioritizing archaeological and historical research in the Arctic for the purpose of supporting and informing the preservation and management of historical resources, would not only provide opportunities for raising the profile of Arctic maritime heritage resource preservation, identifying and developing new collaborations and joint research initiatives, but would also help the scientific community to move, in collaboration with one of the primary funding agencies for this work, toward some consensus on research priorities. This group could also provide expertise in the development of guidance for addressing tourist visitation, as described above, and more generally, the larger challenges related to many of the other expanding human uses. Other organizations, such as the UNESCO International Polar Heritage Committee (IHPC) [68], might be enlisted to lend support, expertise, and experience in this effort.

3.6.2. Expanding National and International Governmental Collaboration on Heritage Protected Areas

The Arctic Council, and the individual Arctic states, have begun processes for the identification of a circumpolar network of marine protected areas [57], which might be encouraged to better integrate place-based historical resource preservation into this initiative. They have already accomplished some related work in the PAME Annex IIc identification of "areas of heightened cultural significance" [38]. Again, international organizations such as UNESCO's IPHC [68] and World Heritage Program [32] could also add much to such a collaboration. However, where the larger potential challenge exists here is establishing and fostering collaboration among the protected area programs of the Arctic states. These programs are critically important as it is under their statutory authorities that any marine protected areas will be established. While the Arctic Council's efforts may potentially be the convening organization for such a collaboration, through their Arctic MPA planning [57], there has not been much apparent progress toward the implementation of this plan as of yet. Support and encouragement by the RCN, discussed in the previous section, might help to speed things along in this regard.

3.6.3. Enhanced Coordination with and Among Tourism Operators, Tourism Organizations, and Local Affected Communities

Clearly, the engagement of these stakeholders would be an essential element of any of the aforementioned collaborations. Tourism operators and their representative organizations possess invaluable on-the-ground expertise in the conduct of Arctic tourism, and it is these operators who will be conducting and overseeing future tourism activities in this region. While local communities and residents are already engaged with the relevant governments, industry, and many scientists conducting relevant research (for example [7,20]), their vision of the future state of the North should be respected and honored.

3.6.4. Visitor Engagement

Expanded visitation to the Arctic is, after all, what is driving this need to address historical resources and place-based preservation. The expectations of visitors, and their experiences in the North, is an active topic of interest to tourism researchers, as demonstrated at the recent International Polar Tourism Research Conference. These studies are critically important in understanding the role and impact of tourism in the Arctic, and collaborations like the RCN could expand and support these valuable research efforts. The other potential role for visitors may be one of "eyes and ears". While the ice may be receding in the Arctic, it remains very remote, and an oversight of what transpires there is a challenging and costly task. With the wider use of social media communication mechanisms, such as Twitter and Facebook, and informed about the guidance with which the tour operators are expected to comply, visitor feedback could be invaluable in determining compliance with this guidance. Such a strategy has been attempted with regard to the whale watching industry in the Northeast United States [69] in a place that is far less remote, but heavily visited.

4. Conclusions

There is little doubt that the Arctic is changing rapidly, creating what is now being characterized as a "new ocean" [70]. While some expanded human uses and resource exploitation activities may occur further in the future than originally projected, Arctic tourism seems to be an exception, and deserves some immediate consideration as to how it will be effectively managed so that the historical resources threatened by this expanded visitation can be preserved for future generations. How the international community of Arctic interests addresses the larger questions of management and preservation of this "new ocean" is a work in progress, involving quintessential examples of "wicked problems" [71] which are identified as difficult to resolve because of incomplete, contradictory, and changing requirements that are often difficult to recognize. Precautionary approaches to resource protection and management may be the most likely effective tool available when confronting such great, and "wicked", uncertainty. In the absence of site-specific resource information, taking a step back and considering the landscape in which those resources are likely to be present is also a strategy for addressing uncertainty, at least until more detailed, place-based resource information can be assembled and analyzed. Additionally, landscape approaches also offer a larger environmental context for resource protection and management, recognizing that place-based natural and historical resources are formed over time, and are likely present because of external influences that may be both natural and the result of human activity. Given the magnitude and complexity, as well as the growing imminence of threats identified, this notion, therefore, of adopting landscape-level, precautionary approaches for preserving the heritage and cultural resources of the Arctic—even as a first step—seems like something worth trying. Certainly, one might argue, it would be preferable to wait for these valued historical resources to be harmed or lost before any action is taken. As Bodansky [50] (p. 4) reminds us, "an ounce of prevention is worth a pound of cure".

Acknowledgments: Many thanks to the organizers of the International Polar Tourism Research Network Conference, where a presentation was made by the author which spawned the idea for this paper. I am deeply grateful to Hans Van Tilburg for his always insightful comments on the draft, and the very helpful comments of two anonymous reviewers. The University Center of the Westfjords provided partial travel support for the author's participation in this conference.

Conflicts of Interest: The author declares no conflict of interest. The founding sponsors had no role in the design of the study; in the collection, analyses, or interpretation of data; in the writing of the manuscript, and in the decision to publish the results.

References

1. Bloom, L. *Gender on the Ice*; University of Minnesota Press: Minneapolis, MN, USA, 1993.
2. Dodds, K. Flag planting and finger pointing: The law of the sea, the Arctic and the political geographies of the outer continental shelf. *Polit. Geogr.* **2010**, *29*, 63–73. [CrossRef]
3. Dittmer, J.; Moisio, S.; Ingram, A.; Dodds, K. Have you heard the one about the disappearing ice? Recasting Arctic geopolitics. *Polit. Geogr.* **2011**, *30*, 202–214. [CrossRef]
4. Arctic Sea Ice Maximum at Record Low for Third Straight Year, National Snow and Ice Data Center. 22 March 2017. Available online: http://nsidc.org/arcticseaicenews/ (accessed on 1 April 2017).
5. Coltrain, D.B.; Tackney, J.; O'Rourke, D.H. Thule whaling at Point Barrow, Alaska: The Nuvuk cemetery stable isotope and radiocarbon record. *J. Archaeol. Sci. Rep.* **2016**, *9*, 681–694. [CrossRef]
6. Historical Resources. California State University. Available online: http://www.csus.edu/hist/centers/ncic/resources.html (accessed on 1 April 2017).
7. Stewart, E.J.; Dawson, J.; Howell, S.E.L.; Johnston, M.E.; Pearce, T.; Lemelin, H. Local-level responses to sea ice changes and cruise tourism in Arctic Canada's Northwest Passage. *Polar Geogr.* **2013**, *36*, 142–162. [CrossRef]
8. Stewart, E.J.; Draper, D.; Dawson, J. Monitoring Patterns of Cruise Tourism across Arctic Canada. In *Cruise Tourism in Polar Regions: Promoting Environmental and Social Sustainability?* Lück, M., Maher, P.T., Stewart, E.J., Eds.; Earthscan: London, UK, 2010; pp. 133–146.

9. Hall, C.M.; Saarinen, J. Tourism and change in the polar regions: Introduction—Definitions, locations, places and dimensions. In *Tourism and Change in Polar Regions: Climate, Environments and Experiences*; Hall, C.M., Saarinen, J., Eds.; Routledge: London, UK, 2010; pp. 1–41.
10. Stonehouse, B.; Snyder, J.M. *Polar Tourism: An Environmental Perspective*; Channel View Publications: North York, ON, Canada, 2010.
11. Kiel, K. More and more Arctic Tourists—but where exactly? *High North News*, 16 February 2017. Available online: http://www.highnorthnews.com/more-and-more-arctic-tourists-but-where-exactly/ (accessed on 31 March 2017).
12. Russia Urged to Boost Polar Cruises. *Maritime Executive*, 9 February 2016. Available online: http://www.maritime-executive.com/article/russia-urged-to-boost-polar-cruises (accessed on 1 April 2017).
13. Royal Caribbean, Hapag-Lloyd Join Cruise Spending Spree. *Maritime Executive*, 10 October 2016. Available online: http://www.maritime-executive.com/article/royal-caribbean-hapag-lloyd-join-cruise-spending-spree (accessed on 1 April 2017).
14. Seeing Double: Two Polar Megayachts in 2018. *Maritime Executive*, 16 March 2016. Available online: http://www.maritime-executive.com/editorials/seeing-double-two-polar-megayacht-in-2018 (accessed on 1 April 2017).
15. Oceanwide Expeditions Orders New Polar Vessel. *Maritime Executive*, 30 November 2016. Available online: http://www.maritime-executive.com/article/oceanwide-expeditions-orders-new-polar-vessel (accessed on 1 April 2017).
16. Crystal Serenity: Mission Accomplished. *Maritime Executive*, 16 September 2016. Available online: http://www.maritime-executive.com/article/crystal-serenity-mission-accomplished (accessed on 1 April 2017).
17. Arctic Cruise Ship First for France. *Maritime Executive*, 21 September 2015. Available online: http://www.maritime-executive.com/article/arctic-cruise-ship-first-for-france (accessed on 1 April 2017).
18. River Cruise Company to Enter Polar Waters. *Maritime Executive*, 18 January 2016. Available online: http://www.maritime-executive.com/article/river-cruise-company-to-enter-polar-waters (accessed on 1 April 2017).
19. All-terrain "Cruise Ship" for the Arctic. *Maritime Executive*, 21 February 2017. Available online: http://www.maritime-executive.com/features/all-terrain-cruise-ship-for-the-arctic (accessed on 1 April 2017).
20. Bystrowska, M.; Dolnicki, P. The impact of endogenous factors on diversification of tourism space in the Arctic. *Curr. Issues Tour. Res.* **2017**, *5*, 36–43.
21. Lemelin, R.H.; Johnston, M.E. Arctic tourism. In *The Encyclopedia of Tourism and Recreation in Marine Environments*; Lück, M., Ed.; CABI: Wallingford, UK, 2008; pp. 32–33.
22. Johnston, M.; Vikrin, A.; Dawson, J. Firsts and lasts in Arctic tourism: Last chance tourism and the dialectic of change. In *Last Chance Tourism: Adapting Tourism Opportunities in a Changing World*; Lemelin, R.H., Dawson, J., Stewart, E.J., Eds.; Routledge: London, UK, 2012; pp. 10–24.
23. Lemelin, H.; Dawson, J.; Stewart, E.J.; Maher, P.; Lueck, M. Last-chance tourism: The boom, doom, and gloom of visiting vanishing destinations. *Curr. Issues Tour.* **2010**, *13*, 477–493. [CrossRef]
24. Murphy, P.; Thackray, D.; Wilson, E. Coastal Heritage and Climate Change in England: Assessing Threats and Priorities. *Conserv. Manag. Archaeol. Sites* **2009**, *11*, 9–15. [CrossRef]
25. Kintisch, E. Arctic shipworm discovery alarms archaeologists. *Science* **2016**, *351*, 901. [CrossRef] [PubMed]
26. Barr, B.W.; Delgado, J.P.; Lawrence, M.S.; Van Tilburg, H.K. The Search for the 1871 Whaling Fleet of the Western Arctic: Writing the final chapter. *Int. J. Naut. Archaeol.* **2017**, *46*, 149–163. [CrossRef]
27. Blankholm, H.P. Long-term research and cultural resource management strategies in light of climate change and human impact. *Arctic Anthropol.* **2009**, *46*, 17–24. [CrossRef]
28. Arctic Council: About Us. Available online: http://www.arctic-council.org/index.php/en/about-us (accessed on 1 April 2017).
29. Barr, B.W. Understanding and managing marine protected areas through integrating ecosystem based management within maritime cultural landscapes: Moving from theory to practice. *Ocean Coast. Manag.* **2013**, *84*, 184–192. [CrossRef]
30. Conservation of Arctic Flora and Fauna (CAFF). *Values of Protected Areas: A Summary*; Parks Canada on behalf of the Conservation of Arctic Flora and Fauna Program: Ottawa, ON, Canada, 2004. Available online: https://oaarchive.arctic-council.org/bitstream/handle/11374/174/Values_Protected_Areas_Summary_2002.pdf?sequence=1 (accessed on 1 April 2017).

31. Rey, L. The Arctic: Mankind's Unique Heritage and Common Responsibility. *Arctic Alpine Res.* **1987**, *19*, 345–350. [CrossRef]
32. United Nations Educational, Scientific and Cultural Organization (UNESCO). World Heritage and the Arctic: International Expert Meeting, 30 November to 1 December 2007, Narvik, Norway. Available online: http://whc.unesco.org/en/arctic (accessed on 22 February 2017).
33. Turner, F.J. *The Frontier in American History*; Henry Holt and Company: New York, NY, USA, 1921.
34. Eccles, W.J. *The Canadian Frontier, 1534–1760*; Revised Edition; University of New Mexico Press: Albuquerque, NM, USA, 1983.
35. Raghavan, M.; DeGiorgio, M.; Albrechtsen, A.; Moltke, I.; Skoglund, P.; Korneliussen, T.S.; Grønnow, B.; Appelt, M.; Gulløv, H.C.; Friesen, T.M.; et al. The genetic prehistory of the New World Arctic. *Science* **2014**, *345*. [CrossRef] [PubMed]
36. Bockstoce, J.R. *Furs and Frontiers in the Far North*; Yale University Press: New Haven, CT, USA, 2009.
37. Barr, B.W. Influencing the contemporary narrative on whaling heritage. In Proceedings of the 2nd Asia Pacific Underwater Cultural Heritage Conference, Honolulu, HI, USA, 12–16 May 2014.
38. AMAP/CAFF/SDWG. Identification of Arctic Marine Areas of Heightened Ecological and Cultural Significance, Arctic Marine Shipping Assessment (AMSA) II-c, Arctic Monitoring and Assessment Programme (AMAP), Oslo, Norway, 2013. Available online: http://www.amap.no/documents/doc/identification-of-arctic-marine-areas-of-%20heightened-ecological-and-cultural-significance-arctic-marine-shipping-assessment-amsa-iic/869 (accessed on 1 April 2017).
39. Barr, W. Discovery of one of Sir John Franklin's ships. *Polar Record* **2015**, *51*, 107–108. [CrossRef]
40. Watson, P. Ship found in Arctic 168 Years after Doomed Northwest Passage Attempt. *The Guardian*, 12 September 2016. Available online: https://www.theguardian.com/world/2016/sep/12/hms-terror-wreck-found-arctic-nearly-170-years-northwest-passage-attempt (accessed on 22 February 2017).
41. Bureau of Ocean Energy Management. *Alaska Annual Studies Plan*; Alaska Outer Continental Shelf Region: Anchorage, AK, USA, 2014. Available online: https://www.boem.gov/uploadedFiles/BOEM/About_BOEM/BOEM_Regions/Alaska_Region/Environment/Environmental_Studies/2014AlaskaStudiesPlan.pdf (accessed on 22 February 2017).
42. Gibson, R.B. In full retreat: The Canadian government's new environmental assessment law undoes decades of progress. *Impact Assess. Project Apprais.* **2012**, *30*, 179–188. [CrossRef]
43. Van Tilburg, H.K. (NOAA Maritime Heritage Program, Honolulu, HI, USA). Personal communication, 2017.
44. U.S. Minerals Management Service. *Chukchi Sea Planning Area Oil and Gas Lease Sale 193 and Seismic-Surveying Activities in the Chukchi Sea, Final Environmental Impact Statement, Volume 1*; MMS 2007–026; U.S. Department of the Interior, Minerals Management Service Alaska Outer Continental Shelf Region: Anchorage, AK, USA, May 2007.
45. Bureau of Ocean Energy Management. *Shell Gulf of Mexico, Inc., Revised Outer Continental Shelf Lease Exploration Plan Chukchi Sea, Alaska, Burger Prospect: Posey Area Blocks 6714, 6762, 6764, 6812, 6912, 6915 Revision 2*; BOEM 2015–20; Alaska Outer Continental Shelf Region: Anchorage, AK, USA, March 2015.
46. Bureau of Ocean Energy Management. 2011 Alaska Shipwreck Database. Available online: https://www.boem.gov/uploadedFiles/BOEM/About_BOEM/BOEM_Regions/Alaska_Region/Ships/2011_Shipwreck.pdf (accessed on 22 February 2017).
47. King, T.F. Cultural heritage preservation and the legal system with specific reference to landscapes. In *Landscapes under Pressure: Theory and Practice of Cultural Heritage Research and Preservation*; Lozny, L.R., Ed.; Springer Science + Business Media: New York, NY, USA, 2008; pp. 243–254.
48. Hutchinson, G. Threats to underwater cultural heritage: The problems of unprotected archaeological and historical sites, wrecks, and objects found at sea. *Mar. Policy* **1996**, *20*, 287–290. [CrossRef]
49. Riitters, K.H.; O'Neill, R.V.; Jones, K.B. Assessing habitat suitability at multiple scales: A landscape level approach. *Biol. Conserv.* **1997**, *81*, 191–202. [CrossRef]
50. Bodansky, D. Scientific uncertainty and the Precautionary Principle. *Environment* **1991**, *33*, 4–5, 43–44. [CrossRef]
51. Sandin, P. Dimensions of the precautionary principle. *Hum. Ecol. Risk Assess.* **1999**, *5*, 889–907. [CrossRef]
52. Sandin, P. The precautionary principle and the concept of precaution. *Environ. Values* **2004**, *13*, 461–475. [CrossRef]

53. Rosenberg, A.A. The precautionary approach in application from a manager's perspective. *Bull. Mar. Sci.* **2002**, *70*, 577–588.
54. Hagen, D.; Vistad, O.I.; Eide, N.E.; Flyen, A.C.; Fangel, K. Managing visitor sites in Svalbard: From a precautionary approach towards knowledge-based management. *Polar Res.* **2012**, *31*. [CrossRef]
55. United Nations, Rio Declaration on Environment and Development. Available online: http://www.unep.org/documents.multilingual/default.asp?documentid=78&articleid=1163 (accessed on 22 February 2017).
56. Collins, J. Preemptive Prevention. *J. Philos.* **2000**, *97*, 223–234. [CrossRef]
57. Arctic Council. *Framework for a Pan-Arctic Network of Marine Protected Areas: A Network of Places and Natural Features Specially-Managed for the Conservation and Protection of the Arctic Marine Environment*; Protection of the Arctic Marine Environment Committee: Akureyri, Iceland, 2015. Available online: http://www.pame.is/images/03_Projects/MPA/MPA_Report.pdf (accessed on 17 February 2017).
58. Abdulla, A.; Obura, D.; Bertzky, B.; Shi, Y. *Marine Natural Heritage and the World Heritage List: Interpretation of World Heritage Criteria in Marine Systems, Analysis of Biogeographic Representation of Sites, and a Roadmap for Addressing Gaps*; International Union for Conservation of Nature (IUCN): Gland, Switzerland, 2013.
59. Speer, L.; Laughlin, T.L. IUCN/NRDC Workshop to Identify Areas of Ecological and Biological Significance or Vulnerability in the Arctic Marine Environment, Workshop Report. Presented at IUCN/NRDC Workshop, La Jolla, CA, USA, 2–4 November, 2010. Available online: https://portals.iucn.org/library/efiles/documents/Rep-2011--001.pdf (accessed on 22 February 2017).
60. Speer, L.; Nelson, R.; Casier, R.; Gavrilo, M.; von Quillfeldt, C.; Cleary, J.; Halpin, P.; Hooper, P. *Natural Marine World Heritage in the Arctic Ocean, Report of an Expert Workshop and Review Process*; International Union for Conservation of Nature (IUCN): Gland, Switzerland, 2017.
61. World Heritage Site Tentative List—Canada. Available online: http://whc.unesco.org/en/tentativelists/state=ca (accessed on 15 February 2017).
62. World Heritage Site Tentative List—Denmark. Available online: http://whc.unesco.org/en/tentativelists/state=dk (accessed on 17 February 2017).
63. Arctic Oil and Gas, 2013, Ernst and Young. Available online: http://ey.com/oilandgas (accessed on 5 November 2013).
64. Sevunts, L. Experts call for collaboration on Arctic fisheries research. *Alaska Dispatch News*, 27 April 2016. Available online: https://www.adn.com/arctic/article/experts-call-collaboration-arctic-fisheries-research/2016/04/27 (accessed on 1 April 2017).
65. Johnston, M.; Dawson, J.; de Souza, E.; Stewart, E.J. Management challenges for the fastest growing marine shipping sector in Arctic Canada: Pleasure crafts. *Polar Rec.* **2017**, *53*, 67–78. [CrossRef]
66. International Maritime Organization. Shipping in Polar Waters: Adoption of an International Code of Safety for Ships Operating in Polar Waters (Polar Code). Available online: http://www.imo.org/en/mediacentre/hottopics/polar/pages/default.aspx (accessed on 17 February 2017).
67. Research Coordination Networks, National Science Foundation. Available online: https://www.nsf.gov/funding/pgm_summ.jsp?pims_id=11691 (accessed on 1 April 2017).
68. UNESCO International Polar Heritage Committee, Welcome to the IPHC. Available online: http://www.polarheritage.com/index.cfm (accessed on 1 April 2017).
69. Whale Watching Guidelines—Northeast Region including Stellwagen Bank. Available online: http://stellwagen.noaa.gov/visit/whalewatching/guidelines.html (accessed on 1 April 2017).
70. Center for Strategic and International Studies. Meeting Announcement. Understanding a New Ocean: The Policy Implications of a Transforming Arctic, September 2016. Available online: https://www.csis.org/events/understanding-new-ocean-policy-implications-transforming-arctic (accessed on 17 February 2017).
71. Skaburskis, A. The origin of "wicked problems". *Plan. Theory Pract.* **2008**, *9*, 277–280. [CrossRef]

resources

MDPI

Article

Evaluating the Role of CSR and SLO in Ecotourism: Collaboration for Economic and Environmental Sustainability of Arctic Resources

Nate Bickford *, Lindsey Smith, Sonja Bickford, Matthew R. Bice and Dustin H. Ranglack

Department of Biology, University of Nebraska Kearney, 1204 11th Ave, Kearney, NE 68845, USA;
Smithll2@lopers.unk.edu (L.S.); Bickfordsh@unk.edu (S.B.); Bicemr@unk.edu (M.R.B.);
Ranglackdh@unk.edu (D.H.R.)
* Correspondence: Bickfordna@unk.edu; Tel.: +1-308-865-8410

Academic Editors: Edward Huijbens and Machiel Lamers
Received: 1 May 2017; Accepted: 31 May 2017; Published: 12 June 2017

Abstract: Major biophysical, economic, and political changes in the Arctic regions during the past two decades has grown business opportunities in the Arctic countries, such as tourism. More specifically, with a focus on sustainability of resources, the industry of ecotourism has emerged and become the fastest growing area within tourism. Ecotourism is a travel experience that embraces environmental conservation and the sustainability of local resources and culture. Ecotourism and related businesses must practice ethical behavior to obtain both government and social permission to conduct and carry out their operations. Government and community acceptance, or gaining a social license to operate (SLO) is key. Being accepted as a part of the community is not a formal agreement or document, but ongoing negotiations, practices, and acts of corporate social responsibility (CSR). For example, in many Arctic regions where tourism occurs, the land and resources have other designated uses such as agriculture, forestry, or fisheries. Added infrastructure grows a smaller community, as revenue generating opportunities bring an influx of people and use the resources and infrastructure, as well as have an impact on the local culture and traditions. Sustaining the local and traditional resources and lands, especially in the Arctic where damage can be unrepairable, becomes a key factor in decisions regarding tourism developments. Thus, the need for responsible businesses with a sustainability focus. The need for practices of CSR and SLO in ecotourism is undeniable. Understanding that businesses hold responsibility and play a role in society, the environment, and the life of the locals is very important.

Keywords: ecotourism; Arctic; corporate social responsibility (CSR); social license to operate (SLO); sustainability

---

1. Introduction

The ecotourism business sector within the tourism industry has grown since mid-1990s. Driving factors include the need for sustainability of a regions natural resources and lifestyles, while capitalizing on the resources present to generate income for the local and/or national community. Three common concepts and criteria for eco-tourism are that the activities and core operations of the business is nature-focused, educational, and sustainable (both economic and social) [1].

The Arctic today differs from the Arctic from 20 years ago and it will continue to change [2]. The major changes in the Arctic region during the past two decades are biophysical, economic, and political. As sea ice thins and disappears, more resources become available and accessible. Alongside that, the economic and political interests in those resources increase. Arctic and nearby remote areas are attracting more attention than ever before, through publicity and through development opportunities because of their abundance of physical natural resources, as well their wilderness environments which have become a major attraction for tourists [3]. The interest from the rest of the world to see and experience the uniqueness of the Arctic is very high. Countries in northern Scandinavia draw people to the area because of the natural environment and tourism was already the most important economic sector since 2009 [4]. Iceland has successfully increased tourism for the northern lights and Arctic experiences during the past decade. The environment, or nature and the natural resources used by the local population and community, is often highly integrated with local traditions and ways of life [4]. For example, in many Arctic regions where tourism occurs it is also used for other purposes such as agriculture, forestry, or fisheries. This leads to the integration of the community with income opportunities, not only in added infrastructure for lodging, restaurants, or shops, but also impacts on nature and the local and traditional ways of life. Sustaining the resources and lands, especially in the Arctic where damage can be unrepairable, becomes a key factor as decisions regarding tourism developments are made.

Corporate social responsibility (CSR) can be defined numerous ways due to its multidisciplinary nature. The underlying principle of CSR, whether for private or public sector, is that the organization in question needs to behave in a socially responsible manner [5]. CSR can thus be thought of as the commitment and actions of an entity to produce a positive impact on society and the environment. This positive image is referred to as a social license to operate (SLO). Corporations will commit to behave ethically, not only to sustain, but to improve the lives that the businesses influence by contributing to economic development [6]. This is very important for business because companies who practice CSR are more successful [7]. CSR and success for business can be measured in many ways, and will range from company to company. A few examples of this success can include financial success, environmental protection, or branding. The actions of the organizations can be categorized as CSR, while the obtaining of a positive image from the stakeholders and the local community is the SLO.

Full legal compliance with state or national regulations have become an increasingly insufficient means of satisfying the community's or society's expectations in regards to industries hosted in local communities [8,9]. Gaining a SLO has been prevalent in the mining industry, but has more recently filtered into other industries where impacts to the local community are present. The SLO is the approval by communities of business operations and emerged in response to the social risk of mining operations in the mid-1990s [10]. It is said to exist when a development project is seen as having broad, ongoing approval and acceptance of society to conduct its activities [9,11,12]. Companies must develop and maintain a quality reputation in order to sustain and grow their business within the local communities. SLO can be a driving factor for how corporations communicate and commit to prioritizing relationships with their stakeholders and local communities. Businesses must practice ethical behavior to obtain both government and social permission to conduct and carry out their business [12]. Government approval comes from the interactions with the public decision makers, such as the local government or agencies involved in the process of deciding on an environmental impact statement for example. However, it must be noted that the community acceptance of the business is not a formal agreement or document, but ongoing negotiation, practices, and acts of CSR with the host community. In many cases, development requires land and land use approval through government approval processes. Land within a municipality can have many uses, such as residential, commercial, agricultural, or community/public lands. Land is important for development, but also for access in a pristine nature. Modern tourism trends emphasize the value of untouched nature [13]. This is where ecotourism has emerged as a balance between revenue generation and the conservation of traditional resources and values.

Ecotourism is a market that has become increasingly popular and is the fastest growing area of tourism [14]. Ecotourism is a combination of two words: 'eco' and 'tourism' [15]. Ecotourism is a travel experience that embraces environmental conservation as well as the sustainment of locals and culture. The concept of ecotourism involves the protection of ecological resources and values, with an emphasis on conservation and the cultural values of the local community [16]. Ecotourism attracts tourists to unique and natural environments where they are introduced to local cultures, traditions, and resources or lands. This promotes a changing of attitudes towards diversity and impressions. Another factor is sustaining the natural setting and the idea of ecotourism improving conservation through education [17]. The rapid growth of ecotourism can be explained due to the appeal of having a satisfying travel experience without disrupting the natural setting. Self-identified ecotourists in West Virginia were found to be more environmentally concerned and responsible, more dedicated to nature, more supportive of tourism accreditation programs, and more likely to patronize businesses with good environmental practices, even at a higher cost [18]. Due to the measures taken for sustainability, ecotourists spend more money than tourists who are not concerned with ecology or conservation efforts. This is an important aspect for the Polar Regions, which can often be expensive locations to get to and are also sensitive to disturbance.

Ecotourism can impact communities in numerous ways, both positively and negatively. Economically, ecotourism can boost economy and supply locals with more job opportunities, especially in developing countries or rural areas. However, attractions, infrastructure, and capital must continue to evolve as tourism grows, or the tourism business will fluctuate. On the negative aspect, this fluctuation serves as an unstable source of income and can severely disrupt the locals and the economy. However, the need for constant changes as well as access for tourist communities deprives locals of access to natural resources, such as hunting and fishing. This can have detrimental effects on the local community and culture, either driving them further away from economic opportunities and modern society, or losing their sense of culture and cultural diversity by entering globalized labor [17].

One of the many reasons people travel internationally is to experience the diversity of different cultures. Ecotourism plays a role in cultural education through sustainable tourism. This way, the culture and locals are not disturbed, while still providing a stage for the public to become more aware and knowledgeable of different cultures and customs. However, without clear guidelines and ethical practices, these cultures can become disrupted and evolve in response to globalization and modernization [19]. Here, we review and summarize key findings from the ecotourism literature, with a focus on CSR and SLO. In the discussion, examples from regions that have a history of ecotourism and CSR practices are noted and discussed, followed by recommendations and best practice examples of CSR and the importance of the attainment of a SLO in the tourism industry.

2. Methodology

For this evaluation of literature in the ecotourism field the ecotourism, publications were reviewed with a special focus on the collection of examples in ecotourism practices of CSR and the attainment or impact of an SLO. This was done with the search terms in Google Scholar and the University Library's journal databases (EBSCO, Gale, LexisNexis, OCLC, Oxford, and/or ProQuest) using the search terms of 'Ecotourism' + 'corporate social responsibility' or 'CSR' and 'Ecotourism' + 'social license to operate' or 'SLO'. In addition, the word 'Arctic' and/or 'Polar' was added to the journal searches. The subject literature was read and analyzed for examples of CSR and SLO. As part of this the authors worked to identify the practices of CSR and attainment of SLO for the Arctic regions. Due to the fact that ecotourism has prevailed as a branch of tourism in the past few decades, we focused our literature review for publications in journals between 1990 and 2017.

3. Key Findings

The key observations and findings from this work is that there is currently no aggregate or collective information on best CSR practices or the attainment of a SLO by tourist operators. More specifically, information is lacking for ecotourism in the Polar Regions, which have a fragile ecology and environment where changes or disturbances can take a very long recovery time. In general, the large positive impacts of tourism for visitors is education and for the locals an increased income and service infrastructure potential. However, the influx of people, infrastructure, etc., can negatively impact on the environment and the culture and livelihoods of the local people. The Arctic environment is more fragile than that of some other regions where disturbance recovery times are faster. Thus, CSR and the relationship building nature of the SLO are key in sustaining the local environment and culture, as well as the tourism industry. There are a few inferences made to both CSR and SLO with regards to tourism [20]. There are, however, many examples of SLO and CSR best practices from energy and mining companies, but relevant CSR and SLO practices for the ecotourism industry are needed. As a result of the literature review, we identified a need for additional work in the area and examples of CSR practices and the reasoning for the attainment and maintenance of a SLO in the ecotourism sector, especially in Artic regions. Examples from areas such as the Caribbean and Spain, which both have a long history of tourism and showcase impacts of tourism on the environment and people, can help us identify relevant and applicable best practices, as well as potential problem areas, for the ecotourism industry of the Polar Region. In addition, this study will also help identify future research areas and topics that will have an impact on the sustainability of the ecotourism industry in the Arctic.

4. Discussion

Ecotourism has influenced the social aspect of communities and countries. Ecotourism is an attractive market because the customer gets more than just a travel endeavor, they get a meaningful experience and a lifetime of memories. To have a successful market in tourism, a country must have a draw that pulls consumers in from all over the world [17]. These attractions include suitable climate, pleasant environment, diverse arts and culture, sufficient security, and low prices, all of which ultimately determine the success of the country's tourism market. In addition, the uniqueness of the country or resources, such as wildlife or nature, can be marketed as sights worth traveling to see and experience. For example, the tourism in Iceland doubled between 2000 and 2012 and it has continued to grow ever since [21]. Iceland has managed to increase their tourism in the past decade by marketing not only its location, but also the resources, such as northern lights, wildlife, and natural wonders. Although tourism is a service, it is necessary to have the infrastructure to support the influx of people. Infrastructure critical to tourism are accommodations in physical capital such as airports, hotels, transportation routes, restaurants, retail, and leisure activities for all social groups. These capitals all generate a substantial amount of revenue in an ideal touristic location and have long lives, but they cannot be changed so easily. Evolving from low tourism numbers to high tourism numbers takes time, and cannot be rushed, or adjustment to the local people and economy can be traumatic [19]. To better understand how CSR and SLO impact the tourism industry and community as collaborative and related business operations work together toward a common goal of sustainable business growth, we look at examples from the Arctic and beyond of how the attainment and maintaining of a SLO and various CSR practices can impact the ecotourism industry.

4.1. Spain & the Caribbean—Without CSR and SLO Practices

Many hot spots in the tourism industry have faced declines due to the market not keeping their responsibility or standards to the community and environment at a high enough level. Spain is a key example of a steady decline in the tourism market with a lack of a SLO. Spain has several important features that draw tourists from around the world. For one, it is a beautiful country with great climate year-round, making it an easy get-away any time of the year. Spain is also the home to diverse culture and customs that make it unique. This initial draw made the tourism market boom. It supplied the country with a more stable economy as well as created thousands of new jobs for locals. However, business CSR and SLO were overlooked when practicing tourism. Tourism was congested on the coast, creating an overpopulation and overdevelopment of beach tourism [19]. This caused several problems, ranging from destruction of natural attractions and environmental degradation to the deterioration and supply of resources. The low-cost and limited-term of the tourism market resulted in cheap repairs and quick fixes, ultimately leading to negative feedback and overall decline in tourism [22].

The Caribbean is experiencing many of the same problems as Spain's tourism industry. The islands are characterized by beautiful beaches and clear water; this was enough to sustain the Caribbean's economy until competition from other countries with similar features stopped their growth. Now, the Caribbean is facing unsatisfactory social responsibility and environmental reports dealing mostly with health and cleanliness concerns from high pollution. This has had detrimental effects on the islands' economy, which is very reliant on tourism [23]. Like Spain, much of the natural setting and biosphere was destroyed in their initial rise in the tourism industry. This region has been strained by inflation and overdevelopment, taking away from not only the tourism experience, but also the locals' lifestyle [24–26]. Polar countries need to be especially concerned with damage to sensitive Arctic regions that require long times to repair damage to the environment.

Spain has increased tourism in 2017, again due to the worldwide political situation, but also by developing better CSR and SLO practices such as education and eco-tours that highlight the unique nature of the country [22]. Spain was able to make a comeback in the tourism market by offering more services based on visitor's expectations. Cultural, rural, sport, city, and ecotourism were all provided in an effort to offer more to the tourist. Spain's model represents how important CSR and SLO are in maintaining a market and reputation [19]. Moving forward, Spain must continue to change their tourism model by reducing congestion, incorporating conservation, increasing education of eco-tourism related topics, and practicing social responsibility.

4.2. Fiji Islands—The Impacts on Local Lifestyle and Traditions from Population Increase & Mixing Cultures

Ecotourism practices led to higher income levels and an increased percentage of educated people in a Fijian village which had initiated tourism compared to an independent community which had not. However, there was also an increase in alcohol related disturbances in the village that was a direct result of ecotourism, as there were no previous problems with alcohol [27]. An increase in the number of facilities and infrastructure had resulted in overdevelopment and crowding of public venues that both locals and tourists must share. The added stress on the local population increased the risk of alcoholism and potentially added tension as the various cultures interact in these same spaces, thus creating change. Similar problems may be occurring in the Polar Regions that have introduced ecotourism.

4.3. Finnish Lapland and Impacts of Education

A big draw for tourists, especially ecotourists, is natural beauty. Having a positive environmental experience is a key part of ecotourism and staying environmentally-friendly in the host community. Ecotourism has helped in conservation considerably through the education of tourists, as well as increasing wildlife and fauna in ecotouristic areas where hunting and other recreational uses of the land has been banned [17]. An increase in wildlife and species diversity can draw even more ecotourists. Officials in these areas see a mutualistic relationship between ecotourist villages and public land, as conservation increases the number of species in both the protected villages and hunting grounds, thus benefiting both the hunter and the economy [17]. However, conservation practices are not always a priority. Deforestation results in soil erosion, floods, and landslides, but is a needed practice for shelter and heat. The larger the population of tourists, the more resources must be used. Although the intent for ecofriendly practices are associated with ecotourism, negative environmental effects still occur [28]. Some countries have taken steps to eliminate excess harm to the environment by limiting the number of tourists and activities in some areas. For example, Arctic Finland has limited the number of people by adapting the space available for certain tours based not only on the available personnel, but also the wear on the environment. This practice not only speaks to the needs and values, but also CSR. Tourists exhibit the strongest interest in sustainable tourism development in the Arctic region. A positive attitude toward cultural preservation is considered the driving force in promoting sustainable tourism operations in Arctic destinations. This positive attitude toward environmental and cultural protection has also prompted stakeholders such as tourist operators and regulators to set limits for tours [29]. Another example from northern Finland is the Ranua Zoo, where the visitors of the zoo walk on a wooden plank walkway that is built above the forest floor to preserve the flora and fauna of the area.

In communities where multiple industries are present there should be a way to cooperate instead of compete for resources. In Kittilä, Finland, the dominant industries of mining, tourism, and traditional reindeer herding are all present. The municipality of about 6500 inhabitants in Arctic Lapland covers about 8264 square km. The area not only includes the town itself and associated infrastructure, but also a part of the river that belongs to the Natura 2000 environmental protection program [30]. Thus, recreation and tourism include a large ski hill and Arctic tourism operators in addition to a gold mine and reindeer herders. The industries of mining, tourism, and reindeer herding can, in some cases, be seen as competing for resources, but with collaboration via CSR practices, education, and communication between the operators and community, a SLO has been obtained by each representative industry. An example of this unique cooperation in this fragile Arctic environment is between a reindeer herding cooperative and gold mine, where while visiting the gold mine, reindeer can be seen enjoying the resources and lands on the gold mine property. In order to promote cooperation and sustained resources and community, they established the Community Liaison Committee in 2013, where representatives from the stakeholder groups in the Kittilä region meet, discuss key issues, and collectively solve problems that arise [31]. The mentioned stakeholders of this group are: the Kuivasalmi reindeer herding co-operative, local villages, Levi Tourist Office, the Kittilän Luonto Association for environmental protection, the local parish, the local government of Kittilä, and Lapland Vocational College.

For ecotourism to succeed, such as in the Kittilä case, ethical practices and responsibility must be upheld towards the environment, community, and society. Ecotourism operators must stress the idea of ecology and economy as sustainable tourism is paired with an experience and education. Effort must be expended in educating awareness of both nature and culture. This will provide a spillover effect around the world as more people are diversely educated on the matters at hand. The practice of CSR, as well as obtaining and maintaining a SLO in the community, is mandatory for ecotourism operators and developers. In order to have a successful ecotourism experience, you must use the idea of CSR and SLO to give back to the community and sustain the culture, as well as follow a set of social and ethical guidelines to conduct the business [32,33]. Becoming a corporate citizen of the community and gaining acceptance for your business in the local community is key for the attainment of the organization's SLO. However, there is a cost–benefit factor that applies to the market of ecotourism. When ecotourism is practiced with CSR and SLO, it is very beneficial to the economy, as costly conflicts between resource users and owners can be avoided [10]. However, if a corporation's social responsibility is not upheld, it can result in negative effects on the business, community, and environment.

Regardless of whether tourists engage in sustainable activities outside of tourism, when surveyed, travelers will choose eco-friendly tourism over the alternative [34]. The demand for ecotourism is at an all-time high, with increased public education of ecology. In order to keep up with consumer demands, suppliers must adopt CSR and SLO practices so that they continue to be viewed as an ethical and good corporate citizen in the local community. Businesses who follow these guidelines and practice responsibility with respect to their customers, locals, and the environment are more successful [7]. Spain, the Caribbean, and other countries struggling to keep up with the demand for tourism must follow CSR and SLO practices. Implementing ecotourism into the economy is beneficial not only for job growth, but also for locals and culture. Tourists travel to a specific location for an experience; to view the diversity of landscapes, natural resources, wildlife, and culture. Overdevelopment and destruction of natural land influences these draws negatively.

Government and local community involvement is essential to CSR and obtaining a SLO in ecotourism, as many industries must cooperate and collectively have an impact on the host community people, lands, and resources. To prevent crowding in coastal areas, the government may limit construction and encourage taller buildings instead of wider. This allows for a more environmentally friendly approach while still increasing economic growth. Another action the government may take is regulating water and energy use in tourism areas. Hotels for example use considerable amounts of resources every year; placing a restriction on overdevelopment of touristic villages will prevent the overuse and waste of essential resources. Many hospitality industries of ecotourism have made changes to lighting and added automatic systems to avoid waste [35]. An example of this is the use of key cards in the main outlet—so when the key card is removed the power of the hotel room is shut off—or the elimination of small disposable cosmetic bottles.

5. Conclusions

The need for CSR practices and obtaining a SLO for the businesses involved in the ecotourism industry is undeniable. Understanding that corporations hold responsibility and play a role in society, the environment, and the life of the locals is very important. The entrepreneurs and business operators of tourist industries, along with those businesses in the value chain, must all work toward the same goal of upholding their values as well as the local values and traditions, behaving ethically, and respecting the consequences of their actions [7]. More specifically, in ecotourism, the corporation must not only be able to meet the demands of the tourists, but they must also give back and aid in the development and sustainability of the society and culture. This is especially important as the industry of ecotourism is very fragmented, composed of a multitude of interrelated and codependent operators such as transportation, lodging, restaurants, retail, and tour operators. This cooperation is accomplished by instilling a tradition of responsibility, demonstrating collaboration between internal and external stakeholders, learning from past successes of other companies or countries through educational programs, and understanding the rules and regulations. It would be advisable to create local stakeholder groups such as the one created in Kittilä, Finland so that the representatives can openly discuss and act on issues as a collective community. To ensure the practices of sustainable tourism for both the environment and culture, there is a need for stricter legislation [36]. It is important to maintain and stay consistent with ethical responsibility in the demanding world of ecotourism, especially in the Artic regions, as the natural environment is fragile and impacts will last much longer than in other parts of the world [37]. Opening the Artic regions for tourists is good for economic development, but must be balanced with sustainable practices for ensuring that the region can support tourism and local businesses into the future. We recommend ecotourism learn from large extractive industries, such as mining, where the developer must obtain the community's approval to operate as part of an environmental impact assessment process [38]. We see examples of this in some Arctic countries and regions and can learn from other regions of the world where ecotourism businesses are prevalent.

6. Future Research

The literature review of CSR practices and the attainment of a SLO in Arctic ecotourism has shown that that there needs to be a comprehensive survey of Artic ecotourism businesses conducted in order to identify best SLO and CSR practices. This would allow for the development of best practice examples that would then aid in attaining and maintaining a SLO developed specifically for the Artic ecotourism industry.

Acknowledgments: We would like to thank The L.E.A.P. group for its tireless effort to educate and research. We also need to specifically thank Tarrah Anne, William Zachary, and Xander Lee for all their support for this project.

Author Contributions: All authors gathered, read, and analyzed the literature. Meetings were held to discuss strategies and plans for the manuscript. All authors have contributed equally in writing of this manuscript.

Conflicts of Interest: The authors declare no conflict of interest.

References

1. Diamantis, D. The concept of ecotourism: Evolution and trends. *Curr. Issues Tour.* **1999**, *2*, 93–122. [CrossRef]
2. Young, O.R. The Arctic council at twenty: How to remain effective in a rapidly changing environment. *UC Irvine Law Rev.* **2016**, *6*, 99.
3. Sæþórsdóttir, A.D.; Saarinen, J. Challenges due to changing ideas of natural resources: Tourism and power plant development in the Icelandic wilderness. *Polar Rec.* **2016**, *52*, 82–91. [CrossRef]
4. Fredman, P.; Tyrväinen, L. (Eds.) *Frontiers in Nature-Based Tourism: Lessons from Finland, Iceland, Norway and Sweden*; Routledge: Abingdon, UK, 2014.
5. Asif, M.; Searcy, C.; Zutshi, A.; Fisscher, O.A. An integrated management systems approach to corporate social responsibility. *J. Clean. Prod.* **2013**, *56*, 7–17. [CrossRef]
6. Baker, M. Definitions of Corporate Social Responsibility—What Is CSR? Available online: http://mallenbaker.net/article/clear-reflection/definitions-of-corporate-social-responsibility-what-is-csr (accessed on 5 February 2004).
7. Goss, A. Corporate social responsibility in the extractive industries. In *Governance Ecosystems*; Palgrave Macmillan: London, UK, 2009; pp. 187–200.
8. Bridge, G. Contested terrain: Mining and the environment. *Annu. Rev. Environ. Resour.* **2004**, *29*, 205–259. [CrossRef]
9. Prno, J. An analysis of factors leading to the establishment of a social licence to operate in the mining industry. *Resour. Policy* **2013**, *38*, 577–590. [CrossRef]
10. Moffat, K.; Zhang, A. The paths to social licence to operate: An integrative model explaining community acceptance of mining. *Resour. Policy* **2014**, *39*, 61–70. [CrossRef]
11. Joyce, S.; Thomson, I. Earning a social license to operate: Social acceptability and resource development in Latin America. *Can. Min. Metall. Bull.* **2000**, *93*, 49–53.
12. Gunningham, N.; Kagan, A.R.; Thornton, D. Social license and environmental protection: Why businesses go beyond compliance. *Law Soc. Inq.* **2004**, *29*, 307–341. [CrossRef]
13. Rajovic, G.; Bulatovic, J. Tourism potential and rural tourism: A case study of the municipality of Andrijevica. *Int. Lett. Nat. Sci.* **2014**, *1*, 33–53. [CrossRef]
14. Wight, P.A. Ecotourists: Not a homogeneous market segment. In *The Encyclopedia of Ecotourism*; CABI: Wallingford, UK, 2001; pp. 37–62.
15. Anomasiri, W. Eastern Philosophy of Ecotourism Management Model in Mae Son Province, Thailand. Master's Thesis, Technology of Environmental Management, Faculty of Graduate Studies, Mahidol University, Bangkok, Thailand, 2004.
16. Aliani, H.; Kafaky, S.B.; Saffari, A.; Monavari, S.M. Determining an appropriate method for the purpose of land allocation for ecotourism development (case study: Taleghan County, Iran). *Environ. Monit. Assess.* **2016**, *188*. [CrossRef] [PubMed]
17. Herbig, P.; O'Hara, B. Ecotourism: A Guide for Marketers. *Eur. Bus. Rev.* **1997**, *97*, 231–236. [CrossRef]
18. Deng, J.; Li, J. Self-identification of ecotourists. *J. Sustain. Tour.* **2015**, *23*, 255–279. [CrossRef]
19. Argandoña, A. Corporate Social Responsibility in the Tourism Industry: Some Lessons From the Spanish Experience. Available online: https://papers.ssrn.com/sol3/papers.cfm?abstract_id=1593592 (accessed on 21 April 2010).
20. Koivusalo, K. Environmental Management in Finnish Tourism Companies. Available online: https://www.theseus.fi/handle/10024/25657 (accessed on 17 February 2011).
21. Jóhannesson, G.T. A Fish Called Tourism: Emergent Realities of Tourism Policy in Iceland. In *Tourism Encounters and Controversies: Ontological Politics of Tourism Development*; Ashgate: Farnham, UK, 2016; pp. 181–200.
22. Vera, J.F. El modelo turístico del Mediterráneo español: agotamiento y estrategias de reestructuración. *Papers de Turisme* **1994**, *14–15*, 131–148.
23. Caribbean Tourist Organization. Caribbean Performance 2007–2008 Caribbean Tourism Board. Available online: www.onecaribbean.org/content/files/IndustryperfOCT08.pdf (accessed on 31 May 2017).
24. Sarlat, E.M.; García, O.; Wood, P. Urban ethno-botanists, storytellers of our cities: An ecotourism initiative from Barcelona, Spain. *J. Ecotour.* **2013**, *12*, 189–196. [CrossRef]
25. Wilkinson, P.F. Strategies for Tourism in Island MicroStates. *Ann. Tour. Res.* **1989**, *16*, 153–177. [CrossRef]

26. Weaver, D. *Mass Tourism and Alternative Tourism in the Caribbean, in Tourism and the Less Developed World: Issues and Case Studies*; Harrison, D., Ed.; CABI Publishing: Wallingford, UK, 2001; pp. 161–174.

27. Scheyvens, R.; Russell, M. Tourism and Poverty Alleviation in Fiji: Comparing the Impacts of Small- and Large-scale Tourism Enterprises. *J. Sustain. Tour.* **2012**, *20*, 417–436. [CrossRef]

28. Tisdell, C. Ecotourism, Economics, and the Environment: Observations from China. *J. Travel Res.* **1996**, *34*, 11–19. [CrossRef]

29. Chen, J.S. Tourism stakeholders attitudes toward sustainable development: A case in the Arctic. *J. Retail. Consum. Serv.* **2015**, *22*, 225–230. [CrossRef]

30. Environment and Nature. Available online: http://www.kittila.fi/en/environment-and-nature (accessed on 12 September 2016).

31. Agnico Eagle. Available online: http://agnicoeagle.fi/sustainability/partnerships/ (accessed on 31 May 2017).

32. Ayuso, S. Comparing voluntary policy instruments for sustainable tourism: The experience of the Spanish hotel sector. *J. Sustain. Tour.* **2007**, *15*, 144–159. [CrossRef]

33. Pérez, M. *Manual del Turismo Sostenible*; Mundi-Prensa: Madrid, Spain, 2004.

34. Travel Industry Association of America. American Travellers Turning Green (but Not at Any Cost), According to New National Survey. Available online: http://www.tia.org/pressmedia/pressrec.asp (accessed on 10 April 2007).

35. International Tourism Partnership. Original Charter and Signatories. Available online: http://tourismpartnership. org/ (accessed on 31 May 2017).

36. Dodds, R. Report for Caribbean Soft Adventure Study. In *Caribbean Regional Sustainable Tourism Development Programme*; Project No. 8 ACP RCA O35; Califorum Tourism Unit: Barbados, UK, 2006.

37. Eagles, P.F.J.; Ballantine, J.L. Defining Canadian ecotourists. *J. Sustain. Tour.* **1994**, *2*, 210–214.

38. Thomson, I.; Boutilier, R.G. The social licence to operate. In *SME Mining Engineering Handbook*; Society for Mining, Metallurgy and Exploration (SME): Englewood, CO, USA, 2011; pp. 1779–1796.

resources

MDPI

Article

The Use of Information and Communication Technology (ICT) in Managing High Arctic Tourism Sites: A Collective Action Perspective

Marta Bystrowska [1,*], **Karin Wigger** [2] and **Daniela Liggett** [3]

[1] Department of Earth Sciences, University of Silesia in Katowice, Bedzinska 60, 41-200 Sosnowiec, Poland
[2] Department of Innovation and Entrepreneurship, Nord University Business School, Universitetsalléen 11, 8026 Bodø, Norway; karin.a.wigger@nord.no
[3] Gateway Antarctica, University of Canterbury, Private Bag 4800, Christchurch 8140, New Zealand; daniela.liggett@canterbury.ac.nz
* Correspondence: mbystrowska@us.edu.pl; Tel.: +48-660-707-290

Received: 3 May 2017; Accepted: 21 July 2017; Published: 25 July 2017

Abstract: Sustainable management of nature-based tourism sites is a pertinent issue in vulnerable Arctic environments. Arctic tourism operators often act collectively to protect their common interests of ensuring the sustainability of tourism sites. Nowadays, information and communication technology (ICT) is increasingly used to support these collaborative efforts, but the remoteness and risks associated with Arctic tourism operations challenge the success of such collective action. This study explores the use of ICT as a management tool for Arctic tourism sites to ensure their sustained quality. Drawing on a case study of an expedition cruise operators' network in Svalbard, we explore how the use of ICT affects collective action and sustainable management of tourism sites. Our findings show that, through increased noticeability, the creation of artificial proximity and the development of new management practices, ICT can help to overcome the challenges for collective action that are posed by the Arctic environment. The use of ICT results in changes in a network's relational and normative structures, which can as much add to as detract from the success of collective action. Our study indicates that the successful application of ICT depends on a high level of social capital, in particular norms, to guide interactions between ICT and network actors.

Keywords: Arctic tourism; collective action; ICT; social capital; common-pool resources; sustainable management

1. Introduction

In the fragile Arctic natural environment, the quality of tourism depends on sustainable management of tourism sites [1–3]. Tourism in the Arctic is mostly nature-based, with untouched wilderness, wildlife and dramatic landscapes being key attractions [4]. Natural resources accessed in Arctic tourism are often non-exclusive, which means that they are open to access by various actors. Prior studies qualify such resources as the commons [4,5] and conclude that the exploitation of common-pool resources (CPR) for tourism purposes can result in environmental depletion and degradation [6,7]. Addressing and minimizing the problem of natural-resource depletion has been traditionally studied from an environmental-policy perspective [8–10]. Scholars in the field claim that governmental regulations alone are insufficient to ensure the environmental quality of tourism sites and recommend involving tourism operators in the management of tourism sites to ensure their sustainability [7,11,12]. In many cases, the management of vulnerable tourism sites requires collective action by tourism operators to sustain tourism activities [11].

Collective action describes spontaneous or organized collaborative initiatives towards common goals, such as sustaining the quality of tourism sites [13]. Studies have shown that formalized tourism industry networks can play a crucial role in achieving common goals; and often the outcome of collective action depends on those networking organizations [11,14].

Arctic tourism sites are characterized by remoteness, short seasons, limited or absent human population and the dominance of multi-national tourism operators who only visit Arctic locations on a short-term basis [15]. These characteristics provide challenges for collective action [16] as there is a limited monitoring capability and control over the behaviour of individual operators and also impeded coordination of action. Advances in information and communication technology (ICT) lead to rapid changes within the tourism industry, and prior studies indicate that the application of ICT can support the sustainable management of tourism sites [15,17,18].

Although prior studies claim that ICT can support the sustainable management of tourism sites, there is little understanding of the exact functions ICT is to assume in this regard [19,20]. Lupia and Sin (2003) [21] highlight that ICT changes communication dynamics in collective action and thus becomes a means for information flow, monitoring and control. The authors show that ICT advances can either facilitate or hamper collective action and call for more research into the use of ICT in collective action. We contribute to the literature on collective action for sustainable tourism sites by studying ICT as a management tool for such sites. Our guiding research question—how does the use of ICT influence collective action to sustainably manage tourism sites?—can be broken down into two subsidiary questions: (1) How are ICT tools used in managing tourism sites? and (2) How does ICT contribute to the success of collective action? Using the example of Arctic expedition cruise tourism, in this paper we will respond to these questions in Sections 4 and 5.

The case of Arctic expedition cruising was selected as it represents a popular form of tourism in the Arctic. Expedition cruising in the Arctic is mostly nature-based and centred around the unique natural resources in a remote and isolated environment [12]. At the same time, Arctic expedition cruise tourism faces issues related to the tragedy of the commons, as it has an undeniable impact on the environment [6,22–24], just like any other human activity. The cumulative impact from tourism operations in the Arctic reduces the sustainability of the respective tourism sites and may also detract from these sites' appeal. Our paper focuses on the archipelago of Svalbard, one of the most visited expedition cruise tourism destinations in the Arctic. As the majority of tourism sites on Svalbard are unpopulated, the paper focuses on the economic-ecological interaction of the sustainability concept, addressing economic growth and environmental constraints, including environmental quality [10]. Negative externalities, such as pollution from ships, noise, soil degradation from walking and shore degradation from anchoring, are a few of the main impacts arising from cruising tourism in Svalbard [25]. To minimize their impact and organize collective action towards preserving fragile Arctic resources, the cruise industry established a formalized network to address the negative externalities and to sustain the environmental quality of the tourism sites.

Our paper consists of three main areas of focus, each of which contributes to the scholarly literature on Arctic tourism, tourism management and collective action networks. Firstly, we assess how vulnerable Arctic tourism sites can be better managed by acknowledging the role of ICT in achieving certain collective goals through a social informatics lens [26,27]. Drawing on Van Bets et al. (2017) [10], we identify ICT as a crucial tool in sustainable Arctic tourism management, while acknowledging the challenges related to the dependence on any network as well as the unreliability of networks in certain conditions. Secondly, we study how human-technology interactions can result in certain sustainability measures in tourism management by focusing on how ICT acts as an enabler for collective action, provided ICT is embedded in the social capital of the collective action network. By stressing the interactions between ICT and social capital in collective action, we gain a new perspective on understanding collective action towards sustainable resource management in tourism. Thirdly, we argue that ICT represents a new factor in collective action networks, whose roles are shaped by network interactions and the wider system of resources [27].

2. Tourism, Common-Pool Resources and Collective Action

Natural resources used for tourism purposes are often referred to as CPR [8,24]. CPR are non-excludable and accessible to all [28]. The exploitation of CPR by one actor reduces the amount available for others or adversely affects the resource quality [28–30]. Persistent overexploitation of those resources, referred to by Hardin (1968) [31] as the tragedy of the commons, leads to resource degradation and directly impacts resource sustainability [4]. Tourism commons include both natural and artificial, material (tangible) and immaterial (intangible), elements [5], which, in the context of Arctic nature-based tourism, includes landscape and wildlife resources.

Overuse of tourism commons can result in crowding in the short term and in resource degradation in the long term [32]. In the case of nature-based tourism, degradation is not an obvious result of the tragedy of the commons, but acts such as trampling, picking flowers, littering, pollution and other kinds of disturbance can reduce the aesthetics of tourist sites and negatively affect their environmental sustainability [6]. Those issues are often considered by the concept of carrying capacity of a tourism site [33], that highlights that increasing tourism demand may challenge sustainability of both natural resources and local communities at visited locations. Nature-based tourism, such as on Svalbard, depends less on hosting communities, but rather on tourism sites that remain relatively pristine to provide a positive tourist experience [34]. Therefore, ensuring the high quality of tourism sites for nature-based tourism activities requires avoiding and minimizing the negative consequences associated with CPR use, and calls for sustainable management practices.

Effective management of nature-based tourism sites is critical, as the disturbance and depletion of natural resources often results from a lack of control and coordination of use [28,35,36]. Despite the existence of official institutions designated to govern the commons [28], Libecap (2005) [37] notes that it is often too costly to (1) place boundaries around a resource; (2) secure agreements to limit individual actions; or (3) obtain enough information to determine a proper course of action to protect the resource. Therefore, scholars emphasize the importance of community-based management to supplement governmental control and monitoring, such as in coastal fisheries, forests, etc. [30,36]. On the community level, local resource users often come together and collaborate to avoid a tragedy of the commons scenario through collective action networks for decision making, control and management [13].

2.1. Collective Action to Manage Common-Pool Resources

Issues related to CPR management can be viewed as a problem of collective action [38]. Collective action occurs when actors agree on decision making arrangements governing CPR use [39] and can be formally defined as any "action taken by two or more people in pursuit of the same collective good" [40] (p. 4). Actors get a higher payoff if they cooperate than if they act independently [31], and the benefits from participating in collective action are greater than any benefits derived from free riding. Free riding refers to the process of deriving benefits from certain goods or services without paying for them and commonly occurs when goods or services are non-excludable or when external costs, such as for ecosystem services, are not being considered. Free riding is problematic as it can result overconsumption of resources [41]. In the case of expedition cruising in Svalbard, free riding could be expressed by certain operators not participating in collective action through the Association of Arctic Expedition Cruise Operators (AECO) or not contributing to information sharing and would result in a reduced ability and effectiveness to coordinate operator activities. The latter could result in unexpected and un-mitigated additional environmental impacts or conflicts between operators or with local authorities, provided that all actors collaborate [42]. For actors performing collective action, transparency, communication and coordination are especially crucial [16]. As challenges for collective action may lie in communication and coordination between individuals [43], actors often establish formalized networks to pursue such action [16].

Collective action is an integral part of CPR management, and a large body of research has been undertaken on this topic [13,14,38,39,44]. The factors determining the outcome of collective action in sustainable CPR management can be categorized as: (1) resource system characteristics; (2) actor group characteristics; (3) institutional arrangements; and (4) the external environment, such as ICT or state [45]. Collective action theory focuses on exploring the conditions that ensure effective collective action [28,45,46]. Effective collective action is often characterized by (1) involving only a small group of actors; (2) well-defined resource boundaries; (3) well-defined group membership; (4) relatively straightforward monitoring and enforcement; and (5) proximity between the locations of users and resources [45]. These design principles for robust institutions [47] tend to be treated as mandatory elements to ensure the success of collective action.

However, most proposed conditions alone are not sufficient to explain or establish successful collective action, especially as they do not consider the contextual characteristics of the collective action environment [39]. Steins and Edwards (1999) [39] argue that "variables linking collective action and the "external world" are remarkably absent," (p. 543) and argue that we need to approach collective action as the result of interactions between actors and contextual factors which emphasize the uniqueness of each collective action setting. In this study, we explore the extent to which the Arctic natural, social and political environment challenges the success of collective action and look at how actors use new technologies in collective action to overcome some of the environmental challenges associated with operating in the Arctic.

2.2. The Application of ICT in Collective Action

Collective action involves not only people, but also a variety of nonhuman resources, such as ICT, and interactions between actors and nonhuman entities [39]. The scholarly literature increasingly recognizes the contribution of technology, especially ICT, in the shaping of social processes, including those related to collective action. Vargo et al. (2015) [48] conceptualize technology as potentially useful knowledge that may offer solutions for new or existing problems. Technology, in general, includes both software, such as processes and methods, as well as hardware [48]. ICT relates mostly, but not exclusively, to the Internet, databases and communication devices [43].

Despite being a part of many collective efforts, the function of ICT in collective action has not been well understood as yet [21]. ICT changes communication dynamics and thereby has the potential to overcome collective action challenges such as free riding [16] or problems of monitoring and coordination [43]. However, it can also cause problems, for example, by making communication more difficult or increasing the relative benefits of free riding [21]. Ongoing debates on how ICT may change the premises of collective action provide evidence of both the success and failure of ICT use in collective efforts [43,49]. However, to date, we lack data on how ICT influences collective action.

To understand the function of ICT in collective action, social informatics [26,27,50,51], which can be defined as "the interdisciplinary study of the design, uses and consequences of information technologies that takes into account their interaction with institutional and cultural contexts" [52] (p. 688), offers some inspiration. In social informatics, ICT is seen as embedded in complex and dynamic social, cultural, organizational and institutional structures [53,54], and a sociotechnical network concept can be applied to understand the function ICT assumes in the actions of an organization [50,55]. A sociotechnical network is an interactive and interdependent network of co-existing human or organizational agents and technology [50]. ICT is thus socially produced, but can also act as an agent influencing its users by reconstituting social ties and redrawing social boundaries [54].

From a social informatics perspective, technology forms part of the social capital that is embedded in a network of actors performing collective action and can modify the network's structure and functioning. Social capital describes the group relations, norms and practices that drive collective efforts and is a widely recognized concept in collective action theory [13,56,57]. Social capital emphasizes the importance of relations and interactions in coordination and cooperation for achieving mutual benefits [49,58]. Networks, trust and norms are often perceived as the essence of social capital [56,59] and reciprocity and exchanges, common rules, norms, and sanctions, as well as connectedness in networks and groups play an important role too [30]. Through social capital, resource users govern resources and perform collective action. Social capital can help people overcome collective action issues, such as free riding, lack of social mobilization or overuse of resources [60].

ICT interacts with the social capital of a group of actors and, consequently, with the resources used and the specific context of their use. As collective action is an outcome of an interaction between a network of actors and environmental resources [45], ICT can be classified as a new actor in a network, which helps the human actors to embrace the complex and dynamic character of mutual relations between the varied components of collective action.

3. Methods

The relative novelty of the studied topic encourages us to use a single case study design [61,62]. Case study methodology allows for the exploration of a complex phenomenon, such as the relationship between ICT use and sustainable management of tourism sites, within a well-defined situational context [63]. Building on the argument that ICT can change the organisational principles of collective action and that it can, thereby, influence the sustainable management of tourism sites [15,19], a single case study approach enables to explore the use of ICT in ensuring the quality of tourism. It also provides room for personal interactions between the researchers and the participants, while giving study participants the opportunity to describe their views on ICT use and sustainable management of tourism sites within the Arctic context they operate [63]. Given the geographical focus on the polar regions in this special issue, we apply the theory of collective action to a unique, and spatially well-defined, polar tourism case study [62]. Through the participants' stories, we are able to explore contextual factors that are relevant to the topic. Therefore, we applied a so-called "extreme case" selection strategy [64], meaning that we have selected a case that demonstrates unusual characteristics of the phenomenon of interest. Consequently, we focused on Svalbard which is a remote location, based on natural attractions, and that is characterized by a relatively developed polar tourism industry.

The network this paper focuses on is the AECO, which was established in 2003 as an industry initiative to promote and practice sustainable Arctic cruising activities. The main objective of the network is to ensure environmentally friendly and safe cruising operations. Collective action within AECO is evident in its self-regulatory tools, which are agreed on between members and are often stricter than governmental regulations. The network has headquarters with administrative and institutional functions and is mainly financed through member fees. Participation is voluntary but necessitates compliance with the organization's goals and values. By 2015, the network had grown to 48 members from a meagre 13 members in 2009 (AECO Annual Report 2015). AECO members include primarily cruise operators but also other international and local organizations, such as ice management service providers, port agents, consultancies and airlines.

The network provides expertise to tour operators and develops operational guidelines. These guidelines define, for example, the minimum distance to wildlife or expected behaviours by both operators and tourists. The network is especially active in Svalbard, where most operators are members. Here, AECO supports programmes such as *Clean Up Svalbard*—an initiative that engages tourists in cleaning up beaches. One of its main tasks in Svalbard is to manage the use of tourism sites by its members. ICT solutions are increasingly used to facilitate the management of tourism sites.

3.1. Data Collection

Our study triangulates [65,66] insights from document analysis, participant observation and interviews with key actors. The primary data were collected between 2014 and 2016. We participated in AECO's annual conferences and thematic meetings, and had access to their annual reports. Other documents, such as official, published thematic reports and conference proceedings were also used. Throughout the meetings we participated in, we took extensive notes on the wide range of presentations and discussions. Applying an ethnographic approach to participant observation, we also duly recorded our personal reflections on the interactions observed.

Moreover, guided by snowball sampling, twelve in-depth interviews (see Table 1) were conducted with ten different network actors, of which five were held in English, six in Norwegian and one in Polish. In interviews lasting between 30 and 131 min, research participants were asked about the management of tourism sites and organization of cruise experience products in Svalbard. The interviews were semi-structured, and we followed a rough interview guide to ensure that a core set of themes and topics were covered in a comparable manner with similar open-ended questions. We then flexibly followed up on certain answers with additional non-scripted questions. This approach allows for significant flexibility in following interesting lines of thought and gave us an opportunity to explore the participants' views in depth, while ensuring that our key questions and topics were covered in each interview [67]. The interviews were recorded and transcribed verbatim, with the transcripts being viewed and approved by the research participants.

The transcripts of the interviews, annual reports and other documents form the network, and the notes from the observation and participation were loaded into NVivo 10 Software (a qualitative data-analysis software, QSR International's, Melbourne, Australia), which functions as a database and facilitates data analysis.

Table 1. Overview of research participants.

Actors	Research Participant	Interview Number
Network secretary 1	1	1 & 2
Network secretary 2	2	3
Product developer 1	3	4
Product developer 2	4	5
Operation manager 1	5	6
Captain 1	6	7 & 8
Captain 2	7	9
Captain 3	8	10
Expedition leader 1	9	11
Expedition leader 2	10	12

3.2. Data Analysis

The data were systematically analysed and iteratively coded jointly by the first two authors following the three coding stages described by Gioia et al. (2013) [68] using QSR NVivo 10, which supports "open" coding and "nested sub" coding [69]. This approach is a hybrid process of inductive data-driven coding and deductive theory-driven thematic analysis to interpret the raw data.

At the first stage, we undertook an initial inductive open coding of the raw data starting without any given coding scheme. New codes were added to NVivo as new elements appeared in the raw data. We compared and discussed the codes, our approach to coding, finding agreement on all codes, while searching for commonalities to group similar codes by adding a new overarching code and grouping the existing codes as "nested sub" codes. The process of grouping and connecting codes was interactive, and through several rounds of discussion and reorganization of the codes in NVivo, common themes and patterns in the data were discovered. Overall, the first step of our inductive data analysis resulted in 26 first-order concepts.

We then used a structural coding approach to identify second-order themes. These second-order themes were developed deductively based on theory from literature on collective action, social informatics and sustainable tourism while drawing on the empirical first-order concepts [70]. At this stage, separate themes were identified, based on the wider scholarly literature relating to our research questions. Seven second-order themes were identified that way.

Finally, further categorisation of second-order themes resulted in the identification of three aggregated dimensions [68] of ICT use in tourism site management, namely increasing noticeability of individual actions, creating artificial proximity and building new management practices.

This study employed the criteria of coding reliability, credibility and confirmability to ensure trustworthiness [65]. Following Campbell (2013) [71], we used an approach involving negotiated agreement to address issues of coding reliability related to the second-order themes and aggregated dimensions. In case of non-agreement, we searched for common themes in the literature to define the codes in a way where they were mutually exclusive, which ultimately enhanced our common understanding of the themes. We achieved credibility through the aforementioned triangulation of methods, which was further enhanced by interviewing actors with different positions in the network. To ensure confirmability related to non-matching patterns and research bias, we followed Gioia et al.'s (2013) [68] analytical approach by combining inductive open coding and structural coding that draws on published research findings. Additionally, the third and most experienced author critically assessed the themes and underlying codes developed by the first two authors to ensure confirmability.

4. Expedition Cruising in Svalbard and the Application of ICT

Svalbard is an archipelago located within 71–81° Northern Latitude and 10–35° Eastern Longitude, approximately midway between the North Cape of Norway and the North Pole. The archipelago consists of islands of a total area of approximately 61,022 km². Around 65% of Svalbard's terrestrial area and about 86% of its territorial waters is under environmental protection [72], because of the archipelago's rich and diverse wildlife which includes various bird colonies as well as mammals such as reindeer, the Arctic fox, polar bears, walrus, seals and whales. At the same time, Svalbard is one of the most northern populated places on earth with a population of around 2500 inhabitants across the capital of Longyearbyen, the Russian mining settlements of Pyramiden and Barensburg, and the research community of Ny-Ålesund [73].

The relative accessibility and developed infrastructure in Svalbard, as well as its abundant wildlife and stunning landscape, make the archipelago appealing for cruising activities [74]. Expedition cruises search for solitude and avoid other ships to ensure a unique Arctic experience in Svalbard. The number of expedition cruise passengers visiting Svalbard increased from 3417 in 2001 to 12,519 in 2014 [75], with Svalbard's visitors exceeding those in neighbouring Greenland, Canada or Russia [74]. However, sailing in such remote areas is challenging due to often rapidly changing or unexpected weather and sea ice conditions.

Tourism and maritime operations are regulated under the umbrella of the Svalbard multi-jurisdictional legal framework, consisting of the Svalbard Treaty, the Svalbard Environmental Act, international and state regulations, as well as the general regulatory framework of shipping, particularly for operations in polar waters [76]. Considering the nature of expedition cruising and its particular operating environment, the complex multi-jurisdictional framework is regarded as being inadequate and insufficient as a governance tool, as it lacks sector-specific elements [12].

In addition to governmental regulation, tourism management in Svalbard is supplemented by AECO self-regulation, e.g., through operational guidelines and a range of tailored technologies to facilitate the pursuit of the network's goals, such as dealing with crowding and environmental degradation.

4.1. ICT Tools Developed by AECO to Perform Collective Action

AECO makes use of two key ICT solutions in support of tourism management, a cruise database and a vessel tracking system, both of which are discussed in greater detail in the following sections. The cruise database features three tools, one for the booking of landing sites, another one to lodge a cruise itinerary, and a third one to upload and manage post visit reports. The vessel tracking system allows for real-time localization and tracking of the expedition cruise vessels of all the network members with a maximum delay of 15 min.

Publicly available ICT, such as an automatic identification system (AIS) for vessel tracking or very high frequencies (VHF) for maritime communication with vessels, supports AECO's in-house ICT management tools. AIS and VHF play crucial roles in terms of ensuring the safety of operations at sea. ICT technologies are constantly evolving to better fit challenging Arctic environment but prior studies as well as research participants note the limitations of ICT use in the Arctic [10,68] due to bandwidth issues and the availability of certain technologies. For instance, research participant 1 stresses that *"some operators have good iridium satellite connections and some do not. And these limitations are real constraints in regard to safety but also communication in regard to other things. So, this area is very important."* Improving communication technologies, such as satellite phones, will enhance communication between vessels. While we acknowledge the importance of ICT in support of safety, which has been the focus of previous research [77], our paper concentrates on AECO's in-house ICT management tools and their use in collective action to address risks associated with environmental degradation and crowding.

4.1.1. The AECO Cruise Database

The AECO cruise database assists in managing tourism visitation to specific sites and, as such, supports the minimization of environmental degradation and crowding. ICT supports planning as well as cruise operation and monitoring. Initially, the cruise database was an Excel spreadsheet for the collection of information on planned operations. In 2009, AECO had an online cruise database custom-built by an information technology (IT) company. However, this tailor-made ICT tool has been criticized as being *"static with very limited areas of use"* (AECO Annual Report 2011/2012). In 2013, an improved cruise database was developed, which better suits AECO's administrative needs and which has been in use ever since.

One of the main purposes of the cruise database is the booking of landing sites (research participant 1). The booking system requires members to register their cruise itineraries before the season starts and book landing sites in advance. The cruise itineraries, or sailing plans, consist of information about where, when and for how long a vessel will visit predefined landing sites. The system ensures that only a limited number of landings can be booked for a specific site and that the operator who booked the landing site will have sole use of the site for a specified period of time, which has environmental benefits in terms of a site's carrying capacity as has been emphasized by research participant 9. Of course, the aspect of being the only operator at any specific landing site is also attractive from a marketing perspective (see also research participant 9, and AECO Annual Report 2014). Figure 1 shows the frequency of bookings for 212 sites (out of a total of 300 sites) by AECO operators in Svalbard.

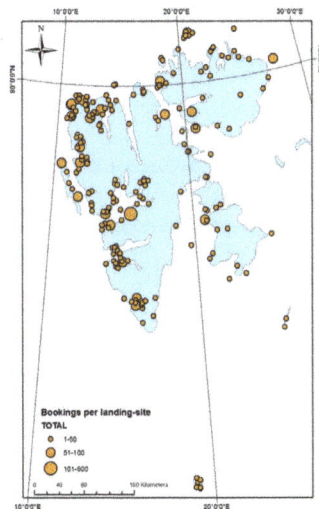

Figure 1. Expedition cruising landing sites in Svalbard 2013–2015. Source: own illustration based on Association of Arctic Expedition Cruise Operators (AECO) data (base map: TM World Borders).

During a pre-defined timeframe, interested AECO members log on to the online system and book landing sites, which they want to visit as a part of a registered sailing plan. The system is open for around three months but there is some degree of competition for the "best" landing sites as research participant 9 noted, "*I need to have all plan in my head (sic), because there are 5 others, who sit and write at the same time. So, this is my decision. If I will be doing this too slow, I may completely lose the spots.*" All AECO members have access to this system and can see each other's itineraries. That way, they also know who else will be in the area and who they can contact for assistance or if ad hoc changes have to be made to the expedition itinerary.

However, the system is not yet integrated into the Governor of Svalbard reporting schemes and currently serves only AECO's collective purposes, which is somewhat problematic as research participant 2 nicely outlined:

> "*We do not have all (cruise operators) in the portfolio. Not everyone is an (AECO) member. There are cruise operators that do not register their activities in the (AECO) database and therefore, we do not have a complete overview of cruise activities in the Arctic*" (translated from Norwegian).

On any given cruise, adverse weather conditions, such as storms, high waves, sea ice or fog, or wildlife migrations, can pose challenges for the execution of the initial itineraries. Therefore, during a cruise, vessel captains and expedition leaders rely on direct communication with other vessels if they wish to change their landing sites or choose more attractive landings. Informal communication between expedition leaders and captains at sea facilitates smooth transitions between planned and actual itineraries and is considered as hugely important in providing a true cruising experience. It depends on whether "*you know other expedition leader, how well do you know each other and then you can say—hey, come on, let's come one hour later, but if it is somebody new, sometimes they do not negotiate with you. And that is a problem. So, the longer you are in the business and the more people of course you know, the easier it is to solve those problems*" (research participant 10). With good communication, vessels at sea can inform each other about current conditions, notable wildlife sightings, or the activities of non-AECO vessels operating in the area. For instance, during the 2011 sailing season, a dead whale on a beach attracted many bears to the area. This information was quickly shared between operators via satellite communication, and many ships visited the area as a result. At the same time, network members organically agreed on a new rule that increased the minimum distance to the bears in the area to minimize adverse environmental impacts through overuse.

4.1.2. AECO's Vessel Tracking System

AECO developed its own vessel tracking system. The system is based on vessel tracking technologies AIS and VTS, and it involves satellite-based surveillance. Based on the information received through AIS or VTS, depending on which of the technologies an operator uses, cruise operators can access information about other operators in the area, including the operators' names, positions, courses and speeds. The vessel tracking adds to the safety management system, but also ensures real-time monitoring of operations.

Additionally, AECO vessel tracking supports communication between the operators at sea. For example, in case of any planned changes to the sailing plan, AECO members are obliged to contact nearby expedition vessels to discuss changes of their initial plans if necessary. Following these procedures helps to reduce uncertainty and the surprise factor related to external changes while supporting the sustainable management of tourism sites. The value of AECO's vessel tracking system has also been highlighted by research participant 1:

> "*By knowing within 15 min where all the other ships are, we can work towards better planning, greater safety, and the avoidance of eventual conflicts at landing sites.*"

5. Results: The Roles of ICT in Collective Action

Our data suggests that ICT can be employed as a management tool which has the potential of playing an important role in the sustainable management of tourism. In particular, our analysis reveals three distinct roles ICT assumes in collective action, (a) building new management practices; (b) increasing noticeability of individual actions; and (c) creating artificial proximity. Drawing on collective action theory and social informatics, we suggest that the use of ICT tools influences the success of sustainable tourism management by facilitating collective action to adjust norms and practices with a focus on sustainability, reduce incentives for free riding and surpass external challenges related to, e.g., the location of sites, weather or the presence of other actors. Figure 2 summarizes these findings.

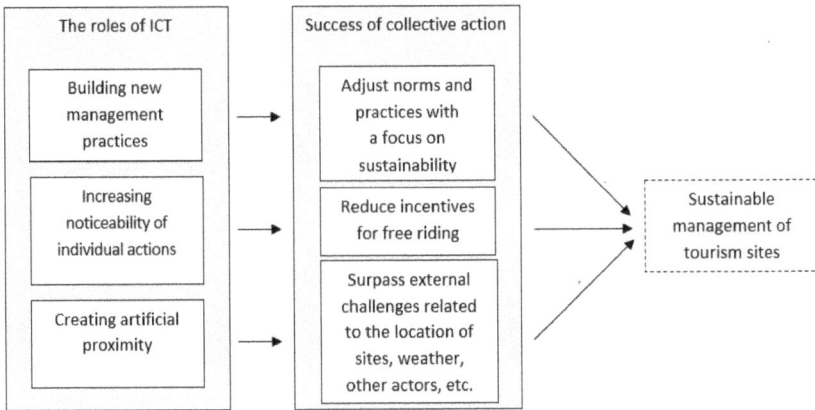

Figure 2. The roles of information and communication technology (ICT) in collective action.

The roles played by ICT in a collective-action context (see Figure 2) are undeniably linked, but for the purposes of clarity in our discussion, we address each of these roles separately in this section. The figures we developed to summarize our findings include, on the left a description of the specific role of ICT in tourism management (in response to our sub-question 1, and on the right an assessment on how ICT contributes to the success of collective action (i.e., our sub-question 2). Our exploration of the roles of ICT (i.e., sub-question 1) follows Gioia et al.'s (2013) [68] approach using first-order concepts, second-order themes and subsequent groupings referred to as "aggregated dimensions".

5.1. Building New Management Practices

The combination of real-time vessel tracking and the utilization of a cruise database builds new sustainable management practices through the sharing of strategic and operational information and flexible management practices (see Figure 3). Shared information enables the coordination of activities on tourism sites and ensures an activity level at, or even below, the predefined carrying capacity of the individual landing sites. New practices are developed as a result of the use of ICT, for example, the booking of landing sites and sharing the information with other AECO members, who often are competitors. Moreover, the use of ICT enables in situ interaction and communication between operators, which enables new practices of managing tourism sites that reduce uncertainty. An example are ad hoc changes to the initial cruise itineraries, which are common because, as research participant 2 explains,

> "Changes can happen due to different reasons. Ice can be one reason. Another reason can be that the expedition leader can get tired of traveling to this place and finds out that they can visit another site. It can be that easy. But according to the agreement between [AECO] members, one shall take

into consideration the plans of other operators. If they change the plans, they first have to check the cruise database that no one else has booked the place. And then they need to make contact or send a message to those that are close by" (translated from Norwegian).

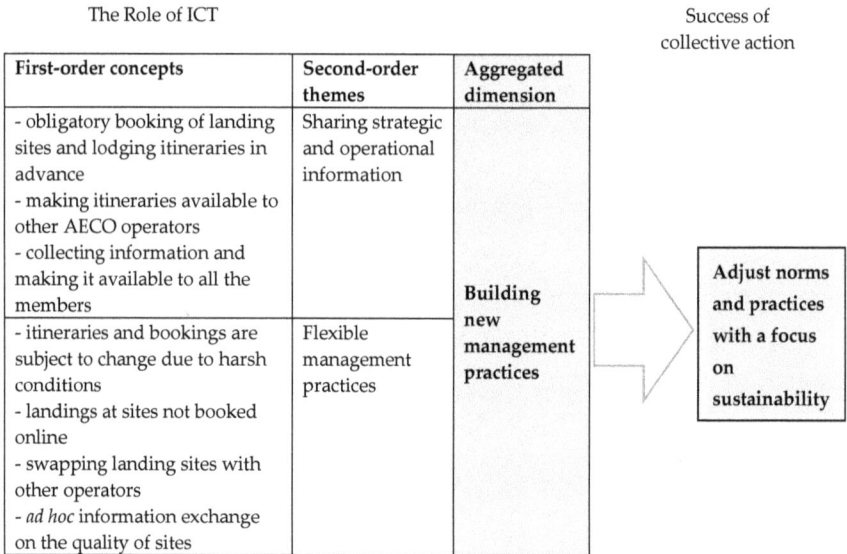

The Role of ICT

Success of collective action

First-order concepts	Second-order themes	Aggregated dimension
- obligatory booking of landing sites and lodging itineraries in advance - making itineraries available to other AECO operators - collecting information and making it available to all the members	Sharing strategic and operational information	Building new management practices
- itineraries and bookings are subject to change due to harsh conditions - landings at sites not booked online - swapping landing sites with other operators - *ad hoc* information exchange on the quality of sites	Flexible management practices	

Adjust norms and practices with a focus on sustainability

Figure 3. Building new management practices.

New management practices related to ICT use are developed through the utilization of social capital. AECO possesses high levels of social capital, evidenced by close ties and frequent communication between members, the willingness to cooperate and shared norms. Social relationships within AECO were especially crucial in adopting and using ICT. High levels of social capital allow a network to apply ICT tools more easily and to adjust its norms accordingly. At the same time, technology reshapes social capital as ICT use forces the modification of existing normative structures. Those norms are comprised of internal regulations, such as obligations for using ICT systems and other common routines, which are socially agreed upon and accepted in the network. New norms had been created in the studied network resulting in certain practices, in particular to ensure flexibility in response to the dynamic Arctic conditions, to maintain activity levels that do not exceed the carrying capacity of individual sites, and to increase the quality of expedition tourism products. ICT facilitates the establishment and adoption of new norms and allows network members to adjust them to changing conditions by easier and faster communication, information exchange, and access to data.

However, ICT can also negatively affect collective action as it is not always reliable in harsh Arctic conditions. The network facilitates operational flexibility, provided formal and informal communication work efficiently and effectively. Using ICT elsewhere and relying on it during Arctic operations may also create complacency with regard to a lack of back-up plans if ICT fails or raise the level of expectation among operators that it will always be available. If limited bandwidth or adverse environmental conditions cause ICT to be unavailable, the network's reliance on ICT may hamper its collective actions.

5.2. Increasing Noticeability of Individual Actions

ICT also plays a role in relation to free riding, which is a common problem of collective action [21] and represents individual behaviours not complying with commonly established norms [28].

If opportunities for free riding exist, at least some of the actors will be tempted to utilize them and pursue individual benefits while not contributing to the collective efforts [16,28]. Opportunities for free riding decrease as information asymmetries are reduced, i.e., as transparency of actions taken by individual network members increases. In AECO, such increased noticeability is enabled by ICT, most notably through the monitoring of cruise traffic, the evaluation of impacts, and awareness about other operators' itineraries (see Figure 4). The noticeability of individual network members' actions is increased through real-time monitoring of cruise vessels, and it is possible to report those who do not comply with existing rules, e.g., by accessing restricted areas.

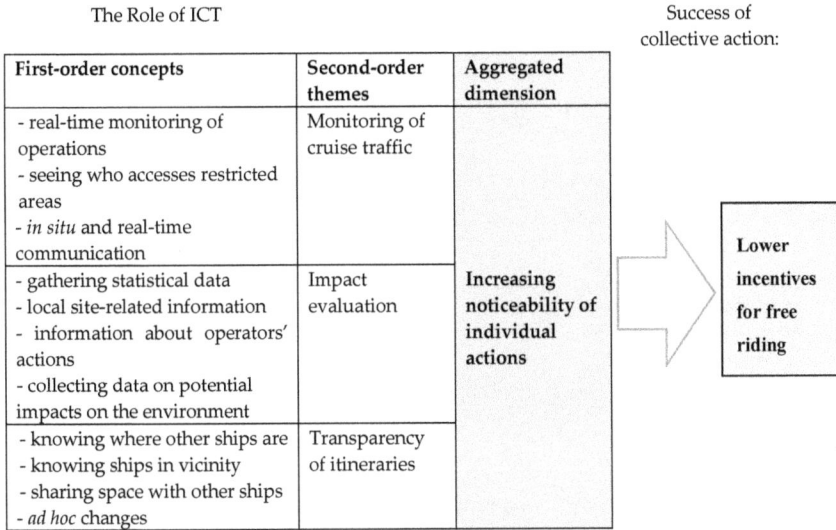

First-order concepts	Second-order themes	Aggregated dimension		
- real-time monitoring of operations - seeing who accesses restricted areas - *in situ* and real-time communication	Monitoring of cruise traffic			
- gathering statistical data - local site-related information - information about operators' actions - collecting data on potential impacts on the environment	Impact evaluation	**Increasing noticeability of individual actions**		
- knowing where other ships are - knowing ships in vicinity - sharing space with other ships - *ad hoc* changes	Transparency of itineraries			

The Role of ICT — Success of collective action: **Lower incentives for free riding**

Figure 4. Increasing noticeability of individual actions.

Increased noticeability enables a network to assess to what extent their norms, as well as governmental regulations, are complied with, which makes free riding less attractive, provided unwanted behaviours can be sanctioned either explicitly or implicitly. Increased noticeability also builds a knowledge base about the individual actions, which can assist in decision-making, e.g., with regard to adjusting existing visitation limits or developing new visitation guidelines. Conversely, increased transparency about cruise itineraries may potentially increase opportunities for free riding as it enables operators to see which landing sites are unutilized at what times and could be accessed without anyone else noticing. Thus, social capital plays a crucial role in terms of creating relationships of trust and peer pressure which can help ensuring that norms are followed.

Further, effective monitoring of cruising activities requires the network to be comprehensive and all resource users to be involved. Challenges arise if one or more resource users are not the part of the network, which is an issue that is also lamented by AECO members: "*I see a problem, though, with people, big ships, that are not member of AECO. They still can do the same as we, but they don't pay anything and they don't have to keep to the rules of AECO*" (research participant 4). Currently, the monitoring of tourism sites in Svalbard only relates to network members and ignores the actions of other resource users. Similarly, social control is limited to the network members, as there is no obligation for external actors to comply with the network's norms.

5.3. Creating Artificial Proximity

ICT builds artificial proximity among a set of spatially dispersed actors in a remote location [78], which strengthens not only informal relations between actors but also the actors' connections to the location. Through artificial proximity, distances between the actors themselves, as well as between the actors and the location are reduced (see Figure 5). Informal contacts and arrangements are a part of network functioning, and the utilization of ICT can create informal proximity.

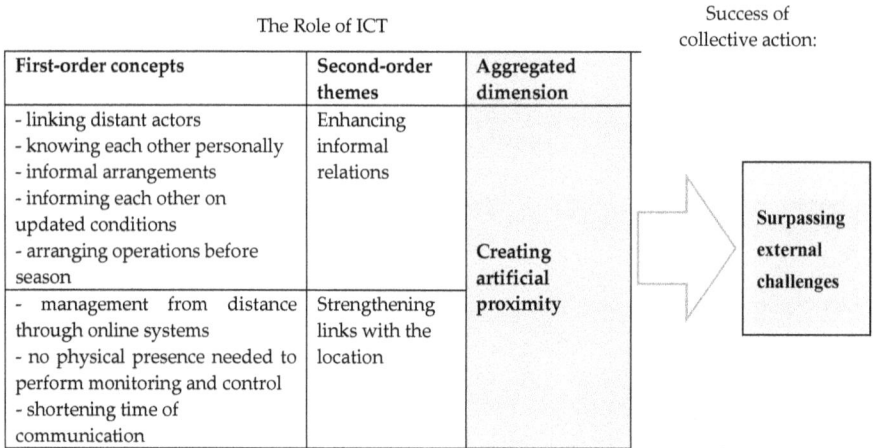

The Role of ICT

Success of collective action:

First-order concepts	Second-order themes	Aggregated dimension	
- linking distant actors - knowing each other personally - informal arrangements - informing each other on updated conditions - arranging operations before season	Enhancing informal relations	Creating artificial proximity	**Surpassing external challenges**
- management from distance through online systems - no physical presence needed to perform monitoring and control - shortening time of communication	Strengthening links with the location		

Figure 5. Creating artificial proximity.

Our findings suggest that network actors can participate in collective action in a location different from where they reside by relying on ICT providing them with up-to-date knowledge about an area and its use. Imposing obligations on network actors to provide data, e.g., submitting their itineraries, not only assigns responsibilities to actors but emphasizes their resource use impact and offers opportunities for electronic monitoring using online resources, e.g., via the vessel tracking system.

AECO network actors are from different parts of the world and operate in Svalbard on a temporary basis, i.e., they usually only spend a few weeks or months each year in the area. Real-time communication facilitated through ICT gives the network actors greater flexibility and swiftness in decision-making, increasing the network's efficiency. In addition, as we highlighted above, the artificial proximity created by ICT supports the formation of stronger relationships between actors, which are a crucial aspect of collective action.

6. Concluding Discussion

Our results show that ICT facilitates collective action by building new management practices, increasing the noticeability of individual actions, and creating artificial proximity between actors in a network. The effective use of ICT has the potential to increase the success of collective action towards sustainable tourism management, especially by offering a way to overcome challenges related to operating in remote locations. However, while the use of ICT can add to the social capital within a network and consequently contribute to the success of collective action [55], social capital goes beyond ICT and is also defined by the relationships between network actors, trust, transparency, interdependence and existing normative systems. Actors can utilize ICT to reshape the relationships within a network, which will have a bearing on their performance [48,79] as well as the efficacy of collective action by the network.

ICT has the potential to reduce free riding and to better coordinate and monitor the actions of culturally and spatially diverse actor networks [21]. By creating artificial proximity and additional avenues for monitoring, ICT can help to overcome challenges in collective action that are common in larger groups. Our study confirms that large and spatially dispersed actor networks are in a position to successfully manage natural resources provided individual actors share the same goals and collective action is possible. Geographical boundaries can be overcome by the use of ICT [45].

Our research has also shown that, in some cases, it is prudent to consider not only the impact and collective action of local residents but also those of external resource users in sustainable tourism management [19]. However, in line with Lupia and Sin (2003) [21], we argue that ICT itself is not sufficient to reduce free riding or increase proximity as actors need to learn how to properly use the respective ICT. We recognize the role of building appropriate management practices drawing on a network's social capital as a necessary element in ensuring the success of ICT use in collective action.

Our work has expanded an ongoing debate on ICT in collective action by highlighting the importance of ICT in addressing challenges related to networks operating in remote locations. In particular, in dynamic polar environments such as Svalbard, AECO uses ICT to overcome location-related constraints to collective action, including issues arising from a tourism site's remoteness, challenging operational conditions, a lack of governmental oversight and monitoring of the activities of individual operators, or the temporary nature of Arctic tourism operations. Overall, the success of collective efforts becomes partly dependent on ICT, with the effectiveness of ICT use being built on the interaction between resource users and the wider environment [45].

The research presented in this paper has implications for the development of practices and policy in a broader context that goes beyond the tourism network. Adopting ICT solutions that are tailored to specific networks and give privileged access to network members excludes other actors from participating in collective action, whilst not restricting their access to common-pool resources. This, in turn, means that the most successful collective action to manage common-pool resources may still result in resource degradation or depletion, if actors operating outside established collective action networks cannot be not excluded from resource use [80] or at least required, e.g., by governmental mandates, to operate in accordance with the rules established by the collective action network. Alternatively, non-member operators could be encouraged to join a network, but this traditionally only works if they already share similar values and backgrounds with an existing network's members, which in turn increases network homogeneity [81]. The latter can also be strengthened by creating dependence on network-specific technologies. However, as Poteete and Ostrom (2004) [35] argue, a certain level of heterogeneity is beneficial for collective action, which would imply that collective action could benefit from making ICT systems available for all users of common-pool resources. On the other hand, access to technologies is an incentive for joining the network and accepting its sustainability goals. Hence, an externally imposed obligation to be a member of AECO to operate commercial cruise tourism in Svalbard could be beneficial for collective action.

ICT creates internal dependence within a network while contributing to its external independence. Currently, AECO's ICT systems are not fully integrated with Svalbard's governmental tourism management systems, and operators have to report through different systems at the same time. This creates confusion among operators and results in trade-offs being made between investing time and resources in reporting on activities and undertaking the actual tourism activities themselves [15]. By providing alternative tools to those introduced by governmental authorities, AECO, as a network of resource users, partially takes over responsibilities of tourism governance and in-situ management [28] and may even be more effective than the government in managing tourism sites. In our case, the introduction of ICT in support of collective action blurs the boundary between the public and private realm [43] by enabling non-governmental organizations, at least partially, to replace government functions with self-regulation.

As we have shown, in the context of Arctic tourism ICT can contribute to the success of collective action by adjusting norms to sustainability goals, decreasing incentives for free riding, creating artificial proximity between geographically dispersed actors, and overcoming some of the challenges of operating in remote places. However, we stress that, while technology is an asset in collective action, it does not automatically guarantee its success. ICT has limitations, e.g., in relation to its versatility, its structural rigidity or the users' ICT capabilities, and a broader suite of social capital is needed to effectively use ICT in collective action.

Besides, many Arctic locations are sparsely populated, but attract economic interest, not only from tourism, but also, e.g., fishing or oil and gas industry. ICT helps to better monitor changes in Arctic environment and enables on-going responses to the observed pressures. In locations far from human settlements, industry monitoring is often the only way to follow environmental changes caused by human activities.

Our study is subject to a number of limitations. Firstly, by taking a case-study approach, our results cannot be easily generalized and are to be viewed within a Svalbard context. More research with different geographical foci is needed to develop a broader, and more generalizable, understanding of the role of ICT in collective action in Arctic tourism operations. Secondly, as the approach we used to study the role of ICT in collective action in tourism is novel, further work is needed before we can conceptualize the role of ICT in relation to the social capital of tourism networks. While ICT is nowadays widely used by the tourism industry, including in the management of nature-based tourism sites, we still only have limited understanding of its roles and impact, which we explored in this study through a social capital lens.

A message that clearly emerges from our research is that ICT has a role to play in sustainable tourism management, especially in remote Arctic environments. Collaborative efforts by the tourism industry and government authorities, both with the support of ICT, could successfully minimize crowding in Arctic tourism destinations. However, with potentially more and more actors operating in the Arctic, within or outside AECO, a fine balance needs to be struck between the quantity and quality of touristic visits as an increasing number of operators may detract from the core ideal of nature-based tourism, which is essentially low-volume and high-value [34].

Acknowledgments: This article is a part of Marta Bystrowska's PhD project realized at the Centre for Polar Studies in Poland. We would like to thank AECO and our informants for sharing their time, experiences and insights.

Author Contributions: Marta Bystrowska and Karin Wigger designed the study and collected and analysed the data. Marta Bystrowska mainly was responsible for the secondary data and Karin Wigger for the interviews. Marta Bystrowska prepared the figures. Both authors contributed to the writing of the paper. Daniela Liggett contributed in the final stages of discussing and analysing the data and of manuscript preparation. Daniela Liggett also contributed to the writing of the paper.

Conflicts of Interest: The authors declare no conflict of interest.

References

1. Mason, P.; Johnston, M.; Twynam, D. The world wide fund for nature arctic tourism project. *J. Sustain. Tour.* **2000**, *8*, 305–323. [CrossRef]
2. Dawson, J.; Maher, P.T.; Slocombe, S.D. Climate change, marine tourism, and sustainability in the canadian arctic: Contributions from systems and complexity approaches. *Tour. Mar. Environ.* **2007**, *4*, 69–83. [CrossRef]
3. Mason, P. Tourism codes of conduct in the arctic and sub-arctic region. *J. Sustain. Tour.* **1997**, *5*, 151–165. [CrossRef]
4. Haase, D.; Lamers, M.; Amelung, B. Heading into uncharted territory? Exploring the institutional robustness of self-regulation in the antarctic tourism sector. *J. Sustain. Tour.* **2009**, *17*, 411–430. [CrossRef]
5. Briassoulis, H. Sustainable tourism and the question of the commons. *Ann. Tour. Res.* **2002**, *29*, 1065–1085. [CrossRef]
6. Duffus, D.A.; Dearden, P. Non-consumptive wildlife-oriented recreation: A conceptual framework. *Biol. Conserv.* **1990**, *53*, 213–231. [CrossRef]
7. Huybers, T.; Bennett, J. Environmental management and the competitiveness of nature-based tourism destinations. *Environ. Resour. Econ.* **2003**, *24*, 213–233. [CrossRef]

8. Kaltenborn, B.P.; Emmelin, L. Tourism in the high north: Management challenges and recreation opportunity spectrum planning in Svalbard, Norway. *Environ. Manag.* **1993**, *17*, 41. [CrossRef]

9. Hall, C.M. Policy learning and policy failure in sustainable tourism governance: From first- and second-order to third-order change? *J. Sustain. Tour.* **2011**, *19*, 649–671. [CrossRef]

10. Nijkamp, P.; Van den Bergh, C.; Soeteman, F.J. Regional sustainable development and natural resource use. *World Bank Econ. Rev.* **1990**, *4*, 153–188. [CrossRef]

11. Erkuş-Öztürk, H.; Eraydın, A. Environmental governance for sustainable tourism development: Collaborative networks and organisation building in the antalya tourism region. *Tour. Manag.* **2010**, *31*, 113–124. [CrossRef]

12. Dawson, J.; Johnston, M.E.; Stewart, E.J. Governance of arctic expedition cruise ships in a time of rapid environmental and economic change. *Ocean Coast. Manag.* **2014**, *89*, 88–99. [CrossRef]

13. Adger, W.N. Social capital, collective action, and adaptation to climate change. *Econ. Geogr.* **2003**, *79*, 387–404. [CrossRef]

14. Vanni, F. Agriculture and public goods. In *Agriculture and Public Goods*; Springer: Dordrecht, The Netherlands, 2014; pp. 1–19.

15. Van Bets, L.K.J.; Lamers, M.A.J.; van Tatenhove, J.P.M. Collective self-governance in a marine community: Expedition cruise tourism at Svalbard. *J. Sustain. Tour.* **2017**, 1–17. [CrossRef]

16. Olson, M. *The Logic of Collective Action*, 4th ed.; Harvard University Press: Cambridge, MA, USA, 2009; Volume 124.

17. Vicky, K. The role of icts in regional tourist development. *Reg. Sci. Inq.* **2011**, *3*, 95–111.

18. Lamers, M.; Pristupa, A.; Amelung, B.; Knol, M. The changing role of environmental information in arctic marine governance. *Curr. Opin. Environ. Sustain.* **2016**, *18*, 49–55. [CrossRef]

19. Dickinson, J.E.; Filimonau, V.; Hibbert, J.F.; Cherrett, T.; Davies, N.; Norgate, S.; Speed, C.; Winstanley, C. Tourism communities and social ties: The role of online and offline tourist social networks in building social capital and sustainable practice. *J. Sustain. Tour.* **2017**, *25*, 163–180. [CrossRef]

20. Lee, B.C. The impact of social capital on tourism technology adoption for destination marketing. *Curr. Issues Tour.* **2015**, *18*, 561–578. [CrossRef]

21. Lupia, A.; Sin, G. Which public goods are endangered? How evolving communication technologies affect the logic of collective action. *Public Choice* **2003**, *117*, 315–331. [CrossRef]

22. Boyle, S.A.; Samson, F.B. Effects of nonconsumptive recreation on wildlife: A review. *Wildl. Soc. Bull. (1973–2006)* **1985**, *13*, 110–116.

23. Tsaur, S.-H.; Lin, Y.-C.; Lin, J.-H. Evaluating ecotourism sustainability from the integrated perspective of resource, community and tourism. *Tour. Manag.* **2006**, *27*, 640–653. [CrossRef]

24. Steven, R.; Pickering, C.; Castley, J.G. A review of the impacts of nature based recreation on birds. *J. Environ. Manag.* **2011**, *92*, 2287–2294. [CrossRef] [PubMed]

25. Evenseth, A.; Christensen, G.N. *Enviromental Impacts of Expedition Cruise Traffic around Svalbard*; Akvaplan-niva: Tromsø, Norway, 2011.

26. Kling, R.; Rosenbaum, H.; Sawyer, S. *Understanding and Communicating Social Informatics*; Information Today Inc.: Medford, NJ, USA, 2005.

27. Kling, R. What is social informatics and why does it matter? *Inf. Soc.* **2007**, *23*, 205–220. [CrossRef]

28. Ostrom, E. *Governing the Commons: The Evolution of Institutions for Collective Action*; Cambridge University Press: Cambridge, UK, 1990.

29. Ostrom, E.; Gardner, R.; Walker, J. *Rules, Games, and Common-Pool Resources*; University of Michigan Press: Ann Arbor, MI, USA, 1994.

30. Pretty, J. Social capital and the collective management of resources. *Science* **2003**, *302*, 1912–1914. [CrossRef] [PubMed]

31. Hardin, G. The tragedy of the commons. *Science* **1968**, *162*, 1243–1248. [CrossRef] [PubMed]

32. Healy, R.G. The "common pool" problem in tourism landscapes. *Ann. Tour. Res.* **1994**, *21*, 596–611. [CrossRef]

33. Lindberg, K.; McCool, S.; Stankey, G. Rethinking carrying capacity. *Ann. Tour. Res.* **1997**, *24*, 461–465. [CrossRef]

34. Valentine, P. Nature-based tourism. In *Special Interest Tourism*; Weiler, B., Hall, C.M., Eds.; Belhaven: London, UK, 1992; pp. 105–127.

35. Poteete, A.R.; Ostrom, E. Heterogeneity, group size and collective action: The role of institutions in forest management. *Dev. Chang.* **2004**, *35*, 435–461. [CrossRef]
36. Agrawal, A. Sustainable governance of common-pool resources: Context, methods, and politics. *Annu. Rev. Anthropol.* **2003**, *32*, 243–262. [CrossRef]
37. Libecap, G.D. State regulation of open-access, common-pool resources. In *Handbook of New Institutional Economics*; Springer: Dordrecht, The Netherlands, 2005; pp. 545–572.
38. Adams, W.M.; Brockington, D.; Dyson, J.; Vira, B. Managing tragedies: Understanding conflict over common pool resources. *Science* **2003**, *302*, 1915–1916. [CrossRef] [PubMed]
39. Steins, N.A.; Edwards, V.M. Collective action in common-pool resource management: The contribution of a social constructivist perspective to existing theory. *Soc. Nat. Resour.* **1999**, *12*, 539–557.
40. Marwell, G.; Oliver, P. *The Critical Mass in Collective Action*; Cambridge University Press: Cambridge, UK, 1993.
41. Albanese, R.; van Fleet, D.D. Rational behavior in groups: The free-riding tendency. *Acad. Manag. Rev.* **1985**, *10*, 244–255.
42. Ahn, T.-K.; Ostrom, E. Social capital and collective action. In *The Handbook of Social Capital*; Castiglione, D., Van Deth, J.W., Wolleb, G., Eds.; Oxford University Press: Oxford, UK, 2008; pp. 70–100.
43. Bimber, B.; Flanagin, A.J.; Stohl, C. Reconceptualizing collective action in the contemporary media environment. *Commun. Theory* **2005**, *15*, 365–388. [CrossRef]
44. Wade, R. The management of common property resources: Collective action as an alternative to privatisation or state regulation. *Camb. J. Econ.* **1987**, *11*, 95–106. [CrossRef]
45. Agrawal, A. Common property institutions and sustainable governance of resources. *World Dev.* **2001**, *29*, 1649–1672. [CrossRef]
46. Wade, R. *Village Republics: Economic Conditions for Collective Action in South India*; ICS Press: Oakland, CA, USA, 1988.
47. Ostrom, E. *Understanding Institutional Diversity*; Princeton University Press: Princeton, NJ, USA, 2005.
48. Vargo, S.L.; Wieland, H.; Akaka, M.A. Innovation through institutionalization: A service ecosystems perspective. *Ind. Mark. Manag.* **2015**, *44*, 63–72. [CrossRef]
49. Norris, P. *Democratic Phoenix: Reinventing Political Activism*; Cambridge University Press: Cambridge, UK, 2002.
50. Kling, R. Learning about information technologies and social change: The contribution of social informatics. *Inf. Soc.* **2000**, *16*, 217–232. [CrossRef]
51. Sawyer, S.; Rosenbaum, H. Social informatics in the information sciences: Current activities and emerging directions. *Inf. Sci.* **2000**, *3*, 89–95.
52. Smutny, Z. Social informatics as a concept: Widening the discourse. *J. Inf. Sci.* **2016**, *42*, 681–710. [CrossRef]
53. Fichman, P.; Rosenbaum, H. *Social Informatics: Past, Present and Future*; Cambridge Scholars Publishing: Newcastle upon Tyne, UK, 2014.
54. Licoppe, C.; Smoreda, Z. Are social networks technologically embedded? How networks are changing today with changes in communication technology. *Soc. Netw.* **2005**, *27*, 317–335. [CrossRef]
55. Sawyer, S.; Jarrahi, M.H. Sociotechnical approaches to the study of information systems. In *Computing Handbook, Third Edition: Information Systems and Information Technology*; Tucker, A., Gonzalez, T., Topi, H., Diaz-Herrera, J., Eds.; Chapman and Hall/CRC: London, UK, 2014.
56. Coleman, J.S. *Foundations of Social Theory*; Harvard University Press: Cambridge, MA, USA, 1990.
57. Jones, S. Community-based ecotourism: The significance of social capital. *Ann. Tour. Res.* **2005**, *32*, 303–324. [CrossRef]
58. Fountain, J.E. Social capital: Its relationship to innovation in science and technology. *Sci. Public Policy* **1998**, *25*, 103–115.
59. Fukuyama, F. Social capital, civil society and development. *Third World Q.* **2001**, *22*, 7–20. [CrossRef]
60. Resnick, P. Impersonal sociotechnical capital, icts, and collective action among strangers. In *Transforming Enterprise: The Economic And Social Implications of Information Technology*; Dutton, W.H., Kahin, B., O'Callaghan, R., Wyckoff, A.W., Eds.; MIT Press: Cambridge, MA, USA, 2005; pp. 399–412.
61. Stake, R.E. Qualitative case study. In *The Sage Handbook of Qualitative Research*; Denzin, N.K., Lincoln, Y.S., Eds.; Sage: Newcastle upon Tyne, UK, 2005; pp. 443–467.
62. Ketokivi, M.; Choi, T. Renaissance of case research as a scientific method. *J. Oper. Manag.* **2014**, *32*, 232–240. [CrossRef]

63. Baxter, P.; Jack, S. Qualitative case study methodology: Study design and implementation for novice researchers. *Qual. Rep.* **2008**, *13*, 544–559.

64. Yin, R.K. *Case Study Research: Design and Methods*; Sage Publications: London, UK, 2013.

65. Guba, E.G.; Lincoln, Y.S. Epistemological and methodological bases of naturalistic inquiry. *ECTJ* **1982**, *30*, 233–252.

66. Gibbert, M.; Ruigrok, W.; Wicki, B. What passes as a rigorous case study? *Strateg. Manag. J.* **2008**, *29*, 1465–1474. [CrossRef]

67. Turner, D.W., III. Qualitative interview design: A practical guide for novice investigators. *Qual. Rep.* **2010**, *15*, 754.

68. Gioia, D.A.; Corley, K.G.; Hamilton, A.L. Seeking qualitative rigor in inductive research: Notes on the gioia methodology. *Organ. Res. Methods* **2013**, *16*, 15–31. [CrossRef]

69. Bazeley, P.; Jackson, K. *Qualitative Data Analysis with Nvivo*; Sage Publications Limited: Beverly Hills, CA, USA, 2013.

70. Saldaña, J. *The Coding Manual for Qualitative Researchers*; Sage: Newcastle upon Tyne, UK, 2015.

71. Campbell, J.L.; Quincy, C.; Osserman, J.; Pedersen, O.K. Coding in-depth semistructured interviews: Problems of unitization and intercoder reliability and agreement. *Sociol. Methods Res.* **2013**, *42*, 294–320. [CrossRef]

72. Lier, M.; Aarvik, S.; Fossum, K.; von Quillfeldt, C.; Overrein, Ø.; Barr, S.; Huberth Hansen, J.-P.; Ekker, M. *Protected Natural Areas on Svalbard*; Norwegian Directorate for Nature Management: Trondheim, Norway, 2009.

73. Eeg-Henriksen, F.; Sjømæling, E. *This Is Svalbard*; Statistics Norway: Oslo, Norway, 2016.

74. Bystrowska, M.; Dolnicki, P. The impact of endogenous factors on diversification of tourism space in the arctic. *Curr. Issues Tour. Res.* **2017**, *5*, 36–43.

75. Governor of Svalbard. *Reiselivsstatistikk for Svalbard 2014 (Travel Statistics for Svalbard 2014)*; Office of the Governor of Svalbard: Longyearbyen, Norway, 2015.

76. Berkes, F.; Colding, J.; Folke, C. Navigating social-ecological systems. In *Building Resilience for Complexity and Change*; Cambridge University Press: Cambridge, MA, USA, 2003.

77. Aase, J.G.; Jabour, J. Can monitoring maritime activities in the European high arctic by satellite-based automatic identification system enhance polar search and rescue? *Polar J.* **2015**, *5*, 386–402. [CrossRef]

78. Kraut, R.E.; Fish, R.S.; Root, R.W.; Chalfonte, B.L. Informal Communication in Organizations: Form, Function, and Technology. In *Human Reactions to Technology: The Claremont Symposium on Applies Social Psychology*; Sage Publications: Beverly Hills, CA, USA, 1990; pp. 145–199.

79. Orlikowski, W.J. Using technology and constituting structures: A practice lens for studying technology in organizations. *Organ. Sci.* **2000**, *11*, 404–428. [CrossRef]

80. Schlager, E.; Ostrom, E. Property-rights regimes and natural resources: A conceptual analysis. *Land Econ.* **1992**, *68*, 249–262. [CrossRef]

81. Carlsson, L.; Sandström, A. Network governance of the commons. *Int. J. Commons* **2008**, *1*, 33–54. [CrossRef]

resources

MDPI

Article

The Forgotten Islands: Monitoring Tourist Numbers and Managing Tourism Impacts on New Zealand's Subantarctic Islands

Emma J. Stewart [1,*], Stephen Espiner [1], Daniela Liggett [2] and Zac Taylor [1]

[1] Faculty of Environment, Society & Design, Lincoln University, P.O. Box 85084, Lincoln 7647, Christchurch, New Zealand; Stephen.espiner@lincoln.ac.nz (S.E.); zac_t87@hotmail.com (Z.T.)

[2] Gateway Antarctica, University of Canterbury, Private Bag 4800, Christchurch, New Zealand; daniela.liggett@canterbury.ac.nz

* Correspondence: emma.stewart @lincoln.ac.nz; Tel: +64-3-423-0500

Received: 2 June 2017; Accepted: 11 August 2017; Published: 15 August 2017

Abstract: Situated to the south of New Zealand in the Southern Ocean are the New Zealand Subantarctic Islands, comprising the Auckland, Campbell, Antipodes, Snares and Bounty Islands. Sometimes referred to as the 'Forgotten Islands', these island groups are among the most remote and hostile within New Zealand waters. Yet, as they harbour some of the country's most unique biodiversity and contain some of the world's least modified landforms, they were recognized in 1998 with the designation of World Heritage Area status. It is not surprising therefore that the Islands have long appealed to visitors wishing to explore and understand the Islands' rich natural and cultural environments. Typically, fare-paying tourists arrive by sea in small- to medium-sized expedition-style cruise vessels, although in recent years, the number of small vessels, such as yachts and sail boats, has increased. The most recent Conservation Management Strategy (2016) proposes developing and implementing a visitor monitoring programme to determine the effects of visitors on the natural and cultural environment, as well as on the visitor experience itself. However, there is only piecemeal data published on visitor numbers (especially since the mid-1990s) upon which to base visitor monitoring, and there is only limited evidence regarding the range of possible impacts visitors may have, including direct and indirect impact on wildlife, soils, and vegetation. In order to address this gap in knowledge, this case study draws on stakeholder interviews ($n = 4$), and a range of secondary sources (including visitor statistics from the Department of Conservation, tour operators and other published works) to provide an overview and update on visitation to the Islands, including site-specific data, an assessment of tourist impacts, and how impacts are currently monitored and managed.

Keywords: New Zealand Subantarctic Islands; tourism; impacts; monitoring

1. Introduction

Throughout the Subantarctic region are widely scattered islands, occurring in ten recognized groups, belonging to six states [1]. The New Zealand Subantarctic Islands are made up of five groups of islands: The Auckland Islands; Campbell Island; Antipodes Islands; Snares Islands; and Bounty Islands (see Figure 1). Often called the 'Forgotten Islands', these islands and their coastal environments are among the most remote and hostile within New Zealand's waters. However, they are home to some of the country's most unique biodiversity and contain some of the least modified landforms in the world. The Subantarctic Islands' climate and geographical isolation from mainland New Zealand, and from each other, has enabled these islands to become a sanctuary for a wide range of biodiversity with a high degree of endemism. These features contributed to their designation as national nature reserves in 1986, one of the highest levels of statutory protection in New Zealand.

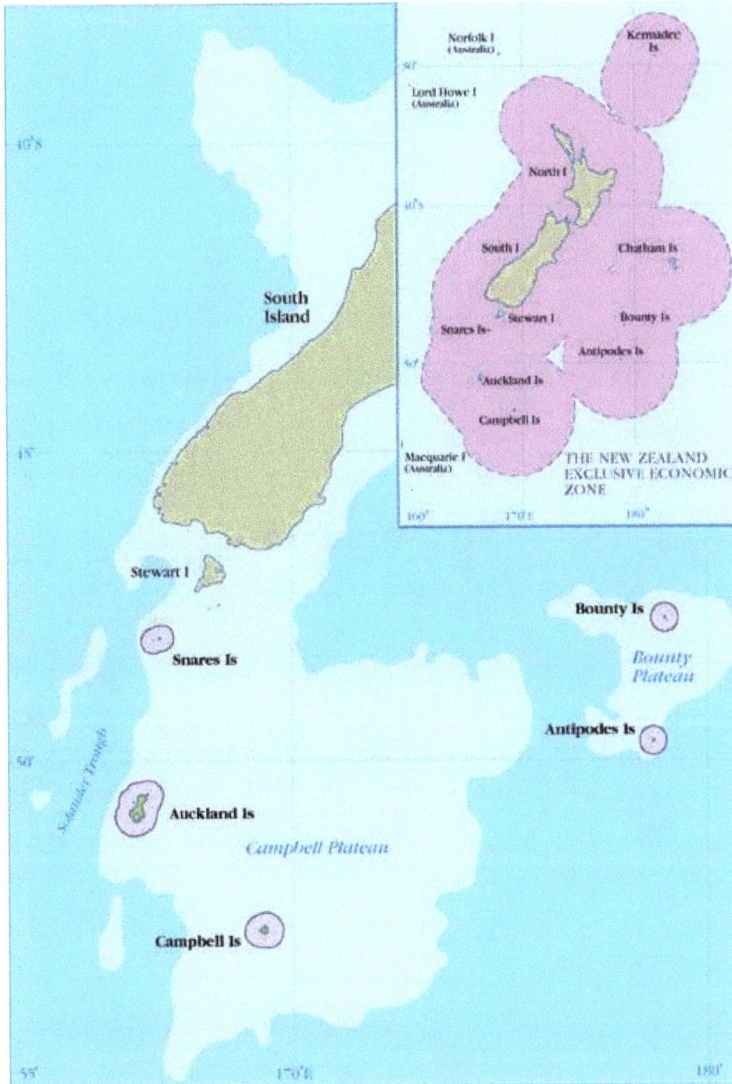

Figure 1. Location of the New Zealand Subantarctic Islands [2].

Furthermore, in 1998, these island groups and their coastlines were internationally recognized as a World Heritage Area due to their outstanding representation of significant ongoing ecological and biological processes and their ability to provide natural habitats for threatened species with outstanding universal value from the point of view of science and conservation (criteria 9 and 10, see The United Nations Educational, Scientific and Cultural Organization (UNESCO) criteria; Department of Conservation, 2014; UNESCO, 1998) (see Table 1).

Table 1. New Zealand Subantarctic Islands and their features [3–6]. DOC: Department of Conservation.

Island Group	Area (ha)	Mean Temp (°C)	Annual Rainfall (mm)	Key Dates	Current Conservation Status	Visitor Access
Auckland Islands	62,560 40 km long, 12 km wide (at its widest)	8	1000–1500	Reserve for preservation of Fauna and Flora 1934. Nature Reserve 1977; under Reserves Act 1977. National Nature Reserve 1986. Marine sanctuary in 1993; under the Marine Mammals Protection Act 1978. Marine reserve in 2003	National Nature Reserve 1986, and World Heritage Area 1998	Landings permitted as part of a guided trip, if a permit is obtained through DOC
Campbell Island	11,331	6		Reserve for preservation of Fauna and Flora 1954. Nature Reserve 1977; under Reserves Act 1977. National Nature Reserve 1986. Marine reserve in 2014	National Nature Reserve 1986, and World Heritage Area 1998	Landings permitted as part of a guided trip, if a permit is obtained through DOC
Antipodes Islands	2097	8 (estimate)	1000–1500	Reserve for preservation of Fauna and Flora 1961. Nature Reserve 1977; under Reserves Act 1977. National Nature Reserve 1986. Marine reserve in 2014	National Nature Reserve 1986, and World Heritage Area 1998	No tourist landings. Cruising permitted
Snares Islands	328	11	1200	Reserve for preservation of Fauna and Flora 1961. Nature Reserve 1977; under Reserves Act 1977. National Nature Reserve 1986	National Nature Reserve 1986, and World Heritage Area 1998	No tourist landings. Cruising permitted
Bounty Islands	135 Depot Island the largest at 800 m long	10 (est)		Reserve for preservation of Fauna and Flora 1961. Nature Reserve 1977; under Reserves Act 1977. National Nature Reserve 1986 Marine reserve in 2014	National Nature Reserve 1986, and World Heritage Area 1998	No tourist landings. Cruising permitted

Since tour operators first began offering commercial cruises in 1967, these Islands have seen an increasing number of tourists [7,8]. Until 1987, only one to two ships visited the Islands annually, bringing with them between 45 and 190 passengers over the duration of each cruise season. Since this time, visitation increased, and a record season between 2008 and 2009 saw 17 vessels bring 1333 passengers to view the New Zealand Subantarctic Islands [8] (the 2008–2009 season also saw record numbers of tourists visiting the Antarctic Peninsula [9]). With such a substantial number of visitors comes the potential for biophysical impacts on these environments, each with varying degrees of significance. Being able to effectively manage these impacts is of utmost importance to the Department of Conservation (DOC), the sole governing body in charge of the management of these island groups. In 2016, DOC published the revised Conservation Management Strategy [10] for the Islands, and proposed a visitor monitoring programme to determine the effects of visitors on the natural and cultural environment, as well as on the visitor experience itself. Critical to the success of the visitor monitoring programme is the availability of reliable data on tourism activities.

However, there is only piecemeal data reported on visitor numbers in the literature (especially since the mid-1990s), and while a knowledge base around the impacts and origins of non-native species in the Antarctic [11,12], and to some extent in the Subantarctic has been established [13] there is limited evidence regarding the full range of possible impacts visitors to the New Zealand Subantarctic Islands may have. In order to address this gap in knowledge, we first need to better understand the patterns and spatial extent of visitation to those islands as well as the impacts that have already been recorded. Responding to these research needs, the objectives of the research upon which this case study paper is based were to: (a) review relevant Department of Conservation visitor management documents and existing visitor data; (b) synthesize summaries of current visitor impact data and identify the range of human impacts occurring on the Islands; and (c) review current strategies for managing tourism to the Islands. As far as we are aware, this is the first time since the mid-1990s that the data on visitation to these islands has been collated, presented and organized at a site-specific scale.

2. Materials and Methods

The research was necessarily exploratory and largely descriptive in nature. In order to gain a holistic perspective on the management of tourism to New Zealand's Subantarctic Islands, a primarily desk-based approach was taken to collate information from a variety of sources, including:

(a) Peer-reviewed articles and prior research about the New Zealand Subantarctic Islands accessed through both internet databases and library catalogues. We used a keyword search of two online scholarly databases (Scopus and Google Scholar) for any articles that had a focus on tourism to the New Zealand Subantarctic Islands.

(b) Four semi-structured interviews, providing first-hand evidence relating to managing and visiting the New Zealand Subantarctic Islands held with a tour guide, a tour operator, a visitor, and a DOC advisor. The interviews focused on topics related to visitor experience, visitor impacts and visitor management. All interviews were transcribed verbatim, and recurring themes and topics were identified and further explored.

(c) A review of policy documents related to the conservation of the Islands and their management in respect of tourism to the Islands. The relevant policy documents were identified in conjunction with DOC and then independently analysed. DOC also provided some site vegetation monitoring data conducted between 2004 and 2013.

(d) An analysis of available data on visitor numbers based on a review of historic visitation (through previously published literature and from tour operators) and more current numbers, including site-specific data (from about 2004 onwards, although data is spotty) that were provided directly by DOC. A spreadsheet was created to show total visitor numbers arriving annually (as well as the number of vessels transporting visitors) in addition to visitation to key landing sites.

3. Results

In order to situate current tourism data, we provide a brief overview of human exploration of the Islands and the early developments in Subantarctic tourism in the following section. We then explore existing tourism data (both published and from DOC sources) to provide an updated overview of visitation to the Islands collectively, but also on a site basis.

3.1. Early Visitors

While early Māori knew of the existence of these islands, the first of the New Zealand Subantarctic Islands to be discovered by Europeans were the Bounty Islands in 1788 [3]. Over the next 22 years, each of the other four island groups were revealed during various European expeditions to this remote corner of the world, concluding with the discovery of the Campbell Islands in 1810 by Captain Frederick Hasselburgh on the Perseverance [3].

Following their discovery by Europeans, the Islands became a place of refuge for ships during the exploration of the Antarctic. As the Islands and their resources became known to the European explorers, permanent whaling bases and camps for sealers were established [6]. Unsurprisingly, by 1827, seal populations throughout southern New Zealand and the Subantarctic region had been severely depleted, although the sealing industry remained (at least in sporadic form) until the last open season on fur seals in New Zealand in 1946 [3].

The first whaling station was established at Port Ross, in the Auckland Islands, in 1850 but lasted less than three years [14]. The second attempt at establishing a permanent whaling station came years later, in Northwest Bay on Campbell Island in 1909, and Northeast Bay, also on Campbell Island, in 1911 [3]. While initially successful, the declaration of the First World War resulted in all resident whalers enlisting and heading to war in 1916 [6].

The decline in whaling and sealing around the Islands, resulted in the abandonment of any permanent settlements, although sheep, pigs, poultry, rabbits, and various vegetables and garden fruits were introduced on the Auckland Islands to serve as an emergency food supply for future castaways [3]. Attempts were made to establish farms on Auckland and Campbell Islands in 1894 and 1895, with the introduction of sheep and cattle. However, neither approach saw success, and the Islands ceased farming within a few decades (Auckland Island in 1910, and Campbell Island in 1931) [3]. Since that time, the Islands and their wildlife, both native and introduced, were largely left alone, other than sporadic scientific voyages. As the scientific knowledge about the Islands grew, they were declared National Nature Reserves in 1986, receiving the highest level of protection available under New Zealand legislation for the preservation of their indigenous biodiversity and natural features.

3.2. Visitor Numbers and Trends

Headland (1994) traces the earliest voyages carrying passengers identified as 'tourists' to Campbell Island and the Auckland Islands (as well the Australian Macquarie Island) to the early 1880s, when ships were commissioned to search for castaways and check the status of provisions deposited on the Islands [15]. However, the modern era of commercial tourism did not start until the 1960s when the Islands witnessed infrequent visitation from commercial vessels, such as the Lindbald Explorer (Lindbald Travel) and World Discovery (Society Expeditions). This era can be regarded as the early days in tourist visits to the Islands, where the total number of visitors between 1967 and 1985 was only 1034 (see Figure 2). A watershed moment came in 1988 when New Zealand-based nature tourism operators Discovery Charters South Seas, Southern Heritage Tours (now Heritage Expeditions) and Pegasus Dive Charters began offering yacht-based tours to the Islands for up to 20 people [5]. As a result, visitor numbers to the Subantarctic Islands dramatically increased, as is illustrated in Figure 2.

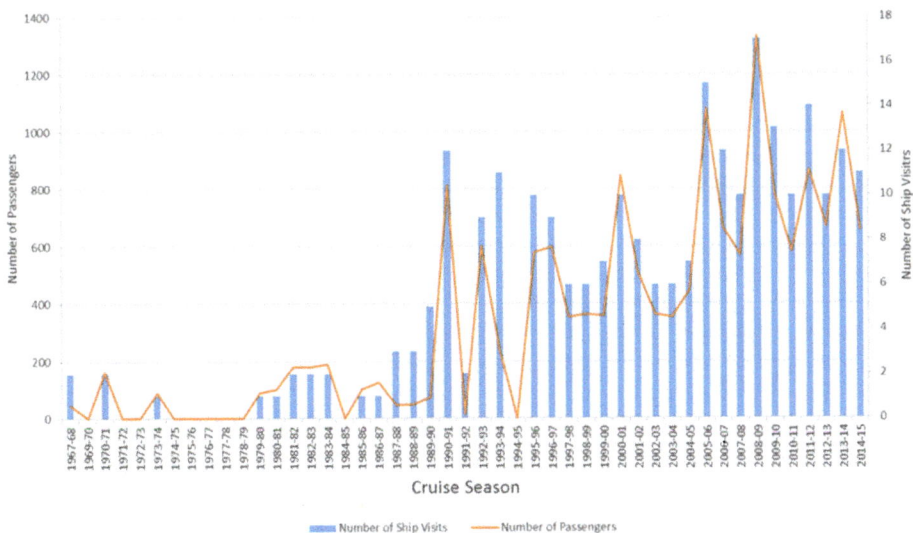

Figure 2. Visitor numbers to New Zealand's Subantarctic Islands 1967–2015 (after: [7,8]).

As the public became more aware of these islands, tourism operators sought to establish regular expedition cruises, allowing the public to experience the Islands and be educated about the unique flora and fauna found there. With these commercial offerings came an exponential increase in visitation, with 1201 visits over the six years spanning 1985 to 1991. This can be seen as the growth stage in tourism to the Subantarctic Islands.

Hall and Wouters (1994) suggest that there were four key reasons behind this initial increase in tourism to the Subantarctic region: (1) increase in public awareness of remote tourism destinations through increased exposure to wildlife documentaries, membership of conservation organizations, and advertising; (2) relative tourist overcrowding of the Antarctic Peninsula, leading some operators to search for more remote destinations that convey an Antarctic experience for visitors without other tourists being sighted; (3) improved ship-transport technology, making travel more comfortable and safer for tourists; and (4) overall expansion of the Antarctic/Subantarctic tourism market [5]. While the overall growth in tourist demand appears to have stabilized since the early 1990s, the volume of tourist visits to the Islands is now established, with 13,890 visits over this period (Figure 2). According to one tour operator:

> " … demand for visitation is currently described as 'flat', for example: The Islands are not a destination in their own right, they are a stop-over on the way, or way back from, Antarctica. If you don't stop at the Subs, it is a long time at sea. Generally there is a fixed number, of which is very small, a lot smaller than projections indicate. Any spikes in demand are due to other ships, taking one-off trips. The demand is flat."

These 'spikes' in demand, seen in seasons 2000–2001, 2005–2006 and 2008–2009, can be attributed to significant calendar events which may draw more passengers than other years, e.g., new millennium, Mawson Centenary, or Scott Centenary. Given that adventure and nature-based travel are two of the fastest growing sectors of the tourism industry [16], it is not surprising that areas such as the Subantarctic Islands have received such sustained visitation over the last 20 years.

Counting ship visits provides a crude overview of visitation. Knowing how many passengers are on each ship offers a better indication of the pressure placed on the environment during each visit. It may also help to explain some unusual trends found in the data, such as in the 2014–2015 season where 11 ships carried 657 passengers, but in the 2013–2014 season, 12 ships brought 1063 passengers. Conversely, a comparison of the seasons 1992–1993 and 1993–1994 shows two more ships in the 1993–1994 season, yet 360 fewer tourists. In order to determine how many passengers landed at each site per vessel, quotas and permits were introduced to help monitor impacts on the environment.

When visiting the New Zealand Subantarctic Islands, tourists have the chance to land on Auckland Island's Main Island and Enderby Island as well as Campbell Island, and to experience the Snares Islands via a zodiac boat (a small inflatable motorized dingy). Each island has specific visitor sites and tracks, allocated by DOC, allowing tourists access to various highlights the Islands have to offer. Research found that tourists visiting the New Zealand Subantarctic Islands and Antarctica were likely to be mature in age, highly educated, affluent, have a high degree of conservation group involvement, and generally very positive about their experiences and satisfactions derived from their visits [7]. Of the limited research conducted on the social aspects of tourism to the New Zealand Subantarctic Islands, the main motivations for going on a trip to these islands include the special settings, wildlife, and remoteness [7].

3.3. Managing Visitors

Tourist landings are only permitted on Auckland Islands' Main and Enderby Islands and on Campbell Island. While it is possible for visitors to observe the coastline of the Snares Island group via zodiac, no landings are permitted [4]. As visits became more frequent, formal management plans were established, for Campbell Island in 1983, the Snares in 1984, and the Auckland Islands in 1987. With these management plans came a quota and permit system, which was introduced by DOC to keep a record of shore landings.

For every shore landing, an entry permit is required per day and per person to cover quarantine and processing costs as well as the Subantarctic Guidebook, which is given to visitors [5]. An entry permit requires a fee to cover both processing of the permit and visitor impact management. Currently, the base fee amounts to NZD 150 per person. In addition, a landing fee of NZD 75 is charged per person and landing at hardened sites, i.e., the Enderby Island Northern Cliffs and Campbell Island Col-Lyall boardwalks. For other sites, the landing fee amounts to NZD 20 per person and day. The permits can be privately obtained, but are most often used by commercial operators who must also obtain a concession to authorize their business activities. A fee is also charged for a concession, which covers both the concession processing fee and a Crown Resources Rental of NZD 12 per day and person, or NZD 6 per half-day and person.

In 1990/1991, a quota of 500 visitors, or four ship visits, per season was set for the Auckland and Campbell Islands [5]. This quota was then increased to a maximum of 600 people to land at any one designated tourism site [5]. Permits are required for all land access, irrespective of purpose (for instance, research, tourism, management, etc.), and visitors are defined as 'people using areas and facilities managed by the Department of Conservation' [4] (p. 221). Although it is technically possible to arrange visits to the Islands independently, typically the Subantarctic Islands are visited using the services of a concessionaire/tour operator. The visitor quota and visitor management regime for the New Zealand Subantarctic Ilands came under revision in 2016 as part of the recent Conservation Management Strategy for the Southland Murihiku region [10].

3.4. Visitor Sites

Within the islands that allow landings, DOC has specified tracks and areas where tourists are permitted to visit (see Figures 3, 5 and 7). These sites are categorized into 'large' and 'small' sites, depending on the number of permits DOC has allocated for these visitation areas (Peat, 2006). Only three 'large' sites exist; Enderby Island, and the Enderby Island settlement/cemetery site in the Auckland Islands, and the Col-Lyall Saddle boardwalk site on Campbell Island. Up until recently, the 'small', more vulnerable sites could receive no more than 150 visitors per season, a number reviewed in the most recent Conservation Management Strategy (2016) [4,10]. Guidelines now identify

17 key visitor areas/or tracks and determine both (a) the maximum number of visitors per day, and (b) the maximum number of visitors per year. The smaller sites allow for 50 visitors per day (and between 50 and 400 visitors annually), while the two large sites, now identified as the Northern Cliffs (Enderby Island) and the Col-Lyall Saddle Track (Campbell Island), permit 200 visitors per day (and 1100 annually). The guidelines also allow for 25 landings per year by non-commercial visitors on small vessels [10].

The following maps (Figures 3, 5 and 7) depict selected landing sites on the Enderby, Auckland and Campbell Islands, and the accompanying charts outline visitation over time to a selection of key landing sites. All figures show the set quota in blue and the activated permits in red. In the past, quotas have been set on an annual basis, and have fluctuated quite significantly as the following figures indicate. The current Conservation Management Strategy (2016) has now fixed these quotas for the duration of the policy document, or until the proposed Subantarctic Visitor Management Plan is implemented (or until visitor facilities are improved to prevent adverse effects) [10].

3.4.1. Enderby Island

One of the most visited areas across the New Zealand Subantarctic Islands are the Northern Cliffs on Enderby Island (Figure 3), and it is here that DOC has installed boardwalks to minimize visitor impacts.

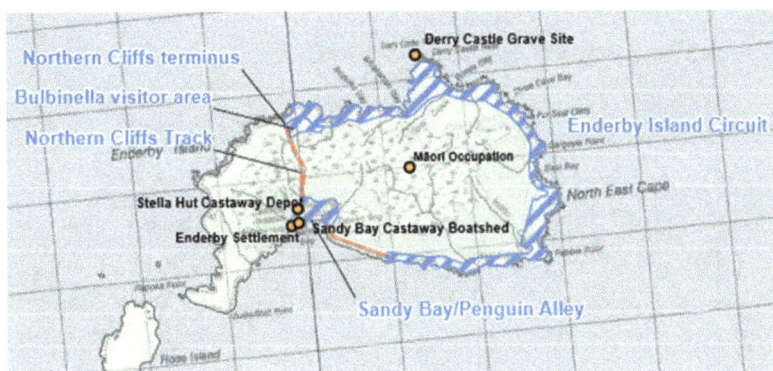

Figure 3. Enderby Island visitor areas, located north of Auckland Island. Blue shows visitor areas and red marks visitor tracks (Image retrieved from [17]) (p. 28).

As Figure 4 reveals, annual visitation to this site has fluctuated from approximately 300 to 750 visitors. It is noted for the 2011–2012 season that the set quota was exceeded for this site, perhaps reflecting a small spike in overall visitor numbers to the Islands (see Figure 2). The current Conservation Management Strategy allows for 200 visitors per day at Sandy Bay/Penguin Alley, Northern Cliffs Track and the Northern Cliffs terminus (Figure 3) and 1100 visitors annually [10]. Based on the historic data (presented in Figure 4), this new guideline more than accommodates existing demand, potentially inviting an increase in visitation to this site in the future.

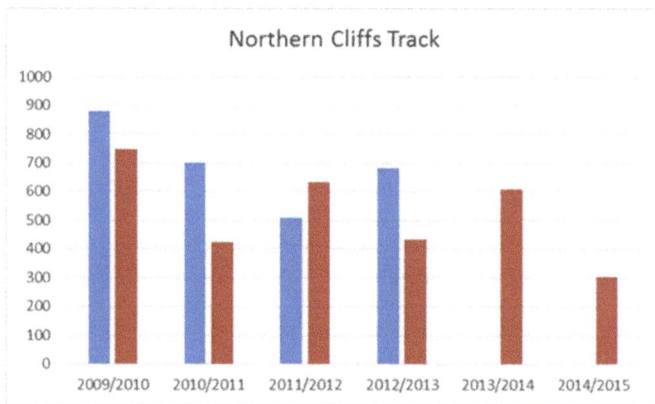

Figure 4. Northern Cliffs track quotas (missing data for 2013–2015) and used permits between years 2009 and 2015 [8]. (The set quota is in blue and the activated permits are in red).

3.4.2. Auckland Islands

In the most recent Conservation Management Strategy (2016) there are nine visitor areas/tracks identified on the Auckland Island, the most among the three visitor-accessible islands. Hardwicke and the Terror Cove visitor area are the most visited sites in the Auckland Islands (Figure 5).

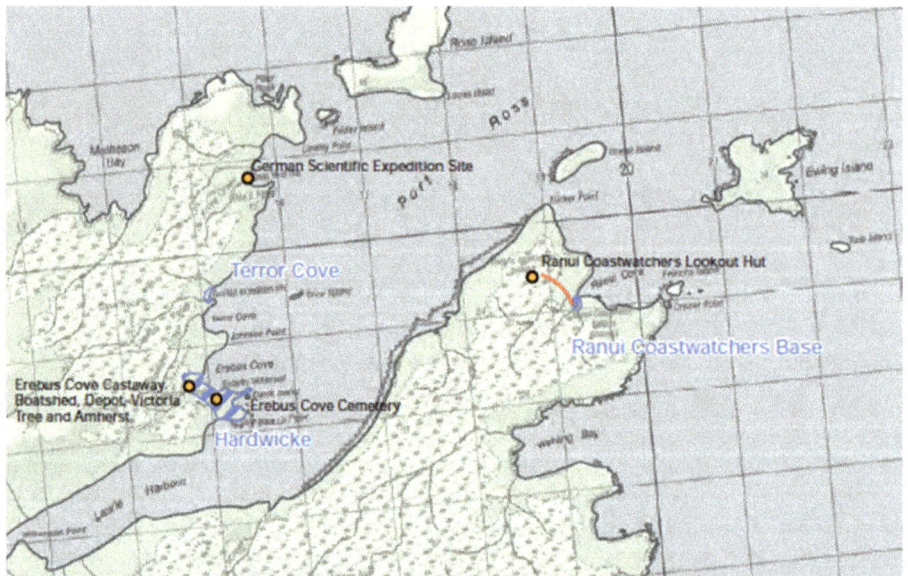

Figure 5. Port Ross visitor areas, located at the northern tip of Auckland Island. Blue shows visitor areas and red marks visitor tracks (Image retrieved from [17]) (p. 28).

The historic visitor data presented in Figure 6 indicates that visitation has not exceeded the stated quota at the Hardwicke visitor site. The most recent guideline allows for 400 visitors per year (with up to 200 per day).

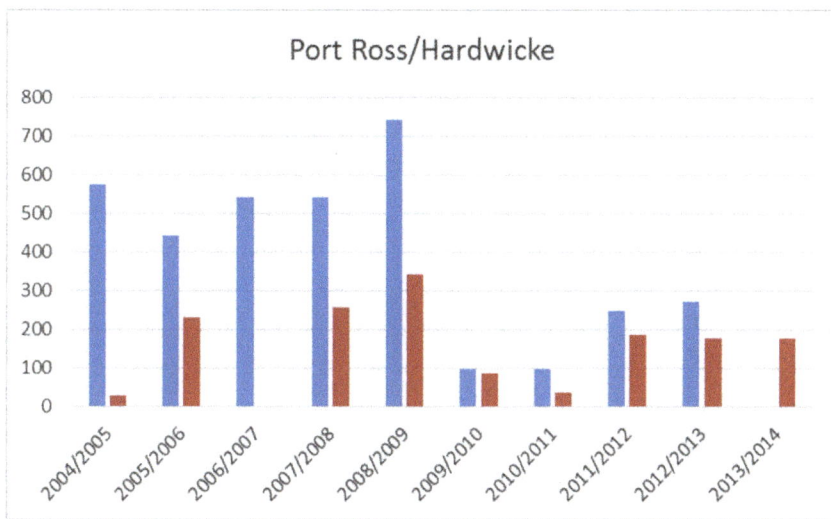

Figure 6. Hardwicke visitor site quotas and permits used from years 2004–2014 (missing data for 2013–2015) [8]. (The set quota is in blue and the activated permits are in red).

3.4.3. Campbell Island

The other most visited site within the Islands is Col-Lyall on Campbell Island (Figure 7).

Figure 7. Campbell Island visitor areas and tracks. Blue shows visitor areas and red marks visitor tracks (Image retrieved from [17]) (p. 27).

As Figure 8 indicates, annual visitation to this site has fluctuated from approximately 250 to 750 visitors since the mid-2000s. In line with the new guidelines set for the Northern Cliffs on Enderby Island, this site on Campbell Island can now allow for 1100 visitors annually and up to 200 daily [10].

Col-Lyall Saddle Boardwalk

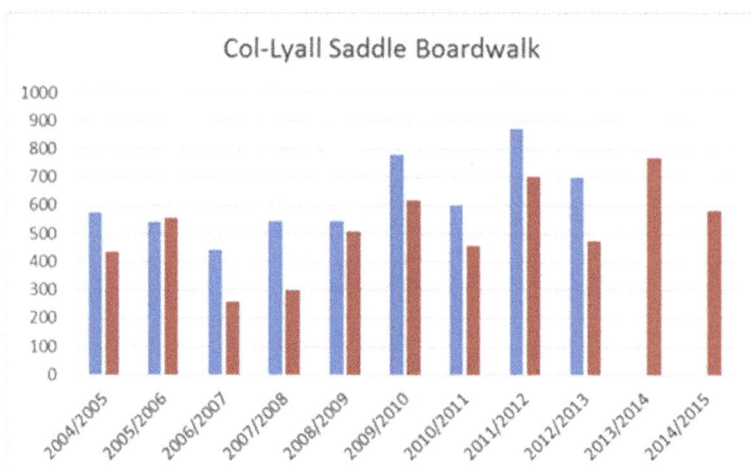

Figure 8. Col-Lyall Saddle Boardwalk quota and permits used between years 2004 and 2015 (missing data for 2013–2015) [8] (The set quota is in blue and the activated permits are in red).

3.5. Quotas and Permits

The choice of areas visited during an expedition are at the discretion of the tour operator and are often tailored to suit the itinerary, e.g., bird watching vs. marine mammal viewing, and are determined by the length of the trip. Consistently popular sites include Enderby Island, Tagua Coastwatcher's base, and the Col-Lyall saddle boardwalk. All of the other sites show sporadic visitation over the last ten years. Despite their allocated quotas, these less-visited sites often receive only half of their allocated quota—generally because these sites are not easily accommodated in the itinerary implemented by the expedition, and due to the significant influence of the weather and ocean conditions in determining which landing sites can be used, as well as the length of time spent ashore. When asked about the factors that influence visitation, a tour operator stated that:

"The weather is the largest contributing factor. At times there is a 50% chance of bad weather, dramatically impacting visitation. If it was a flat run to the subs, which could be done in pleasure boats, there would be a lot more people going there".

Simply knowing what permits are used does not necessarily imply knowledge of actual visitation, as "a ship may have a permit for 100 people to do the walk, but due to weather or track conditions, only 4 people will do the walk. Gaining a permit does not reflect actual landings of people on the Island. Of the 350 passengers to go in one year, if 140 do the full walk on Enderby Island, and 210 just do the boardwalk, the resulting impact would be different, so too would be the time spent on the Island. If the weather is bad, trips will be quick, with minimal participation" (Tour operator).

When examining the quota and permit data, it is clear that site quota numbers have changed from year to year for many sites. While the reason for this remains unknown (this appears to have been remedied in the recent Conservation Management Strategy), it is imperative that for these quotas to be effective at minimizing the impacts associated with visitation, they must be informed by some form of monitoring to build the evidence base for establishing a threshold. One tour operator indicated that, over the last four years, they have had an average of seven vessel visits to the Subantarctic Islands per year plus two Antarctic itineraries which included visits to the Subantarctic Islands, with a capacity of 50 people per trip. These visits would likely be spread throughout the season, bringing an estimated 350 people to the Islands. Alternatively, it is possible for one larger cruise ship with a capacity of 200 passengers to make two trips, bringing 400 people to these islands in a relatively short space of time. Not only would these larger cruises bring more people, and hence more noise, to the Islands at any one time, but temporally proximate visits of large groups would also reduce the amount of time the environment has to recover from any resulting impact on vegetation and wildlife.

3.6. Tourism Impacts

Internationally, obtaining and managing visitor data is an essential component of protected area management. Common data obtained includes information on visitor numbers, behaviour and attitudes [18]. This data can provide comparative information on the use of resources by visitors and help managers prioritize investment decisions. Quotas and permits are the current method used by the Department of Conservation for the management of visitors to the New Zealand Subantarctic Islands [4]. Due to the Islands' protected status and their associated values, any access to the Islands requires permits. This includes those accessing the Islands to maintain the facilities of the Meteorological Service of New Zealand and researchers and other visitors travelling to the Islands. The intent in utilizing such a rigorous permitting process stems from a precautionary approach, aiming to avoid potential adverse effects of research and visitor access by limiting the number of visitors per site [4].

While permits help monitor visitor use, and quotas enforce restrictions on visitor numbers per site to help minimize impacts associated with their visitation, these specific impacts can only be measured if sufficient information on the original status of the landscapes and their flora and fauna is available, against which observed changes can be assessed. The latter also implies that regular vegetation and wildlife surveys are undertaken to notice and record any changes. The data collected through regular monitoring should include physical and biological data, but should also extend to the cultural values of a site and information about social and land-use history, visitor use, non-recreational uses, socio-economic costs and benefits, and infrastructure and facilities [18]. While it may be challenging to obtain data on all of the above for all sites, a robust set of accurate and comprehensive site-specific baseline information is crucial when attempting to identify what may be the cause of any changes in an environment.

It is well documented that visits to pristine natural environments will create some impact [19,20] but it is possible to minimize many of these impacts through effective management. To be managed effectively, these impacts must first be identified, measured, and evaluated [21]. Table 2 gives an overview of potential impacts, their possible causes, and options for management wishing to mitigate or minimize these impacts.

These impacts associated with island visitation are compounded by the relatively small size of each island and their unique evolutionary development [16]. Their relative isolation from population centres, unique climatic and physical conditions, and distinctive biodiversity found there are the Islands' greatest conservation assets, but their fragility means minute changes brought about through human impacts may have major long-term impacts on ecosystem stability [5]. The reason for this is that "the specialization of island biota makes them more vulnerable to external disturbance and environmental change, particularly human-induced impacts, and the extinction of species is particularly common on islands when new competitors or physical conditions are introduced" ([5], p. 359). Table 3 shows how impacts associated with human visitation have already been addressed by DOC.

Table 2. Actual/potential environmental impacts from human visitation (Amended and updated from [5,18]).

Impact Category	Impact	Cause	Management Options
Biophysical	Soil erosion or soil compaction	Walking on/off tracks Established tracks create channels where water flows more frequently	Restrict access Dictate track route Harden site Instate quotas Monitoring
Biophysical	Vegetation trampling	Walking on/off tracks	Restrict access Dictate track route Harden site Monitoring
Biophysical	Souveniring	Visitors taking flora/fauna/objects	Legislation Education Supervision
Biophysical	Littering	Visitors leaving rubbish/possessions behind (mostly accidental)	Legislation Education Supervision
Biophysical	Pollution	Ships dispose of waste (either purposefully or accidently) Oil/fuel spill	Legislation Rules regarding ship design
Biophysical	Alien species introduction	Seedlings/organisms introduced on clothing or equipment	Legislation Education Quarantine procedures Boarder security
Biophysical	Wildlife disturbance	Noise pollution Visitors interacting with/getting too close to fauna Visitation during peak breeding periods Overflights	Restrict access Dictate track route Legislation Education Supervision
Cultural	Damage to historic sites	Gradual change through visitation (increased CO_2, changed moisture content, movement of dirt) Souveniring Direct damage (e.g., through graffiti or vandalizing)	Restrict access Legislation Education Visitor guidelines Supervision
Social	Diminished visitor experience	Overcrowding	Restrict access
Social	Interference with other activities, e.g., research	Visitors going outside of designated visitor sites and tracks	Restrict access Dictate track route Legislation Education Supervision

Table 3. Solutions instated by DOC to address impacts associated with tourism.

Impact	Solution
Trampling	Hardening of two popular sites, set track routes and visitor areas, and set quota numbers for these areas
Souveniring	Established code of practice through legislation, education of visitors by tour operators, and having a DOC representative present on all voyages to ensure compliance
Littering and pollution	Introduced legislation, enforce through education and supervision of visitors through guide ratios
Introduction of alien species	Thorough quarantine checks before and after leaving the ship, educate visitors prior to their trip so they are aware of procedures, and having a DOC representative present on all voyages to ensure compliance
Wildlife disturbance	Guide to visitor ratios and education of visitors prior to their visit, as well as briefing on board the ship prior to shore landings
Overcrowding	Quota system to reduce diminished visitor experience and guidelines set in the CMS stating how many people may visit a site in one day and how many ships may be present at stated landing sites

It is because these islands are so vulnerable to potential biophysical impacts associated with visitation that they must be managed with extreme care, not only for the sake of their endemic flora and fauna, but also because nature-based tourism in island settings relies on ecologically intact and well-managed ecosystems [16]. Research conducted on the impacts of hiking on soils and vegetation has shown that there are a variety of factors that influence the overall resulting impact: frequency of use; type and behaviour of use; season of use; environmental conditions; and the spatial distribution of use. The primary management tools involve manipulation of these factors [22]. Generally, it has been shown that in Subantarctic environments trampling benefits introduced vascular species, such as *Poa annua*, and that lichens and bryophytes prefer undisturbed environments [23]. It is also known that the relationship between the amount of use and the amount of impact is curvilinear, or asymptotic, suggesting it is best to concentrate use and impact at sites which already have established visitation, and to disperse use and impact in relatively pristine places [22]. The latter has also been emphasized by Tejedo et al. [24], who have found that soils in maritime Antarctica that are subject to limited exposure from foot traffic, which they define as generally fewer than 100 passes per year, can generally recover relatively quickly, and that therefore dispersal of foot traffic on these soils is advised. Frequently visited areas with high foot traffic are not recovering quickly enough, and Tejedo et al. suggest that single-track use of these areas be the recommended modus operandi [24].

Many sites within the New Zealand Subantarctic Islands are restricted by quotas to receive between 50 and 200 visitors annually, but the two most visited sites within the New Zealand Subantarctic Islands, the Northern Cliffs on Enderby Island and the Col-Lyall Saddle on Campbell Island, are now able to receive 1100 visitors annually. This is made possible due to boardwalks being installed in an effort to minimize vegetation trampling associated with visitation (see Figure 9). While this has certainly altered the vegetation found beneath the boardwalks, it is a compromise to allow sustained visitation into the future in a way that restricts the spread of vegetation trampling and any associated erosion [19].

Figure 9. Boardwalks on New Zealand Subantarctic Islands (Source: Heritage Expeditions New Zealand Ltd (Christchurch, New Zealand)).

Alongside quotas and permits and site hardening interventions (such as boardwalks), the DOC has introduced several other means of visitor impact mitigation for these islands, such as minimum visitor-to-guide ratios, biosecurity procedures, minimal impact codes and a government observer scheme, which requires departmental representatives/observers to be present on every voyage that has people landing in the Islands [4]. The minimal impact codes are set by the DOC as a tool for managing the impacts related to visitation, but the physical effects of visitation on the environments cannot be known without sufficient and ongoing monitoring [19].

Between 2004 and 2013, DOC undertook vegetation trampling and soil erosion monitoring at a number of sites, on tracks commonly used by tourists throughout Campbell Island and Enderby Island [25]. Longitudinal photo points were used to allow comparison with previous years in a bid to illustrate any change. A desk-based analysis of this monitoring in 2013 did not show any significant observable change in physical impact at the sites monitored [25]. It was noted, however, "that as track surfaces start to deteriorate, they will continue to do so quite rapidly, as track surface and vegetation recovery is expected to be slow in the harsh Subantarctic conditions" ([25], p. 2). The first year that monitoring was conducted 'pre-season' in December was in 2013, and the pre-season monitoring results suggest that some track surfaces do recover over the winter [25]. Such replicable monitoring informs DOC about whether the visitor quotas set for the previous season are sufficient. Upon comparison of the recent photos, it appears that repeat visitation to the sites monitored has not caused significant observable changes in the soil and vegetation cover at the sites monitored, and where any vegetation damage has occurred, it has not occurred to an extent where that vegetation could not recover naturally [25].

The most recent Conservation Management Strategy (2016) proposes to develop and implement a visitor monitoring programme to determine the effects of visitors on the natural and cultural environment, as well as on the visitor experience itself. The DOC indicates that if the effects are more than minor (or if a site's values are vulnerable to degradation), the number of site permits may be reduced (or a site may be closed entirely to visitors). Any concerns arising will be addressed with interested parties, including concessionaires [10]. However, it remains unclear how this proposed monitoring programme, and the proposed Visitor Management Plan, will be developed and implemented.

4. Conclusions

From their European discovery in 1788, through commercial exploitation of whales and seals during the 1800s into the early 1900s, the attempts at colonization from 1894 to 1931, to the beginnings of commercial cruises in 1967, these unique island habitats have witnessed increasing visitation from humans. While visitors' motivations for travelling to these islands have undeniably changed over the course of their human history, the Islands continue to fascinate and intrigue anyone who is exposed to their wild, isolated, natural environments [26–28].

While visitor numbers are small compared to many other tourist destinations, to ensure continued protection of the natural conservation values, meaningful policy frameworks and conservation management strategies must be in place to facilitate sustainable tourist visits to these pristine environments. The DOC now implements practices learnt from previous experience and examples from overseas to help sustain functional ecosystems for the Islands' unique biodiversity, and their notably high degree of endemism, while allowing particular islands and sites to be visited by nature-seeking tourists. Allowing tourism within these islands comes with an undeniable risk to the environments found there, but with effective communication, a robust programme of visitor research (including a site-specific assessment of visitor impacts; as well as impacts associated with cruise travel to the Islands themselves), education, legislation and supervision, these risks may be mitigated, eliminated, or at least minimized, ensuring managers meet conservation goals while providing appropriate opportunities for the public to appreciate these once 'forgotten islands' and the wonders found there.

Resources **2017**, *6*, 38

Acknowledgments: The research was funded via the Royal Society of New Zealand for a summer scholarship project examining visitor impacts on the New Zealand Subantarctic Islands. The authors acknowledge the Department of Conservation for support and especially the guidance and encouragement from the staff at the Southland Conservancy. Staff at Heritage Expeditions New Zealand Ltd. are also thanked for their kind assistance.

Author Contributions: Emma J. Stewart, Stephen Espiner and Daniela Liggett conceived, designed and supervised the summer scholarship project. Zac Taylor analyzed the data and drafted the initial report in conjunction with his supervisors. Emma J. Stewart, Stephen Espiner and Daniela Liggett wrote the paper in conjunction with Zac Taylor.

Conflicts of Interest: The authors declare no conflict of interest.

References and Notes

1. Hall, C.M.; Johnston, M. *Polar Tourism: Tourism in the Arctic and Antarctic Regions*; John Wiley & Sons: London, UK, 1995.
2. Department of Conservation. *Subantarctic Islands Research Strategy: Background*; Department of Conservation: Wellington, New Zealand, 2005.
3. Department of Conservation. *New Zealand's Subantarctic Islands*; Reed Books: Auckland, New Zealand, 1999.
4. Department of Conservation. *Southland Murihiku Conservation Management Strategy 2015–2025*; Department of Conservation: Wellington, New Zealand, 2014.
5. Hall, M.; Wouters, M. Managing Nature Tourism in the Sub-Antarctic. *Ann. Tour. Res.* **1994**, *212*, 355–374. [CrossRef]
6. Peat, N. *Subantarctic New Zealand: A Rare Heritage*; Southland Conservancy, Department of Conservation: Invercargill, New Zealand, 2006.
7. Cessford, G.R.; Dingwall, P.R. *Tourist Visitors and Their Experiences at New Zealand Subantarctic Islands*; Science & Research Series 96; Department of Conservation: Wellington, New Zealand, 1996; pp. 1–66.
8. Department of Conservation supplementary data.
9. International Association of Antarctica Tour Operators. IAATO overview of Antarctic tourism: 2008–2009 Antarctic season and preliminary estimates for 2009–2010 Antarctic season, IP 85, XXXII. In Proceedings of the Antarctic Treaty Consultative Meeting, Baltimore, MD, USA, 6–17 April 2009.
10. Department of Conservation. *Conservation Management Strategy: Southland Murihiku, Volume 1*; Department of Conservation: Wellington, New Zealand, 2016.
11. Hughes, K.A.; Convey, P. Determining the native/non-native status of newly discovered terrestrial and freshwater species in Antarctica—Current knowledge, methodology and management action. *J. Environ. Manag.* **2012**, *93*, 52–66. [CrossRef] [PubMed]
12. Tsujimoto, M.; Imura, S. Does a new transportation system increase the risk of importing non-native species to Antarctica? *Antarct. Sci.* **2012**, *24*, 441–449. [CrossRef]
13. Whinam, J.; Chilcott, N.; Bergstrom, D.M. Subantarctic hitchhikers: Expeditioners as vectors for the introduction of alien organisms. *Biol. Conserv.* **2005**, *121*, 207–219. [CrossRef]
14. Department of Conservation. *Subantarctic Islands Heritage: Nomination of the New Zealand Subantarctic Islands by the Government of New Zealand for Inclusion in the World Heritage List*; DOC: Wellington, New Zealand, 1997.
15. Headland, R.K. Historical development of Antarctic tourism. *Ann. Tour. Res.* **1994**, *21*, 269–280. [CrossRef]
16. Newsome, D.; Moore, S.A.; Dowling, R.K. *Natural Area Tourism: Ecology, Impacts and Management*; Channel View Publications: Bristol, UK, 2013.
17. Department of Conservation. *New Zealand's Subantarctic Islands: Tourism Policy*; Department of Conservation: Wellington, New Zealand, 2013.
18. Chape, S.; Spalding, M.; Jenkins, M. *The World's Protected Areas: Status, Values and Prospects in the 21st Century*; University of California Press: Berkeley, CA, USA, 2008.
19. Cessford, G.R.; Dingwall, P.R. *An Approach to Assessing the Environmental Impacts of Tourism*; Conservation Advisory Science Notes No. 247; Department of Conservation: Wellington, New Zealand, 1999.
20. Higgenbottom, K.; Green, R.; Northrope, C. A Framework for Managing the Negative Impacts of Wildlife Tourism on Wildlife. *Hum. Dimens. Wildl.* **2003**, *8*, 1–24. [CrossRef]
21. Wearing, S.; Neil, J. *Ecotourism: Impacts, Potentials and Possibilities*; Elsevier: Oxford, UK, 2009.
22. Cole, D.N. Impacts of hiking and camping on soils and vegetation: A review. *Environ. Impacts Ecotour.* **2004**, *41*, 60.

23. Scott, J.J.; Kirkpatrick, J.B. Effects of human trampling on the Subantarctic vegetation of Macquarie Island. *Polar Rec.* **1994**, *30*, 207–220. [CrossRef]

24. Tejedo, P.; Pertierra, L.R.; Benayas, J.; Convey, P.; Justel, A.; Quesada, A. Trampling on maritime Antarctica: Can soil ecosystems be effectively protected through existing codes of conduct? *Polar Res.* **2012**, *31*, 10888. [CrossRef]

25. Visser, C. *Subantarctic Visitor Impact Monitoring Results 2013*; Department of Conservation: Wellington, New Zealand, 2013; pp. 1–53.

26. Sanson, L. An Ecotourism Case Study in Subantarctic Islands. *Ann. Tour. Res.* **1994**, *21*, 244–254. [CrossRef]

27. Cessford, G.R.; Dingwall, P.R. Tourism on New Zealand's Subantarctic Islands. *Ann. Tour. Res.* **1996**, *21*, 318–332. [CrossRef]

28. Orams, M. Experiences of adolescents on an expedition to New Zealand's sub-Antarctic: Results from the use of photo-elicitation. *Polar J.* **2015**, *5*, 446–465. [CrossRef]

resources

MDPI

Article

Expedition Cruising in the Canadian Arctic: Visitor Motives and the Influence of Education Programming on Knowledge, Attitudes, and Behaviours

Brittany Manley [1], Statia Elliot [1] and Shoshanah Jacobs [2,3,*]

[1] School of Hospitality, Food & Tourism Management, University of Guelph, Guelph, ON N1G 2W1, Canada; brittany.manley@gmail.com (B.M.); statia@uoguelph.ca (S.E.)
[2] Department of Integrative Biology, University of Guelph, Guelph, ON N1G 2W1, Canada
[3] College of Biological Sciences, Office of Educational Scholarship and Practice, University of Guelph, Guelph, ON N1G 2W1, Canada
* Correspondence: sjacob04@uoguelph.ca; Tel.: +1-519-824-4120 (ext. 58096)

Academic Editors: Machiel Lamers and Edward Huijbens
Received: 30 April 2017; Accepted: 19 June 2017; Published: 23 June 2017

Abstract: Cruising is a segment of tourism that is increasing at a faster rate than other kinds of leisure travel, especially in the Arctic region. Due to changing environmental conditions in recent years, cruise ships have been able to access more regions of the Arctic for a longer operating season. We investigated the cruiser motivations for polar expedition cruising and the educational dimensions of expedition cruising. Motivations of cruisers were identified using entrance surveys prior to embarking on four separate itineraries ($n = 144$). We conducted semi-structured interviews, $n = 22$), made participant observations while on board the vessel for one trip to support survey findings, and followed up with a post-trip survey to assess attitudinal changes ($n = 92$). We found that, unlike mainstream cruisers, expedition cruisers are motivated by opportunities for novel experience and for learning. Subsequently, the educational programming offered by expedition cruise companies is an important component of the cruise experience. We found that this programming has positively impacted cruiser attitudes, behaviours, and knowledge post-cruise. These findings will encourage cruise companies to improve their educational offerings (i.e., preparedness, program quality, level of engagement) to meet the expectations of their clientele, thereby transferring critical knowledge of environmental stewardship.

Keywords: Arctic; expedition cruising; knowledge transfer; eco-tourism

1. Introduction

Cruising is a high growth segment of tourism that is increasing faster than other formats of leisure travel [1], particularly in the Arctic and Antarctic regions in the past two decades [2,3]. Due to increasingly milder environmental conditions and the subsequent earlier breakup of ice [4–7], cruise ships are able to access more of the polar regions for a longer operating season ([8], but see [2]) and growing participation in "last chance tourism" is projected to cause a further increase in visitors [9–16]. According to the International Association of Antarctica Tour Operators (IAATO), the 2016–2017 Antarctic cruise operating seasons saw 44,402 tourists compared to 7547 in 2002–2003 [17], a 580% increase.

Expedition cruising as we know it today came to the Arctic in 1984 with the MS Explorer [18,19]. Expedition cruising is unique compared to other forms of mainstream cruising; with relatively small ships that hold up to 200 cruisers, the specific intent is to offer rich experiences with shore landings via inflatable boats that access remote locations. Onboard programming focuses on a comprehensive educational experience, usually for a highly educated clientele. Expedition cruising is a specialized niche requiring considerations beyond the cruiser experience. Operators are required to consider the unique challenges of passenger and ship safety, ship logistics, environmental sustainability, and—of specific interest here—knowledge transfer and education of the cruisers. While research has studied cruising from an environmental and operational perspective (i.e., [20]), few studies have addressed the motivations of cruisers to embark on expedition cruising and the educational dimensions (but see [21,22]).

Based upon internal cruiser exit surveys, expedition cruising companies assume that cruisers are motivated to buy a ticket because of the educational aspects of the proposed itineraries, in addition to the opportunity to explore an extreme environment and see the expanse of ice before it melts. Consequently, Arctic and Antarctic expedition cruise lines have developed a range of educational programs to address the presumed desire of cruisers for an educational and immersive experience. Pre-embarkation packages might include a variety of resources including company-specific handbooks and websites and suggested reading lists. On board, programs of specialized lectures on destination-appropriate topics are offered during time at sea or poor weather conditions. Guides are employed to lead excursions on shore such as guided walks and interpretation with flora and fauna identification. Whether at sea or on land, the guides are constantly scanning for wildlife. Upon disembarkation cruisers often leave with packages of information and photographs provided by the cruise company.

While educational programming is offered in practice, there is little research on the motivations and expectations of the cruisers, or the effectiveness of knowledge transfer from the programming to the cruiser. Therefore, we investigated the motivations of cruisers to take an Arctic expedition cruise and examined the impacts of the educational programming on cruisers' subsequent attitudes and conservation behaviours.

1.1. Motivations

In the 30 years that expedition cruise ships have been travelling to Canada's Arctic regions [18,23], there has been a steady increase in the companies involved and itineraries offered [13]. A few studies have investigated the motivations of cruise passengers more generally [24,25], but none have studied the motivations of cruisers who choose expedition cruises to the Arctic.

Studies on motivations for cruising have focused on factors such as pleasure, control, and novelty [26,27], and it has been found that pleasure is correlated with cruisers' value perceptions, that cruisers are swayed by social influences, and that cruisers are loyal to a company from which they have previously purchased trips [28]. Mainstream cruisers are motivated by the opportunity for relaxation, enhancement of kinship relationships or friendships, and convenience [24].

While participating in educational programs is not a top motivating factor in mainstream cruising, Hung and Petrick (2011) suggest that cruise ship programming should include opportunities to learn and discover. They recommend specific activities such as "Be a chef/captain/cast member today", or shipboard tours in addition to off-ship activities offered at the various ports of call. While it is noteworthy that mainstream cruisers are often interested in learning and discovery, it is likely that their educational expectations are different from those of the expedition cruisers.

We hypothesize that learning and discovery are the primary motivators for Arctic expedition cruisers and is based upon the observation that expedition cruise companies have focused on nature-based excursions that are included in the price of the cruise package and the offering of educational programming.

1.2. Attitude Change Theory Model

The Elaboration Likelihood Model (ELM) was used as the basis for this research because this is the predominant method used within the educational tourism context [21,29] and it is used to investigate how a persuasive message can change attitudes.

There are two routes of persuasion: central processing and peripheral processing [30]. The route of persuasion that the cruiser takes when involved with an educational program is important to map because it predicts the strength of change in attitude [29]. Central processing refers to the individual being an active participant such that s/he would need to contemplate the message from the educational programming, consider the implications, and relate information to her/his own knowledge and values. Motivation and ability are the two main influences that would dictate the cruiser's route of attitude change. If the topic is not of interest to the cruiser then there is a lack of motivation to achieve central processing. If the educational program is poorly designed and the message is unclear, the cruiser will be unable to achieve central processing [29]. However, if the message is clear, well presented and meaningful to the cruiser, s/he can then be motivated to process the information and will have a high level of cognitive involvement. Petty et al. (1995) found that long-term and short-term attitude changes are often developed from the central route and peripheral route, respectively [31].

The second route is relevant when the cruiser has little or no interest in the subject. S/he will focus on everything but the actual message such as: qualifications of the guide, whether the tone of the guide's voice and body language demonstrates authority, and/or the degree to which the messages are supported by credible sources. In this context, the cruiser decides if the information offered through the educational programming is worth accepting.

ELM relates best to understanding Arctic cruisers' attitudes toward the environment and the impacts of education related to the cruise experience because it posits that the more the information regarding pro-environmental attitude provokes the cruiser to think about their own attitudes, the more they create personal meanings about the topic. It therefore predicts that the cruiser is more likely to act on the information presented [21].

1.3. Expedition Cruise Ships

Expedition cruise ships can carry up to 200 cruisers, and offer an educational experience delivered by discipline-specific guides on board [21]. An important feature of expedition cruising is that companies search for new and unvisited locations with either a natural or cultural appeal ([32], p. 251) such that cruisers have the opportunity to develop a deeper connection with a novel environment [29,33]. In the Arctic, this is achieved by Zodiac boat trips to view wildlife, kayak excursions in sea ice, hikes on the tundra, and cultural programming offered in remote ports of call. The quality of the interaction between the environment and the cruiser therefore varies depending on the individual's personality, the effectiveness of the guide [34], and the presence of wildlife.

This study explored four questions:

Q1. Are motivational factors for engaging in Arctic expedition cruising different from other cruising motivations?

Due to the highly specialized nature of expedition cruising, we hypothesized that expedition cruising attracts cruisers with different motivations than mainstream cruises. We predicted that expedition cruisers are more motivated by educational factors.

Q2. What on-ship cruising activities is the expedition company offering to meet presumed cruiser's educational expectations?

Q3. Do on-ship cruising activities for cruisers correspond to pre-cruise motivations?

Q4. What is the impact of the educational experiences on attitudes post-cruise?

It was hypothesized that cruiser engagement with destination-based educational programming has an effect on attitudes and behaviours. Based on the learning-focused motivations and expectations of the cruiser, and the onboard multi-day exposure to the Arctic environment, it was predicted that some knowledge will be retained post-cruise and will result in modified environmental behaviour.

2. Methods

We investigated the motivations, engagement with the educational programming, and subsequent knowledge transfer, attitude changes, and behavioural changes of expedition cruisers on an Arctic expedition cruise ship within the region of Nunavut, Canada and western Greenland during the 2014 summer sailing season. A research ethics approval certificate was received for all described protocols (see Supplementary Materials). The expedition cruise company Adventure Canada was selected because it is a Canadian cruise company that sails within the preferred locations and this increased the probability of contact with English-speaking cruisers as research participants. Adventure Canada provided a reduced rate for room and board for one of the researchers to conduct cruiser interviews and act as a participant observer. Pre-cruise surveys ($n = 383$) were distributed to cruisers on each of the four Adventure Canada trips. Post-cruise surveys ($n = 272$) were sent electronically three months after the trip. Three months was the selected timeframe to allow participants to return to their daily routines while still feeling a sense of group belonging to the pool of research participants. This time frame was also used in the Powell's 2008 Antarctic expedition study [35].

2.1. Pre-Cruise Survey—Cruiser Motivations and Current Knowledge and Attitudes

A pre-cruise survey was distributed to expedition cruisers while on board the charter flight at the beginning of their itinerary. This survey assessed motivations, knowledge, and attitudes about the Arctic and resource management, general views about the natural environment, and engagement in environmentally conscious behaviours. The specific factors assessed and the questions asked were based upon Powell's 2008 study on Antarctic expedition cruisers [35]. Modifications were made when necessary to reflect the difference in destination. Our survey tools are available in the Supplementary Materials. Of the 383 surveys distributed to potential participants, 144 pre-trip surveys were completed and returned for analysis (38% response rate).

2.2. Assessment of Educational Programming

Information relating to the educational programming was collected via participant observation. This methodology, and the research generally, was introduced to all guides and cruisers during the technical stop of the charter flight. Cruisers received a letter of information, consent form, and pre-cruise survey. All cruisers and resource staff were informed of their right to be excluded from observation and from the study. A researcher attended all programming, excursions, and participated in many small group conversations while on board. Note taking was used to record information. This was done discreetly during the programming or immediately following the activity so as not to disrupt the cruiser experience. Being on board allowed the researcher to develop a relationship of trust with the cruisers and guides because they travelled together, ate together, and shared the same space for 10 days. This allowed the cruisers and guides to become accustomed to the researcher aboard and understand the intentions of the study. The educational programming offered by the company was recorded and characterized according to the location offered, duration, and nature of the offering.

2.3. Semi-Structured Interviews with Cruisers

The researcher conducted open-ended, semi-structured interviews with participants randomly selected from the ship's manifest near the end of the expedition to obtain detailed insight about the cruiser's experience (see Supplementary Materials). To ensure the sample of interviewed cruises was representative, the researcher interviewed 14 cruisers [36], which was also the maximum number that could be interviewed given the time constraint. Participants were asked to share how they felt about the educational programming on board and what effect the presentations had on their attitudes about various topics. The analysis looked at features of the educational programming and explored what potential benefits were likely. Finally, the interviews elucidated which aspects of the programming had personal significance to the cruisers and whether or not this changed their attitudes.

2.4. Semi-Structured Interviews with Guides

During the 2014 Arctic expedition season, the expedition company employed between 12 and 15 expedition guides per itinerary. The guides varied in specialization including historian, geologist, culturalist, naturalist, or archaeologist. The researcher interviewed the eight guides who were responsible for topics related specifically to the natural environment (see Supplementary Materials). The data collected were used to help answer both the second and third research questions.

2.5. Cruiser Interaction with the Educational Programming

Expeditions to the Arctic offer a wide variety of educational themed activities to appeal to the cruisers and guides and cruisers interacted regularly. Observational data on guide interpreted information were collected during presentations and daily meetings. The researcher specifically observed the level of engagement that the cruisers had with the educational programming and guides by documenting the number of participants per activity and the frequency and quality of the questions posed during lecture sessions relating to the environment. A manifest content analysis of the questions posed during lecture sessions was measured against an adapted Bloom's Taxonomy scale [37].

2.6. Post-Trip Survey: Effectiveness of Knowledge Transfer and Impact of the Expedition

All cruisers were sent a link to a post-cruise survey three to four months after their cruise (see Supplemental Material). A modified Dillman (2000) approach was used [38]. This consisted of a cover letter with the survey, a subsequent email sent out three weeks after the initial email and a final reminder email to non-respondents five weeks after initial contact. The researcher did not collect email addresses from the pre-trip survey—the expedition company used their database to email each cruiser on behalf of the researcher using software to show the researcher's email address as the sender. Ninety-two cruisers completed the post-cruise survey that was used to determine whether there had been changes in cruiser attitudes. Therefore, it consisted of the same questions asked in the pre-cruise survey. Two sections were added to gain further information on the cruisers knowledge gain and educational impact from the expedition.

To better understand the educational benefits of participation in an Arctic expedition, cruisers were asked to self-report knowledge gain in five areas. The questions in this section have been adapted from Powell's (2008) survey with the addition of ornithology [35].

In an open-ended question, the post-cruise survey asked cruisers to share, what impact the expedition had on them.

2.7. Data Analysis

NVivo was used for the qualitative data analysis that required coding. All returned surveys were coded and the data were entered for quantitative analysis using the statistical program SPSS (Statistical Package for the Social Sciences). *T* tests were used to determine whether there were significant differences in means and G tests were used to determine whether there were significant differences in distributions. Statistical significance was identified at $p < 0.05$.

3. Results

3.1. Arctic Cruiser Profile

Most of the participants were Canadian or American, living in large urban areas, between the ages of 61 and 80 years old, with post-secondary education. Most were inexperienced travellers to the Arctic but had previously participated in nature-based travel (see Table 1).

Table 1. Summary of Arctic visitor profile (*n* = 144).

Demographic Variable	Summary
Gender	56.9% female, 42.4% male
Age	Mean age is 61–70 years
Previous Arctic Experience	43.8% of participants had participated in an Arctic tour before
Previous Nature experience	25.7% of participants had not participated in a nature trip before. The mean number of previous nature tours is 4. 33.6% had participated in 4 or more
Residence Description	57.7% of participants reside in a city or suburb
Country of citizenship	63.9% of participants live in Canada
Formal education	88.9% of participants either completed a college or university degree or have graduate from professional or graduate program

Q1. Are motivational factors for buying an Arctic expedition cruise different from other cruising motivations?

Motivational factors for buying a ticket for an Arctic expedition are different from the motivations associated with mainstream cruising motivations. "Seeing a beautiful landscape" and "seeing beautiful and unique wildlife" are the most common motivators for cruisers, with a combined 89.6% and 88.2%, respectively, of cruisers identifying it as being either extremely important or very important. The third greatest motivator is "exploring new places" with a combined percentage of 86.1% (extremely important and very important). An additional motivation that is worth noting is "Learning about the natural history of the Arctic", with a combined percentage of 72.2% (extremely important and very important). The item with the lowest reported motivation was "Socializing with friends and family" (see Table 2).

In Hung and Petrick's (2011) study of motivations to cruise, they found "escape and relaxation" to be the strongest motivator, contributing the most to intentions to cruise [24]. In addition, in-depth interviews of participants did not report "exploration and education" as a motivation. The main motivations for expedition cruisers are therefore different compared to mainstream cruisers. Expedition cruisers are interested in being immersed within the Arctic environment; they want to learn, experience, and see the landscape and wildlife that are unique to the area.

3.2. Open-Ended Survey Question

To more fully understand cruiser motivations, an open-ended question asked: "Please explain in your own words why you chose to go on this expedition". The responses are categorized into four main motivational traits: learning/discovery, novelty/thrill, social recognition/prestige, and escape/relaxation with 15 sub-traits, for a total of 19 categories (Table 3—top three motivation categories identified).

In support of the quantitative findings, these responses indicate experiencing the landscape as the prime motivation to travel in the Arctic. What also emerges is the extent of the knowledge and previous travel experience held by expedition cruisers. Some participants mentioned a specific location: "most especially to see the Ilulissat Ice field" (AS-9) or referenced a specific landscape feature such as icebergs: "more iceberg scenery" (AS-23) and "to see the natural environment—wildlife, icebergs" (Q-80).

Responses also indicated that seeing Arctic wildlife was a primary motivation to visit the Arctic. A number of the responses were general, such as: "to see the wildlife" (AS-6) and: "to experience the wildlife" (AS-8). However, many responses referred to specific animals: "To see unusual wildlife like narwhals and polar bears" (AS-9); "I chose the trip to see the Arctic—hoping to see whales, muskoxen and polar bears" (Q-94); and "Bird watching" (Q-107).

Table 2. Percent distribution of importance for 14 possible cruiser motivations for Arctic cruising (pre-trip survey; $n = 144$).

Motivation	Mean * (Out of 7)	Extremely Important	Very Important	Important	Slightly Important	Not Very Important	Not at All Important	No Opinion
Seeing a beautiful landscape	6.4	59.7	29.9	8.3	1.4	0.7	0.0	0.0
Seeing unique wildlife	6.4	57.6	28.5	11.8	1.4	0.0	0.0	0.0
Exploring new places	6.4	57.6	28.5	11.8	1.4	0.0	0.0	1.4
Seeing beautiful or interesting wildlife	6.4	54.2	31.9	12.5	1.4	0.0	0.0	0.0
Learning about the natural history of the Arctic	6.1	44.4	27.8	22.2	4.9	0.7	0.0	0.0
Learning about the human history of the Arctic	5.9	40.6	25.9	24.5	8.4	0.0	0.7	0.0
Adventuring in the wilderness	5.8	38.9	22.9	27.8	8.3	1.4	0.7	0.0
Learning about environmental issues and conservation	5.6	29.2	31.3	26.4	9.0	2.8	1.4	0.0
Seeing the Arctic before it melts away	5.5	38.5	17.5	24.5	11.2	2.1	3.5	5.6
Capturing photographs	5.2	28.7	23.1	23.8	15.4	4.2	4.2	1.4
Experiencing a spiritual connection with nature	4.6	18.3	19.0	25.4	14.8	9.2	9.2	6.9
Following in the footsteps of the great explores	4.4	18.9	12.6	25.2	26.6	11.9	4.2	1.4
Relaxing & escaping from everyday life	4.1	8.4	11.9	34.3	20.3	12.6	10.5	4.2
Socializing with family and friends	3.3	11.2	7.0	19.6	12.6	14.7	32.9	4.2

* Scale: 7 = Extremely important to 1 = not at all important.

Table 3. Top expedition cruiser motivations for Arctic expedition cruising (*n* = 144) identified in an open-ended survey question. Some examples provided.

Landscape	AS-8 To experience the landscape. AS-17: Fascinated by scenery. AS-20: Hoping to see magnificent vistas.
Wildlife	AS-9: To see unusual wildlife like narwhales and polar bears. AS-16: … the chance to see wildlife found nowhere else in the world. AS-4: Seeing unique wildlife of the Arctic. Interested in birds and their birthing places in the Arctic. Q-84: Iconic animals.
Exploring new places	AS-7: To be able to reach remote communities. AS-17: Do something interesting and different; I like to go to the end of the road kind of thing.
	AS-31: We normally don't take or like cruises but this is the only practical way to see the Canadian north. One of the few areas in Canada and the USA that we have not explored.
Learning	Q-45: I want to learn about the Arctic because I am Canadian and if we claim sovereignty over it I should have some knowledge about it.
	Q-48: To learn about cultural history of the Inuit people. Q-76: I am excited to learn more about our Canadian Arctic ecology. Q-82: My first choice for travel is always a new experience, one where I am learning every day.

Cruisers were motivated not only to experience the novelty of the landscape, but also to simply experience novelty. Common across all participants was a desire to experience a new place. This is identified in responses such as: "Do something interesting and different; I like to go to the end of the road kind of thing" (AS-17); "The Arctic is the only area in Canada that I have not visited" (Q-34); and "To explore a part of Canada, territory that I have not previously visited while I can still enjoy. The level of adventure required to get in/out of zodiacs, climbing, hiking, etc. to fully participate" (Q-47).

Though the cruisers were interested in seeing wildlife and landscapes, they also indicated a strong desire to learn. This is supported by responses such as: "To see and learn over 10 days" (AS-19) and: "My first choice for travel is always a new experience, one where I am learning everyday" (Q-82). Motivation to learn about a broad topic is reported: "I am excited to learn more about our Canadian Arctic ecology" (Q-76). One respondent had specific interest in "being with resource staff that can educate me regarding plants" (Q-117).

3.3. Semi-Structured Interview

During the semi-structured interview, the researcher asked, "Could you share with me your reasons for taking an expedition cruise to the Arctic?" Seeing or experiencing the landscape as a motivation was apparent again. These one-on-one verbal responses correspond to the top motivation categories identified earlier, and they reveal deeper motivations, reflective of the cruisers' aspirations and life dreams.

Cruisers talked about seeing and learning about the Arctic—the landscapes and wildlife. These themes are supported with comments such as the "landscape was a motivation of mine to go to the Arctic and certainly had a connection with nature while I was up there. To see polar bears where they live and how they live" (AM-13). This is further identified when another participant shared "I think it was always something I wanted to do because I was drawn to the beauty of the north and felt a connection to it" (CA-12). The strength of the many affective responses—"I have been interested in going to the Polar Regions since I was a child", "we've gotta see this", "I was drawn to the beauty" (AC-14)—are evidence of the depth and meaning of the expedition experience to these cruisers.

Q2. What on-ship cruising activities is the expedition company offering to meet presumed cruisers' educational expectations?

Expedition cruisers seek educational opportunities, specifically regarding the Arctic landscape. The expedition cruise company responds to these expectations by providing a diverse educational program with many opportunities for cruisers to engage.

3.4. Expedition Guides

The expedition company always hires a geologist, archaeologist, marine biologist, naturalist, culturalist, historian, and photographer. All of the guides have formal and informal education relating to their area of specialization and a personal connection to the Arctic region ranging from 10 to 55 years. As an indication of the high level of their expertise, all 15 on board had university degrees, including three with PhDs and four with Master's degrees, with an average of 26 years' experience.

3.5. Planned Educational Programming

With the option to attend a variety of the educational presentations and the ability to interact with guides throughout the 15-day expedition, the cruisers were able to draw upon the knowledge of the guides to address their educational expectations.

The activities offered by the expedition company covered a wide range of Arctic topics, including history and culture; geography and landscape; and environment and wildlife. Most programming was offered on board during one-hour sessions presented by an experienced guide. Off-ship experiences were longer, typically 2 to 3 h, in which cruisers took part in a range of activities often relating to the most recent one-hour presentation.

The ship made several stops at natural sites with no human presence. Cruisers were offered the opportunity to go on a guided hike according to their level of fitness. Locations for hiking were selected based on likelihood of unique wildlife viewing, known Inuit archaeology and/or European explorer history sites, and stunning landscapes. Observing plants, rocks, animal tracks, droppings, and bones was usually guaranteed.

Visits to Arctic communities consisted of guided walks with stops at the school gymnasium or cultural centre for drum dancing and throat singing presentations, Arctic games demonstrations, traditional Inuit fashion shows, and country food tastings. There were also opportunities to visit museums and historical sites. While exploring, cruisers had the chance to see plants, birds and marine creatures, and enjoy magnificent views.

The majority of the cruisers attended the daily recap held by the guides. During the one-hour meeting, the events of the day were discussed and plans for the following day were presented. This was followed by a few fun facts shared by the guides and photos taken throughout the day.

In total, over the 14-day trip, 88 h of formal educational programming were provided to the cruisers. On average (excluding the arrival and departure days), there were 6.5 h of formal programming offered per day. The 88 h were allocated to on-ship presentations, workshops, briefings, and recaps. There was a change in the itinerary due to heavy ice, which resulted in two full consecutive days of only onboard programming. As planned, one full day sailing across the Davis Strait was allocated for onboard programming. The remaining 44 h of programming were provided during off-ship excursions.

Q3. Do on-ship cruising activities for cruisers correspond to pre-cruise motivations?

3.6. Cruiser Interaction with the Educational Programming

Assessing the attendance of educational activities provided information about the cruisers' behaviours. We found that attendance was highest at activities that corresponded to the general cruisers' pre-cruise motivations: learning about a new place, its landscape and wildlife.

The landings and Zodiac cruises were well-attended. On any given excursion, between two and 10 of the 82 cruisers opted out. A resource staff shared "They are at them, most of them are going ashore, on the zodiac rides, despite some pretty terrible weather." (CG-03). The recap and briefings at the end of each day were well attended; participation was consistently in the high 70% range. Presentation attendance varied depending on topic and ranged from the mid 50% range to the high 70% range. There does not appear to be a correlation between the presentation or workshop topic and the number of participants. Several workshops were offered concurrently to allow cruisers' a variety of options that appealed to different interests. Some workshops had limited space or a maximum number of cruisers. "What I see in our passengers in general is that for a variety of reasons they are lifetime learners, really motivated, want to get the most out of everything, the vast majority of them will attend every lecture and will make every landing. We've got older people who had extremely full days in the outdoors and what have you and they are still up for whatever social programming we are having so this is a group of people who know how to most out of life and are really keen to do that. Whatever the lecture topics are they are keen to learn for the first time or learn to a deeper knowledge." (DN-01).

Based on participant observations, some cruiser behaviours did not correspond to the identified pre-cruise motivations. These exceptions were likely due to cruisers' age, physical mobility and energy levels. Some days the weather was challenging and cruisers chose to remain on the ship instead of disembark. Of note, there were two cruisers who chose to only disembark at a single location, remaining on board the ship for the remainder of the trip. The cruisers choosing not to partake in a landing was puzzling to the guides as the cruisers' were paying a significant amount of money to "be here". One guide shared in the semi-structured interview: "When would they be back here? Never! Why not bundle up and go for a bit?" (DR-07).

3.7. Questions Posed during Lectures

The vast majority of the questions posed by cruisers during or after presentations (see Supplemental material) were comprehension-based. The cruisers were using the information presented to ask further questions such as "What causes polynya?" and "How does the fox avoid becoming food for the polar bear, since they follow behind?" Comprehension questions can be found across all topics presented, including climate change, wildlife, and geography. The "application" questions that cruisers asked included: "With El Niño pushing the jet stream, could that have an effect (on the climate)?" and "How will climate change impact the vegetation (in the Arctic)? More bugs? Wildfires?"

Climate change was important to many cruisers, as indicated by the open-ended survey and interview responses. Many of the cruisers connected their experiences during the expedition with the onboard presentations to gain a better understanding. There were no questions asked during the presentations that would be considered analysis or synthesis. There were several opportunities for informal learning during meals, unscheduled time on board, and zodiac rides.

3.8. Cruiser Engagement as Reported by Expedition Guides

To gain a deeper understanding of cruisers' behaviour on ship, the researcher asked the guides for their observations. The comments from guides show further evidence of the cruisers' interest in learning and absorbing all that the expedition itinerary had to offer. This was reinforced by comments from guides that support cruiser behaviours such as asking questions, attending presentations, and participating in activities despite the weather. "I've had some keeners that have been veracious in terms of asking questions and consuming new knowledge, that's always great" (CH-06) and "There has been great attendance at all of the presentations, they are at the recaps, sometimes people are bailing on the recaps but they are at them. Most of them are going ashore, on the zodiac rides, despite some pretty terrible weather" (CG-03). Another guide refers to the cruisers' desire to learn more about a specific area: "I feel like the people in this group are a bit more serious about learning. There is usually a small general interest in plants and there are a half dozen that are really keen" (CM-05). Another guide mentioned the overall attitude and engagement of the cruisers, "On this trip there is no one who is down, they are a very bubbly, happy, engaging group of folks" (MM-04).

The cruisers' motivations are further supported by the following comments from the guides. "What I see in our passengers in general is that for a variety of reasons they are lifetime learners, really motivated, want to get the most out of everything. The vast majority of them will attend every lecture and will make every landing. You know, we even saw, late in the evening we've got older people who had extremely full days in the outdoors and what have you and they are still up for whatever social programming we are having. So this is a group of people who know how to get most out of life and are really keen to do that" (DN-01).

Another guide touched on the continued motivation to learn and behaviours during informal times on ship, "They are all really great. They are motivated to learn, and every day, all through the trip, the lecture hall has been pretty much full. And I'm really impressed, everybody comes away from the lecture super charged and enthusiastic, tons of questions, not just after the lecture, but as they interact with us out on the land, over dinner, in the hallways, it's a very high level of enthusiasm" (RB-02).

The expedition cruisers' behaviours on ship correspond to pre-cruise motivations. The cruisers are keen to be immersed in this novel destination and to take it all in despite some unpleasant weather. They interact with the guides to gain more knowledge about the wildlife and landscape.

Q4. What is the impact of the educational experiences on post-cruise attitudes?

3.9. Arctic Knowledge

Participants were asked questions concerning their general knowledge of the Arctic environment. Note that the pre and post-trip surveys were not linked by participant. In the pre-trip survey ($n = 144$), high scores were achieved by only 2% of respondents, who answered 12 of 15 questions correctly. The mean score of the pre-trip participants was 5.9 correct answers and shows an even distribution of answers with a median score of 6/15. Six percent of respondents were only able to manage one correct answer.

The same questions were asked in the post-trip survey ($n = 92$). While the subject matter of the questions was not necessarily addressed during the expedition, scores improved. One participant achieved a perfect score. The post-trip survey mean score for all participants increased by 0.6 points to 6.4 and the median value improved by 2 points to 8/15. Those who could only manage a single correct answer were reduced to only 2% of participants.

There was a statistically significant difference in the scores for pre-cruise ($M = 5.9$, $SD = 3.1$) and post-cruise ($M = 7.5$, $SD = 2.9$) conditions ($t_{234} = 4.5$, $p < 0.001$). The overall average increased by 10%, as cruisers answered one to two more questions correctly in the post-trip survey. In particular, there were six questions where performance increased significantly. Questions #1 on climate, #4 on culture, #10 on human history, #11 and #12 on geography and #13 on oceanography (see Figure 1). This quiz was assembled pre-season; therefore, it was not guaranteed that the content of questions would be addressed during the expedition, making this result even more significant. Results suggest that there is an increase in knowledge that occurs after participation in an Arctic expedition.

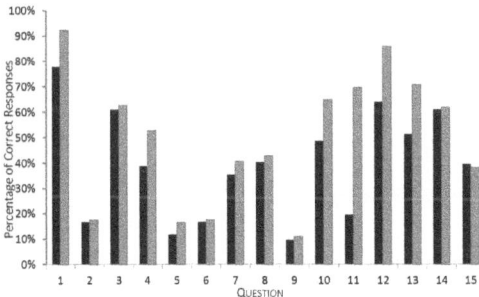

Figure 1. Results of pre-trip (dark grey bars) and post-trip (light grey bars) survey response by question.

3.10. Self-Reported Knowledge Gain

To better understand the participants' view on potential educational benefits from participation in an Arctic expedition, they were asked: "Please indicate how much you think this trip has increased your knowledge in the areas listed below", using a Likert scale with "5 = A great deal" and "1 = none" (see Table 4).

Table 4. Percent distribution of cruisers' self-reported knowledge gain by topic ($n = 92$).

	Mean (of 7)	A Great Deal	A Moderate Amount	Somewhat	A Little Bit	None
General awareness of the natural environment	4.6	65.6	30.1	3.2	1.1	0
Natural History	4.31	40.9	48.4	8.6	1.1	1.1
Environmental conservation	4.3	43	46.2	8.6	2.2	0
Marine Biology & Oceanography	3.8	15.1	54.8	21.5	7.5	1.1
Ornithology (Bird biology)	3.59	11.8	44.1	32.3	10.8	1.1

The post-trip participants indicated that their knowledge gain about the natural environment was high. Natural history and environmental conservation followed closely behind. However, the more science-related topics such as marine biology and oceanography had lower scores. Therefore, participants learned a moderate to high amount in three areas: general awareness of the natural environment, natural history, and environmental conservation. Combining these data with the results from the "knowledge of the Arctic" section suggests there was a positive impact on expedition cruiser knowledge.

3.11. Knowledge Gain Reported by Cruisers

To more fully understand the impact of educational experiences offered by the expedition cruise company, an open-ended question in the post-trip survey ($n = 92$) asked: "Has the expedition to the Arctic had an impact on you? Please explain". Supporting the quantitative findings, responses indicated that the cruisers made gains in general knowledge. Responses such as: "Gives me more knowledge of the world around us" (PS-04), and "We very much appreciated the interaction with the staff and high educational quality of lectures and sharing of knowledge" (PS-64).

Arctic-specific knowledge as indicated by: "Expanded knowledge and appreciation of that part of the world" (PS-59), "Increased knowledge about the Arctic" (PS-32), "Greater understanding of the eastern coast of Canada and the people and wildlife that inhabit it" (PS-16), and one respondent shared "Definitely! Since the expedition I have been reading about the Arctic, listening to discussions and watching video. Because I am more knowledgeable, I have more interest in and am more concerned about the issues affecting the environment, the wildlife and the Inuit way of life. I feel a personal connection to the Arctic. I have a better understanding of the impact of global warming on the Arctic environment and certainly on the people living there. I have also stayed loosely connected with some of the people that I met on the voyage. It is all such a positive memory, a once in a lifetime experience" (PS-58).

Responses also indicated an increase in knowledge about climate change: "This trip reinforced my views on Global warming as a very big problem" (PS-41), and "Made even more aware of climate change" (PS-54). "Instilled a better awareness of the negative effects of human activities that pose a threat to the balance of nature (animal and environmental) throughout the globe" (PS-55).

Knowledge gain regarding the Inuit culture was outside the scope of this research. However, responses on this topic did surface: "Gave me a much better understanding of issues regarding the Inuit" (PS-19), and: "A greater understanding of Arctic communities and culture" (PS-44), "Have a better understanding of the difficulties of the local residents and the Northern Nutrition program, which has had a lot of negative publicity lately, needs review at a high level (we did some window shopping/pricing in the Northern store)" (PS-64).

3.12. Attitudes about Arctic Resource Management

Prior to departure on the itinerary, cruisers agreed with many of the environmental resource statements. However, their agreement increased further after the trip (see Table 5). Although support for all conservation measures included in the survey received a high level of support, responses to questions #1 and #9 indicated that cruisers became more supportive of conservation measures that limit the activities of future tourists in the Arctic. The category of "no opinion" was selected 5.7% of the time pre-trip. This decreased to 0.7% in the post-trip survey, showing an over 90% decrease of "no opinion" responses.

The results suggest that participation in an Arctic expedition had only a slight impact on cruiser attitudes toward environmental and management issues facing the Arctic. However, when interpreting the results, consideration should be given to the low number of "no opinion" responses and respondents' high base level of agreement with these issues.

Table 5. Attitudes toward Arctic resource management pre- and post-survey.

	Question	Mean Pre (n = 144)	Mean Post (n = 92)	G (df =6)	p-Value (Two-Tailed)
1	Limiting the number of tourists that visit the Arctic	5.3	5.5	21.8	<0.001 *
2	Setting aside large pieces of land in the Arctic as protected areas that limit human use	6.0	6.1	4.4	0.62
3	Conserving wildlife in the Arctic by limiting human access to important breeding areas	6.4	6.5	1.5	0.96
4	Regulating the use of long lines for fishing in the Arctic, which accidently kills seabirds	6.1	6.1	5.6	0.47
5	Setting aside large sections of the Arctic Ocean as marine protected areas where economic uses like fishing and drilling are excluded	6.0	6.1	8.4	0.21
6	Monitoring cruise tourism's impact in the Arctic	6.4	6.5	3.6	0.73
7	Regulating greenhouse gas emissions in an effort to curb global warming	6.1	6.3	14.0	0.03 *
8	Regulating the commercial fishing of krill within the Arctic	6.0	6.3	85.4	2.7
9	Developing stricter regulations on field excursions in an effort to minimize negative impacts	5.9	6.1	21.2	0.001 *

* Significant at $p < 0.05$.

3.13. General Views about the Natural Environment

Similar to the responses about Arctic resource management, the pre-trip survey indicated strong opinions that became even more pronounced after the trip (see Table 6). Comparing answers from the pre- and post-trip surveys to questions #2, #6, #11, and #12 more closely, the respondents' attitudes regarding the environment shifted by the conclusion of the trip. Question #2, addressing a spiritual connection, showed significant change post-cruise, with no participant indicating "no opinion", and a 16% increase in those who felt a stronger connection with nature. Over 20% more participants indicated post-trip that they strongly agree that seeing the physical grace of a whale conveys to them a sense of the beauty of the natural world. There was also a significant increase in how participants felt about their relationship to wildlife in the Arctic, with 16.5% more participants indicating a stronger connection.

Question #13 looked at the level of agreement that participants had with the expedition company's mandatory Discovery Fee of US$250. Prior to the trip, 43.8% of participants indicated that they strongly agree with a fee that is used to support environmental efforts to the areas visited. About 5% of participants did not have an opinion. However, the post-trip survey shows that 64.5% of participants thought of the Discovery Fee favourably and the number of those with no opinion of the fee dropped to zero.

An overall pattern that emerges from the responses is a deeper connection to nature and an interest in learning more about the wildlife and environment. The items that showed a statistically significant increase related back to cruiser motivations. After experiencing the Arctic first-hand the participants indicated support for the protection of the Arctic environment in the form of stricter visitor guidelines and monetary fees to assist with restoration.

Table 6. Pre-trip and post-trip comparison of general views toward the natural environment.

	Question	Mean Pre (n = 144)	Mean (Post) (n = 92)	G (df = 6)	p-Value (Two-Tailed
1	I enjoy the thrill of sailing across a wild place like the Davis Strait	5.76	6.31	37.5	1.41
2	I don't have a particularly strong spiritual connection with nature	3.03	2.58	29.5	<0.001 *
3	I approve of seal hunting for aboriginal subsistence	5.72	6.14	15.7	0.015 *
4	If large oil reserves are found in a wildlife refuge, I believe drilling should be approved so long as efforts are made to protect the environment	3.16	3.03	2.0	0.92
5	I am not particularly interested in bird-watching	3.1	3.17	4.8	0.57
6	Seeing the physical grace of a whale conveys to me a sense of the beauty of the natural world	6.1	6.43	25.1	<0.001 *
7	I am morally opposed to the hunting of seals for sport	5.53	5.54	7.7	0.26
8	I can accept the harvesting of a small number of unthreatened animal species in fishing nets if it keeps the price of fish at a reasonable price for consumers	4.08	4.4	22.8	<0.001 *
9	I think the environment is important but protection measures should not hurt the local or national economy	3.2	3.28	7.5	0.27
10	I would enjoy reading a book on the ecology of the Arctic	5.28	5.78	26.1	<0.001 *
11	I feel a strong connection with the wildlife that I see	5.59	6.08	23.9	<0.001 *
12	I participate in tours like this one primarily to see beautiful scenery and wildlife	6.06	6.43	16.5	0.01 *
13	I support the expedition company's $250 fee for restoration and protection of the Arctic environment	6.2	6.56	23.2	<0.001 *
14	Mandatory visitation guidelines are needed for the protection of the Arctic environment	6.28	6.42	3.6	0.73
15	While approaching a group of muskoxen to photograph them, they show signs of agitation. As long as they don't run, it is okay to photograph before moving away	3.25	3.68	11.9	0.07
16	In order to get a better photo of the sleeping walrus, it is acceptable to toss a small stone or make a noise to awaken the walrus	2.08	2.15	4.1	0.67
17	Visitors to the Arctic should follow the guidelines designed to protect the wildlife and vegetation	6.48	6.8	19.5	0.003 *

* Significant at p < 0.05.

3.14. Attitude Change Reported by Cruisers

The open-ended question in the post-trip survey asked: "Has the expedition to the Arctic had an impact on you? Please explain." Many of the responses show a reinforcement of pre-trip attitudes. The common theme found in the responses that support their attitudes regarding the Arctic environment was indicated by: "Yes, it reinforced my appreciation for this part of Canada and the need to preserve it" (PS-08), "I enjoy the north country, the landscape is unlike other parts of the world. Seeing the strength and at the same time the fragility of the country, makes me more aware of why everyone needs to become stewards of this great land" (PS-17), "It has given me a greater appreciation of the 'wild areas' that are still left on our planet. The great solitude of the Arctic is a precious resource that we cannot waste" (PS-35), and "Have an even greater concern about the environment in terms of energy, waste, and disposal of products of our consumer society" (PS-38).

There were also a few responses noting the connection with the natural environment and Inuit culture: "the importance of restricting commercial exploitation without negatively affecting the aboriginal population's ability to do more than just survive" (PS-46) and "Yes, I am more appreciative of the fragile environmental impact of global warming, and natural resource explorations and its impact on the land and its people" (PS-60).

The strong baseline of attitudes reported in the pre-trip survey align with cruisers' post-trip attitudes toward the environment.

3.15. Behaviours

Participants expressed a slight increase in some environmentally-oriented behaviours (Table 7). Prior to the cruise, there was already a high level of engagement in the nine items identified on the survey. Results indicated that participants modified their behaviours in ways that showed a new interest in donating time or money to an organization, attending meetings in the community about the environment, or voting for elected officials that support environmental protection. However, these behaviours most likely would not influence daily activities that influence, for example, consumer decisions.

Table 7. Comparison of pre-trip and post-trip behaviours.

	Question	Mean Pre ($n = 144$)	Mean Post ($n = 92$)	G (df = 9)	p-Value (Two-Tailed)
1	Donating money or time to organizations concerned with the protection and restoration of the Arctic	2.62	2.87	19.4	<0.001 *
2	Voting for elected officials that support environmental protection	3.68	3.9	10.9	0.03 *
3	Becoming a member of organizations concerned with the environment	3.19	3.15	3.9	0.42
4	Avoiding the use or purchase of certain products because of their environmental impact	3.88	4.01	3.6	0.46
5	Contributing waste to a recycling program	4.71	4.84	7.3	0.12
6	Making efforts to reduce your consumption	4.45	4.35	27.6	<0.001 *
7	Finding ways to reuse materials	4.38	4.41	1.5	0.83
8	Reading about the environment	4.01	3.96	0.9	0.92
9	Attending meetings in the community about the environment	2.9	3.24	10.4	0.03 *

* Significant at $p < 0.05$.

4. Discussion

The increase in cruise tourism within the last decade, especially within Canada's Arctic Region, has created a demand for better understanding of how cruisers' attitudes toward the environment are affected as a result of their expedition experiences. This will help inform the debate on whether there is value in supporting a tourism industry in an ecologically sensitive region. We examined cruiser motivations to take an Arctic expedition to determine whether the educational programing had any impact on cruiser knowledge, attitudes, or behaviour.

Pro-environmental attitudes of cruisers can be positively affected by the incorporation of well-designed educational programming [29,35,39,40]. There has been debate, however, regarding the effectiveness of knowledge transfer within nature-based tourism [41]. In a cruise context, this is because it has been hypothesized that a cruiser's motivation to take a cruise is based upon seeking relaxation and comfort and is therefore at odds with focused learning. Regardless of the intentionality of the educational programming, it may have little to no lasting effect on attitude or behavioural change toward the environment.

The first question of this study assessed if motivational factors for engaging in Arctic expedition cruising differed from motivational factors for mainstream cruising. Our results indicated that expedition cruisers are motivated by opportunities to learn. Specifically, expedition cruisers are motivated to gain a deeper understanding of the unique landscape and wildlife found in the Arctic. Our results also indicated that cruisers are eager to experience the novelty associated with visiting the Arctic. Therefore, expedition cruisers have different motivations compared to those that travel on a mainstream cruise line to Caribbean-type destinations. It is therefore highly likely that they also have different expectations of the cruise company, the programming, the comfort of the accommodations, and of the excursions.

According to the ELM, the results indicated that expedition cruisers are in the first stage of central processing. The expedition cruiser was motivated to think about the message that is being conveyed, as evidenced by the open-ended survey responses. For example: "My first choice for travel is always a new experience, one where I am learning everyday" (Q-82), "I am excited to learn more about our Canadian Arctic ecology" (Q-76), and "Being with resource staff that can educate me regarding plants" (Q-117).

Expedition cruisers already have a high level of environment-related knowledge and engagement in pro-environmental behaviours, indicating that they likely have the ability to process the information being presented on-ship as it complements their prior knowledge. This is an important result because the central route of persuasion strengthens a change in attitude [42].

The ELM further suggests that if the educational program is designed properly, with a clear message, is well-presented, and is meaningful to the cruiser, it is likely that s/he will have a high level of cognitive involvement. Our results indicated that the expedition company is providing a meaningful and intentional educational program to the cruisers. Over the 15-day trip there was on average 6.5 h per day of planned educational programming and the expedition company's knowledgeable, interactive, and enthusiastic guides provided interesting lectures that appealed to cruisers' interests and learning expectations. In addition, cruising is conducive to continued or repeated exposure as cruisers are immersed in pro-environmental messaging for the duration of the Arctic trip. This further supports the likelihood of change in attitudes as there is a combination of immersive nature-based experience, information from guides, and relevant educational activities. An important aspect of central processing and long-lasting change in attitudes is the opportunity to contemplate the information being provided. Hiking or sitting on outer decks to enjoy the view are just two examples of activities that provided the cruisers with the opportunity and sufficient time for careful reflection of the messages provided.

Our results indicated that cruisers' pro-environmental attitudes strengthened from pre-trip to post-trip. The participants' knowledge of the Arctic region increased on several of the questions, in particular those related to geography and climate and culture and history. There was very little improvement in the biology- and science-focused questions, though the cruisers self-reported a large increase in their general awareness of the natural environment, natural history, and environmental conservation.

Attitudes about Arctic resource management issues showed a slight increase in stronger opinions. However, consideration should be given to the cruisers' high base level of agreement toward resource management and the Arctic environment in general. Open-ended interview responses also indicated a reinforcement of attitudes. For example, "this trip reinforced my views on global warming as a very big problem" (PS-41) and "it reinforced my appreciation for this part of Canada and the need to preserve it" (PS-08).

After traveling to the Arctic, participants indicated a positive change in some behaviours. More money or time were donated to organizations concerned with the protection and restoration of the Arctic, and participants indicated that they have a stronger belief that voting for elected official that support environmental protection is important. Given the profile of this study's expedition cruisers, these behaviours and level of engagement with environmental issues was already quite high. The fact that any changes in behaviour were documented post-trip is, therefore noteworthy and suggests that educating less informed group of cruisers (i.e., mainstream cruisers) could have a greater influence on behaviour. These results are similar to Walker and Moscardo's (2006) results on expedition cruising in Australia [21]. They noted that attitude change increases when there is a combination of immersive nature-based experience, information provided from the field staff, and activities offered through educational programming.

With an increase in cruise tourism to Canada's Arctic region comes a need to better understand the cruise experience and its long-lasting impacts. To the authors' knowledge, this is the first quantitative and qualitative study addressing cruiser motivations to take an expedition cruise in the Polar regions, and one of few to study the impact of educational programming on cruisers' attitudes toward environmental conservation.

From a managerial perspective, cruise companies can benefit from this research by gaining market insights. Customer retention is important and Arctic expedition cruisers who value environmental programming are likely to make informed choices in the future, due to the high expenditure of time and money spent on the Arctic expedition.

The data collected from this study indicated that expedition cruising currently caters to a narrow demographic with a specific motivation to learn and an already high level of engagement in environmentally conscious behaviours. Recently, a mainstream cruise company has begun operating in the Arctic Regions of Canada, offering a Northwest Passage cruise for 32 days from Alaska to New York with 1080 passengers. They are catering to the comfort- and kinship-motivated mainstream cruiser by providing a variety of entertainment options on board and offering select off-ship activities [43]. While in the Arctic Region (26 days) the cruisers have only nine days allocated for off-ship activities as only a limited number of ports are able to accommodate a large ship. All nine stops are within communities and only two are made within Canada. It is highly unlikely that cruisers on a mainstream cruise will have the same environmentally focused knowledge and experience as those travelling on an expedition ship but the potential for knowledge transfer and encouraging behavioural changes may be higher as a result.

5. Conclusions

On board, expedition cruisers connect with nature, appreciate and expect knowledgeable resource staff, seek unique experiences, and engage in lectures and other educational experiences. Post-cruise, they are more knowledgeable about climate, geography, history, and culture but feel as though they are more knowledgeable about the environment, natural history, conservation, biology, and ornithology. Notably, the respondents are highly likely to continue their interest in learning about the Arctic after the trip has finished.

This research provides valuable insight into the educational motivations of expedition cruisers. Learning opportunities are an important component of the cruise experience, which has the potential to positively impact cruiser attitude and knowledge post-cruise. These findings will encourage cruise companies to improve their educational offerings (i.e., preparedness, program quality, level of engagement) to meet the expectations of their clientele, thereby transferring critical knowledge of environmental stewardship.

Supplementary Materials: The following are available online at http://www.mdpi.com/2079-9276/6/3/23/s1, Research Ethics Certificate, Pre-cruise survey, Post-cruise survey, Semi-structured interview questions for guides, Semi-structured interview questions for cruisers, List of questions posed by cruisers during educational programing.

Acknowledgments: We would like to thank Adventure Canada for kindly allowing us to conduct research on their operation. The Northern Scientific Training Program provided an award to Brittany Manley to offset the costs of research in the North.

Author Contributions: Shoshanah Jacobs and Brittany Manley conceived on the project. Brittany Manley, Shoshanah Jacobs, and Statia Elliot designed the methodology. Brittany Manley collected the data. Brittany Manley, Shoshanah Jacobs, and Statia Elliot analysed the data. Brittany Manley wrote an MSc thesis on the topic. Shoshanah Jacobs drafted the article.

Conflicts of Interest: The authors declare no conflict of interest. Adventure Canada does not expect a right of first refusal, a preview approval of any publications, ownership, nor to set the direction of the research.

References

1. Douglas, N.; Douglas, N. Foreword. In *Cruise Tourism in Polar Regions: Promoting Environmental and Social Sustainability*; Earthscan: London, UK, 2010; p. xx.
2. Stewart, E.J.; Howell, S.E.L.; Draper, D.; Yackel, J.; Tivy, A. Sea Ice in Canada's Arctic: Implications for Cruise Tourism. *Arctic* **2007**, *60*, 370–380. [CrossRef]
3. Maher, P.T.; Meade, D. *Cruise Tourism in Auyuittuq, Sirmilik and Quttinirpaaq National Parks*; Technical Report—ORTM Publication Series 2008-02; UNBC ORTM Program: Prince George, BC, Canada, 2008.
4. Stirling, I.; Parkinson, C.L. Possible effects of climate warming on selected populations of polar bears (Ursus maritimus) in the Canadian Arctic. *Arctic* **2006**, *59*, 261–275. [CrossRef]
5. Serreze, M.C.; Holland, M.M.; Stroeve, J.C. Perspectives on the Arctic's shrinking sea-ice cover. *Science* **2007**, *316*, 1533–1536. [CrossRef] [PubMed]
6. Arntsen, A.E.; Song, A.J.; Perovich, D.K.; Richter-Menge, J.A. Observations of the summer breakup of an Arctic sea ice cover. *Geophys. Res. Lett.* **2015**, *42*, 8057–8063. [CrossRef]
7. Feng, Z.; Ji, R.; Campbell, R.G.; Ashjian, C.J.; Zhang, J. Early ice retreat and ocean warming may induce copepod biogeographic boundary shifts in the Arctic Ocean. *J. Geophys. Res. Oceans* **2016**, *121*, 1–22. [CrossRef]
8. Dawson, J.; Johnston, M.E.; Stewart, E.J. Governance of Arctic expedition cruise ships in a time of rapid environmental and economic change. *Ocean Coast. Manag.* **2014**, *89*, 88–99. [CrossRef]
9. Lück, M. *Nautical Tourism: Concepts and Issues*; Cognizant Communication: Putnam Valley, NY, USA, 2007; pp. 75–82.
10. Lemelin, R.H.; Johnston, M. Northern protected areas and parks. *Parks Prot. Areas Can. Plan. Manag.* **2008**, *3*, 294–313.
11. Dawson, J.; Stewart, E.J.; Maher, P.T.; Slocombe, D.S. Climate Change, Complexity and Cruising in Canada's Arctic: A Nunavut Case Study. In *Natural Resources and Aboriginal People in Canada*, 2nd ed.; Anderson, R., Bone, R.M., Eds.; Captus Press Inc.: Concord, ON, Canada, 2009; pp. 414–439.
12. Lemelin, H.; Dawson, J.; Stewart, E.J.; Maher, P.; Lück, M. Last-chance tourism: The boom, doom, and gloom of visiting vanishing destinations. *Curr. Issues Tour.* **2010**, *13*, 477–493. [CrossRef]
13. Lück, M.; Maher, P.T.; Stewart, E.J. *Cruise Tourism in Polar Regions: Promoting Environmental and Social Sustainability*; Earthscan: London, UK, 2010.
14. Johnston, A.; Johnston, M.; Stewart, E.; Dawson, J.; Lemelin, H. Perspectives of decision makers and regulators on climate change and adaptation in expedition cruise ship tourism in Nunavut. *North. Rev.* **2012**, *35*, 69–95.

15. Dawson, J.; Stewart, E.J.; Johnston, M.E.; Lemieux, C.J. Identifying and evaluating adaptation strategies for cruise tourism in Arctic Canada. *J. Sustain. Tour.* **2016**, *24*, 1425–1441. [CrossRef]
16. Johnston, M.; Dawson, J.; De Souza, E.; Stewart, E.J. Management challenges for the fastest growing marine shipping sector in Arctic Canada: Pleasure crafts. *Polar Rec.* **2016**, *53*, 1–12. [CrossRef]
17. IAATO (International Association of Antarctica Tour Operators). Tourism Overview. 2013. Available online: http://iaato.org/tourism-overview (accessed on 20 May 2017).
18. Jones, C.S. Arctic ship tourism: An industry in adolescence. *North. Raven* **1999**, *13*, 28–31.
19. Marsh, J.; Staple, S. Cruise tourism in the Canadian Arctic and its implications. In *Polar Tourism: Tourism and the Arctic and Antarctic Regions*; Hall, C.M., Johnston, M.E., Eds.; John Wiley and Sons Ltd.: Chichester, UK, 1995; pp. 63–72.
20. Maher, P.T.; Stewart, E.; Lück, M. Moving forward. In *Cruise Tourism in Polar Regions: Promoting Environmental and Social Sustainability*; Earthscan: London, UK, 2010; pp. 227–232.
21. Walker, K.; Moscardo, G. The Impact of Interpretation on Passengers of Expedition Cruises. In *Cruise Ship Tourism*; Dowling, R.K., Ed.; CABI: Wallingford, UK, 2006; pp. 105–114.
22. Green, G. Students on Ice: Learning in the Greatest Classrooms on Earth. In *Cruise Tourism in Polar Regions: Promoting Environmental and Social Sustainability*; Earthscan: London, UK, 2010; pp. 93–105.
23. Snyder, J.; Shackleton, K. *Ship in the Wilderness*; Dent and Sons: London, UK, 1986.
24. Hung, K.; Petrick, J.F. Why do you cruise? Exploring the motivations for taking cruise holidays, and the construction of a cruising motivation scale. *Tour. Manag.* **2011**, *32*, 386–393. [CrossRef]
25. Jones, R.V. Motivations to cruise: An itinerary and cruise experience study. *J. Hosp. Manag. Tour.* **2011**, *18*, 30–40. [CrossRef]
26. Petrick, J.F. The role of quality, value, and satisfaction in predicting cruise passengers' behavioral intentions. *J. Travel Res.* **2004**, *42*, 397–407. [CrossRef]
27. Li, X.R.; Petrick, J.F. Examining the antecedents of brand loyalty from an investment model perspective. *J. Travel Res.* **2008**, *47*, 25–34. [CrossRef]
28. Petrick, J.F. Are loyal visitors desired visitors? *Tour. Manag.* **2004**, *25*, 463–470. [CrossRef]
29. Ham, S. From interpretation to protection: Is there a theoretical basis? *J. Interpret. Res.* **2009**, *14*, 49–57.
30. Petty, R.E.; Cacioppo, J.T. *The Elaboration Likelihood Model of Persuasion*; Springer: New York, NY, USA, 1986; pp. 1–24.
31. Petty, R.E.; Haugtvedt, C.P.; Smith, S.M. Elaboration as a determinant of attitude strength: Creating attitudes that are persistent, resistant, and predictive of behavior. *Attitude Strength Anteced. Conseq.* **1995**, *4*, 93–130.
32. Ellis, C.; Kriwoken, L.K. Off the Beaten Track: A Case Study of Expedition Cruise Ships in South-west Tasmania, Australia. In *Cruise Ship Tourism*; Dowling, R.K., Ed.; CABI: London, UK, 2006; pp. 251–260.
33. Powell, R.B.; Brownlee, M.T.; Kellert, S.R.; Ham, S.H. From awe to satisfaction: Immediate affective responses to the Antarctic tourism experience. *Polar Rec.* **2012**, *48*, 145–156. [CrossRef]
34. Stern, P.C.; Dietz, T.; Kalof, L. Value orientations, gender, and environmental concern. *Environ. Behav.* **1993**, *25*, 322–348. [CrossRef]
35. Powell, R.B.; Kellert, S.R.; Ham, S.H. Antarctic tourists: Ambassadors or consumers? *Polar Rec.* **2008**, *44*, 233–242. [CrossRef]
36. Guest, G.; Bunce, A.; Johnson, L. How many interviews are enough? An experiment with data saturation and variability. *Field Methods* **2006**, *18*, 59–82. [CrossRef]
37. Murrant, C. *Blooming 101: How to Use the Bloom's Taxonomy Metric to Assess Course Learning Expectations*; University of Guelph: Guelph, ON, Canada, 2014.
38. Dillman, D.A. *Mail and Internet Surveys: The Tailored Design Method*; Wiley: New York, NY, USA, 2000; Volume 2.
39. Lück, M. Education on marine mammal tours as agent for conservation—But do tourists want to be educated? *Ocean Coast. Manag.* **2003**, *46*, 943–956. [CrossRef]
40. Walter, P.G. Theorising visitor learning in ecotourism. *J. Ecotour.* **2013**, *12*, 15–32. [CrossRef]
41. Hollinshead, K. Surveillance of the worlds of tourism: Foucault and the eye-of-power. *Tour. Manag.* **1999**, *20*, 7–23. [CrossRef]

42. Perloff, R.M. *The Dynamics of Persuasion: Communication and Attitudes in the Twenty-First Century*; Routledge: New York, NY, USA, 2010.
43. Crystal Cruises. Northwest Passage. Available online: http://www.crystalcruises.com/northwest-passage-cruise (accessed on 10 November 2015).

resources

MDPI

Article

Strategic Development Challenges in Marine Tourism in Nunavut

Margaret E. Johnston [1,*]**, Jackie Dawson** [2] **and Patrick T. Maher** [3]

[1] School of Outdoor Recreation, Parks and Tourism, Lakehead University, Thunder Bay, ON P7B 5E1, Canada
[2] Department of Geography, Environment, and Geomatics, University of Ottawa, Ottawa, ON K1N 6N5,
    Canada; jackie.dawson@uottawa.ca
[3] School of Arts and Social Sciences, Cape Breton University, Sydney, NS B1P 6L2, Canada; pat_maher@cbu.ca
* Correspondence: mejohnst@lakeheadu.ca; Tel.: +1-807-343-8377

Received: 30 May 2017; Accepted: 26 June 2017; Published: 30 June 2017

Abstract: Marine tourism in Arctic Canada has grown substantially since 2005. Though there are social, economic and cultural opportunities associated with industry growth, climate change and a range of environmental risks and other problems present significant management challenges. This paper describes the growth in cruise tourism and pleasure craft travel in Canada's Nunavut Territory and then outlines issues and concerns related to existing management of both cruise and pleasure craft tourism. Strengths and areas for improvement are identified and recommendations for enhancing the cruise and pleasure craft governance regimes through strategic management are provided. Key strategic approaches discussed are: (1) streamlining the regulatory framework; (2) improving marine tourism data collection and analysis for decision-making; and (3) developing site guidelines and behaviour guidelines.

Keywords: marine tourism; cruise ships; pleasure craft; Nunavut Territory; management; impacts; Arctic Canada

---

1. Introduction

Marine tourism in the Arctic has been growing as tourism demand increases and accessibility is improved [1–3]. Much of this activity involves smaller expedition cruise ships and the larger vessels common in more accessible cruise destinations. Sailboat and luxury yacht travel has also grown. But there are distinct differences in tourism within the Arctic region that reflect particular geographic and political contexts. It is important to consider these particularities in order to understand sustainable tourism and natural resource protection as it relates to marine tourism development in the Arctic.

The entire Canadian Arctic, in comparison to the European Arctic, is at a geographic disadvantage that is largely related to its remoteness from major population centres; as a result, total numbers of cruise visitors to this area are much lower. Planning and investment in cruise tourism infrastructure in Greenland over the past decade has resulted in strong tourism numbers [4–6], while Iceland has experienced a dramatic boom linked to planning and a favourable geographic position (see [7,8]). Svalbard, likewise, has benefited from good planning and management, as well as proximity to large markets. Marine tourism is slowly developing in Russia where present military activity and past military nuclear waste has resulted in large areas being off-limits for commercial purposes. The area available to cruise tourism in Russia is advantaged by robust infrastructure that supports the maritime sector in general. However, cruise tourism in Russia remains limited because of the aging fleet of cruise vessels in use, an inconsistent regulatory system, and competition from other polar cruising regions [9]. Development of the Russian Arctic National Park in 2009 has been an attraction to cruise vessels and more recently the protected area also attracts pleasure craft [10].

The ice regime in Arctic Canada has meant that until recently the region has not been reliably accessible for marine tourism. Changes in ice cover and distribution across the region have resulted in greater accessibility for all vessel types [11–13] and this has been particularly beneficial for Nunavut where the marine tourism sector has seen a relatively rapid increase in vessel numbers [14–16]. Pleasure craft, typically sailboats and motor yachts, are now the fastest growing shipping sector in Nunavut, while passenger vessels (both large and expedition cruise ships) are the fourth fastest growing sector in the region [16–18]. The Northwest Passage, known for its rich history and scenic beauty, has emerged as the most popular area to visit with transits increasing dramatically [18,19]. The greater accessibility of the Northwest Passage has meant more vessels are travelling into and through Nunavut; the discovery of the *Erebus* and the *Terror*, the two ships lost in the region during the 1845 Franklin Expedition, is a new factor increasing the draw for tourists and providing opportunities for the tourism industry [18].

Nunavut's position in the Canadian Arctic has meant that, of the three territories, it has seen the greatest growth in marine tourism, creating both challenges and opportunities for the territory, communities and businesses (Figure 1). There are distinct cultural and environmental attractions in Nunavut, but the vast geographic extent of the region is a disadvantage in terms of the provision of infrastructure and services needed in the development of the sector. In addition, there is a regulatory barrier across the various jurisdictions of the Canadian Arctic (the federal government, the territorial governments, provincial governments, and the Inuit and Inuvialuit organizations) that affects the development of cruise tourism particularly.

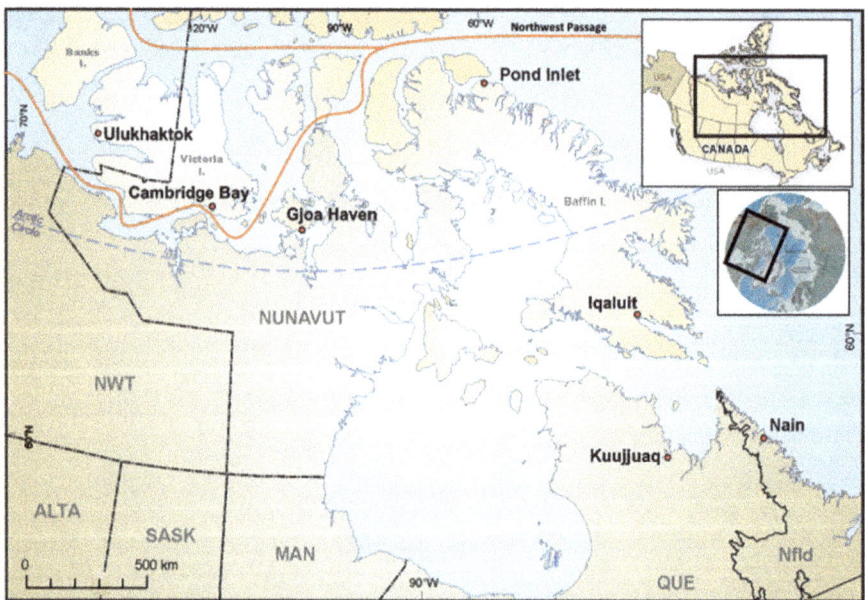

Figure 1. Map of Nunavut in the context of the Canadian Arctic.

There is hope that the increased activity will bring tourism benefits to Nunavut, but there is also concern about the risks involved. Researchers and government departments have described both the benefits (e.g., economic development, promotion of history and culture, community and infrastructure development) and the risks (e.g., human safety and security, environmental impacts, local costs) (see, for example, [15,19–24]).

Thus far, the region has a strong history of safe operations with only a few notable mishaps that include several ship groundings, requests for search and rescue assistance, and inappropriate or illegal behaviour of visitors [15,25–31], but the number of incidents is expected to increase as the numbers of vessels, voyages and passengers increase [32] and with new and/or unprepared entrants to the region [15,30]. Questions remain about the contribution of marine tourism to local economic development, especially given the capacity of cruise vessels to be completely self-contained [21,24,33]. The most recent Nunavut Tourism visitor exit survey [34] shows that, despite the high income of passengers and high prices paid for Arctic cruises and airfare, cruise visitors only spend an average of $700 each on shore during their entire cruise. This echoes data presented by Maher [21] and by Nunavut Tourism [35] showing that cruise tourists to Nunavut spend less than $50 CDN per day in Nunavut.

Despite the lack of visitor spending, the Government of Nunavut does want to develop marine tourism in an appropriate way, seeing the need for culturally-compatible economic development at a scale that is manageable in the small communities. The successful examples of cruise tourism development in Greenland, Iceland and Svalbard provide possible approaches, as do the best practices of sustainable tourism in other jurisdictions. Nunavut Territory is part way along its planning journey: it has a tourism strategy, a marine tourism management plan, an exit survey, a cruise readiness program, and the intent to resolve problems through cross-jurisdictional discussions. Nunavut is considering marine tourism management in an inclusive and integrated fashion, addressing both the cruise ship and pleasure craft categories together, an approach that has not been used until recently in the territory. At this point in its planning, Nunavut is seeking to develop effective management for the sector that both regulates and supports marine tourism development. This paper outlines current cruise and pleasure craft trends in Nunavut, describes the context, development, and strengths and weaknesses of the regional cruise management regime, and presents recommendations for enhancing the strategic management of the sector.

2. Growth in Marine Tourism

Marine tourism in Nunavut largely involves tourists travelling as cruise ship passengers or on small pleasure craft such as motor yachts and sail boats. Regulatory definitions help distinguish the two categories of vessels and these distinctions have important implications for management. Vessels with passengers who pay for their voyage fall into the commercial category, while non-commercial vessels carry no passengers, that is, the persons on board have not paid for or provided any remuneration for their transport. Both types of travellers are counted as tourists, though much emphasis has been on understanding the cruise segment, in particular, of the marine tourism industry in Nunavut. Those visitors travelling in pleasure craft might be termed "independent" travellers, while those on cruise ships might be termed commercial or package tourists. Both commercial and independent marine tourism involve the potential for positive and negative impacts in Nunavut, but they have different needs and ways of interacting with residents, communities, government agencies and the environment; consequently, there are different strategic challenges associated with each category.

Cruise tourism in Nunavut has followed the expedition cruising style popularized in the Antarctic by Lars-Eric Lindblad [22], which is founded upon exploration and education: "Experiences take three forms: using the ship as an observation platform (e.g., for whale watching), small boat cruising (e.g., along scenic coastlines, to view icebergs) and landings ashore. Throughout the cruises, both afloat and ashore, passengers are guided by experienced staff and naturalists, with lectures given en route between destinations. The guides also ensure visitors behave in a way that causes minimal or no disturbance to the natural environment" ([36], p. 106). Expedition cruising provides tourists with "off the beaten path" experiences in remote parts of the world that are often only accessible by sea [37,38]. These smaller ships do not require the infrastructure of conventional cruising such as docks and other facilities as shore access is typically by inflatable rubber boats [39].

Polar expedition cruise passengers generally are older in age, well-educated, well-travelled, in good health, and have successful careers or are retired; therefore, they usually have high levels of disposable income and time [21,22,40,41]. Expedition cruising, with its focus on adventure and education, appeals to these travellers, typically motivated by "finding new unspoilt, previously unvisited locations with a strong natural or cultural appeal" ([37], p. 251). Exit surveys undertaken of visitors in Nunavut confirm the typical polar expedition cruise demographic profile [34]: 90% are from Canada, the US and Europe, most are over age 65, 58% are female, and travel parties are often family and friend, and have an average size of 4 people. Cruise visitor are typically well-educated (60% have a graduate degree), and have a high household income (75% of respondents have a household income above $100,000; 30% above $200,000), yet the average spend on shore is only $700.

Little is known about the demographic profile, spending patterns, and motivation of pleasure craft tourists in the region. Vessels range from small sailboats with two persons aboard to luxury yachts with more than 50 people aboard. Pleasure craft tourists set their own itineraries and have the capacity to access landings virtually anywhere in Nunavut. While cruise visits are concentrated at a moderate number of communities and desirable historic, cultural or landscape sites, pleasure craft visits are substantially more dispersed. This form of travel was limited in the past largely to niche adventurers attempting to reach untouched and untraversed seaways of the Canadian Arctic, but it has now evolved into a regular form of tourism to the region. Because the pleasure craft sector is new and dispersed, and because vessels fall below regulatory thresholds for mandatory reporting, very little is known about these tourists. It is likely that there are at least two distinct sets of travellers, based on the type of vessel used and the motivation to visit the region. The adventurers in sailboats are likely different in many ways from the wealthier individuals who travel in luxury yachts (see [1,2]).

Table 1 illustrates a decade of changing patterns in marine tourism in Nunavut from 2005 to 2015. The year 2005 marks the beginning of a stable cruise tourism industry in Nunavut. The number of vessels increased over the next three years and since has fluctuated between a low of 18 and a high of 30 vessels. In recent years, the size of cruise vessels has increased and thus the number of passengers arriving has also increased. The actual number of kilometers traveled by cruise ships has fluctuated over time, peaking in 2008 and 2010 with a slight decline in more recent years. Table 1 also shows the development in pleasure craft tourism, which has increased steadily over the same decade, reflecting the opening up of the Canadian Arctic as a new destination region for both luxury and adventure travellers ([15], see also [1]. Pleasure craft are now the fastest growing category of all ship types in the Canadian Arctic [15]. The westward shift in cruise ship activity noted by Stewart and Dawson [29] is mirrored in the spatial patterns of pleasure craft travel, reflecting enhanced accessibility of the Northwest Passage [15]. Although the actual number of vessels is low compared to other more southern cruising regions, the increase in kilometres traveled is particularly striking. The distance traveled by pleasure craft in kilometers increased by 148% during the 2010–2015 time period compared to 2005–2010 and current distances traveled are close to that of traditional cruise ships. Pleasure craft are also moving into more northerly parts of the region and average length of visit has increased dramatically [15].

The table data arise from advertised cruise itineraries and Canadian Coast Guard NORDREG, a database established through the vessel reporting system in Canada that is non-mandatory for pleasure craft and for cruise ships under 300 tonnes. It is likely that all cruise ships and most pleasure craft voluntarily report because this provides access to services (e.g., weather reports, SAR), but a degree of non-reporting does exist in the pleasure craft sector [15].

While marine tourism in Nunavut is comprised almost exclusively of expedition cruise tourism and pleasure craft tourism, the exceptions are quite noteworthy because they present distinct strategic management issues. For example, in 2016 the largest cruise ship to ever enter the Canadian Arctic sailed into Nunavut. The *Crystal Serenity*, a vessel ten stories high, traversed the Northwest Passage over 32 days, covering 7297 nautical miles and bringing more than 1000 guests and 600 crew to the small hamlets of Cambridge Bay (population 1766) and Pond Inlet, Nunavut (population 1617). The luxury vessel is now becoming a regular in the region, with plans to visit again in summer 2017 [42,43].

Table 1. Passenger Vessel and Pleasure Craft Trends across Nunavut (2005–2015).

Year	Passenger Vessel Voyages	Estimated Number of Persons on Passenger Vessels	Kilometres Traveled	Pleasure Craft Voyages	Estimated Number of Persons on Pleasure Craft	Kilometres Traveled
2005	11	1045	69,621	9	25	9394
2006	23	2200	84,519	3	5	N/A
2007	24	2496	75,981	7	21	5757
2008	26	2962	85,973	7	21	22,871
2009	25	2738	59,225	12	70	26,475
2010	24	2628	87,704	11	103	25,749
2011	18	1890	43,728	20	104	44,754
2012	22	2582	33,503	26	175	51,510
2013	26	3002	62,673	23	152	54,048
2014	25	2880	62,557	30	240	72,569
2015	30	3680	68,127	21	139	54,068

Another large vessel that visited the region in 2012, the *World*, has proven hard to categorize using regulatory definitions. The *World* is a luxury condominium ship with 165 units on board valued at up to $13 million each. The *World*'s trip to Nunavut included disembarking its 508 passengers in two Nunavut communities to experience local culture [44].

The *Octopus*, categorized as a pleasure craft, is a super luxury yacht that can accommodate more than 50 guests. The vessel features a glass bottom swimming pool, cinema, recording studio, hangar for two helicopters, a submarine, wood burning fireplace, and full spa and exercise room. Owned by Microsoft co-founder Paul Allen, it has travelled in the Canadian Arctic on numerous occasions, often stopping in Pond Inlet, Nunavut to purchase supplies and make donations to the local visitor centre [45].

Overall, the marine tourism sector in Nunavut has been steadily growing since 2005 and is expected to continue to increase at least moderately into the future. The numbers of vessels in the region are much smaller than other popular Arctic cruising areas such as Svalbard, Norway, Iceland and Alaska. However, the territory of Nunavut in Arctic Canada is unique in its governance (settled land claim area combined with territorial and federal oversight) and thus warrants focused research and management attention.

3. Marine Tourism Management Context

As cruise tourism has grown in Nunavut, attention has been given to understanding the negative and positive aspects of this change from the perspectives of decision-makers, industry, the tourists themselves, and residents (e.g., [19,21,22,46–51]). One of the key areas of concern has been the challenges associated with the development of marine tourism policy and an appropriate management regime [18]. In particular, three areas of concern are significant: a complicated regulatory framework, a lack of data and monitoring capability, and insufficient control over tourist behaviour.

Concerns with the regulatory framework were identified in an exploration of cruise tourism policy needs in protected areas [23]. Stakeholders in the study were concerned about poor communication and industry fragmentation, and its effects on tourism development and control. The creation of a central organization to develop guidelines and represent the Arctic cruise industry was desired by the respondents in the study and, in particular, the International Association of Antarctica Tour Operators (IAATO) model of self-regulation was viewed as providing a good example that could be emulated in the Canadian Arctic. These themes were explored further in an analysis of cruise vessel governance in Arctic Canada [30]. This research highlighted the need for a dedicated authority to oversee management, to streamline licensing procedures and to develop guidelines and best practices.

A coordinated approach to effective governance would aid development by both controlling and supporting the growing cruise tourism industry.

Regulatory concerns also arose in research on cruise industry operator perspectives regarding decision-making and expectations about operations in Arctic Canada [49,50]. While operators were concerned about ice hazards and a lack of infrastructure, they were also concerned about additional costs incurred by operators related to following Canadian legislation and permitting. Lasserre and Têtu [50] concluded that growth in cruise tourism in the Canadian Arctic would be limited unless these regulatory challenges were addressed. The role of this barrier is further addressed by Dawson, Johnston & Stewart [18] who recommended that the overly complex system of permitting should be replaced with a streamlined and coordinated approach by government agencies and that more attention be paid to collecting appropriate data needed for decision-making. This reinforces the point made 10 years earlier by Marquez and Eagles [23] that a lack of data was hindering policy development.

The territorial approach to tourism is linked with a wide number of other bodies that, as a whole, provide the regulatory framework for marine tourism. Currently there is a multi-level framework for vessel traffic aimed at ensuring safe and secure operations that protect the natural environment, preserve local culture and traditions, and encourage economic development for the region. The general principle of the governance approach is to manage the cruising industry through both regulation and development support [30]. An overview of the regulatory and permitting process is outlined by Transport Canada in a document titled 'Guidelines for the Operation of Passenger Vessels in Canadian Arctic Waters' [52], currently under revision (see [18]).

Of particular note is the oversight and support provided by the Canadian Coast Guard. Vessels of 300 gross tonnage or more must register with NORDREG, the Canadian Coast Guard Marine Communications and Traffic Services, upon entering the Canadian Arctic and thereafter report their daily location in compliance with the zone date ice regime system. Further, operators of passenger vessels entering Canadian waters in Nunavut are required to arrange for and cover the costs of Canadian Border Services agents coming to the port of entry (typically Pond Inlet) in order for all passengers and crew to clear customs. For pleasure craft entering Canadian waters in Nunavut it is the responsibility of all persons on board to clear customs through the local Royal Canadian Mounted Police office.

Territorial specific regulations, licenses and operating permits include those related to doing business in Nunavut, as well as those established for environmental assessment through the Nunavut Impact Review Board, for supporting Inuit guides through the Inuit Heritage Trust, and those that are itinerary specific, such as permits to enter National or Territorial Parks. Permission is also required to access Inuit owned land. Pleasure craft operators are not required to seek permits related to commercial standards, expectations and responsibilities that are required for passenger vessels. An area of concern for both federal and territorial authorities is the possibility that commercial vessels with paying passengers are operating as pleasure craft, therein avoiding relevant regulation [15].

In addition to the complicated and multi-jurisdictional system of laws and permits, there is a concern that the current territorial licensing framework through the Department of Economic Development and Transportation does not sufficiently cover cruise vessels or smaller commercial craft. Neither of the two current licensing options is relevant for cruise operators. The tourist establishment licence had been in use until the Nunavut Department of Justice determined that the Government of Nunavut did not have the authority to use this licence to regulate cruise ships. More recently, the second licence has been used—the outfitter's licence. This licence is relevant for local tour operators engaging in marine based activities such as kayaking, fishing and canoeing, but the definitions of an outfitter might not apply to a cruise operator depending on how the cruise activities are taking place. This two-licence system in the *Travel and Tourism Act* originated in a largely land-based tourism context and no revisions have occurred to reflect the dramatic changes evident with increasing marine tourism. It is vital that the legislation and regulations that support licensing activities be revised to accommodate the needs of a growing and changing marine tourism sector. Consultations have taken place on needed changes in this act, of which the licensing issue is a part [53].

That tourism has resided in the Department of Economic Development and Transportation relates to its being seen primarily in economic terms. While commercial marine tourism should be licensed in relation to economic development and/or economic impacts, this situation has meant that less attention has been paid to non-commercial forms of tourism such as pleasure craft tourism and to impacts of cruise tourism that are not economic in nature. The absence of reliable and consistent marine tourism data exacerbates the challenges associated with monitoring industry growth and fulfilling the territorial obligations to safeguard the region's natural environment and cultural heritage. It also makes it difficult to support the industry and to facilitate locally desired economic development pathways. Currently some effort is made to collect data through regular visitor exit surveys (conducted in 2006, 2008, 2011, and 2015) and through the permitting process [34,35,54]. However, neither system yields sufficient or reliable data for decision-making related to cruise and pleasure craft tourism. More effective systems for collecting tourism statistics on cruise tourism exists in other Polar destinations (see [55–57]). Where these data collection systems are built directly into tourism permitting and industry self-regulation procedures they are more effective. In these systems cruise operators are required to provide pre-trip information on the intended voyage, as well as post-trip information that identifies the location of all shore landings and number of passengers disembarking at those locations. The current pre/post-trip reporting forms in Nunavut for cruise vessels are focused on community disembarkations and on economic benefits, reflecting the mandate of that department [58], and so do not provide the complete record of disembarkations. Further, given the dispersed and unregulated nature of pleasure craft travel, there is little information about the activities of this sector other than what can be obtained through voluntary reporting of location or through examination of internet sites for particular voyages (see [59]). The increase in marine tourism leaves Nunavut Territory, its residents and its environment vulnerable to impacts without sufficient information to address problems. While control of cruise tourism is a regulatory and an industry responsibility, there is little oversight of the far more dispersed and independent pleasure craft now taking advantage of the increased access afforded by changes in the ice regime.

In an exploration of adaptation strategies for managing the increased tourism opportunities and risks in the context of climate change, Dawson, Stewart, Johnston and Lemieux [32] concluded that "there is a strong need for appropriate adaptation and management strategies to be implemented across Arctic Canada that allow local residents and regional communities to benefit from climate-induced development. Instead of passively observing economic change in the region, it is vital that development trajectories are directed via locally dictated desires and through evidence-based decision-making. Thus, policy- and management-focused research is necessary in order to better understand the particular adaptive strategies that are needed to ensure that a sustainable and desired tourism economy is facilitated in light of climate change." (p. 15).

Though much of the research on marine tourism management has focused on cruise vessels, Johnston, Dawson, De Souza and Stewart [15] surveyed decision-makers and managers in industry and government in order to assess the management concerns related to pleasure craft tourism. They grouped these concerns related to pleasure craft growth as comprising four categories: visitor behaviour; services, facilities and infrastructure; control; and, planning and development. They recommended that research on the sector, the development of effective regulations, and a strategic approach to development be prioritized. While their research demonstrates some overlap with the concerns identified in relation to cruise tourism, distinctions are important and must be addressed in management.

In Nunavut, tourists are able to disembark at any location (assuming they have permits for certain protected sites, Inuit lands and permission from communities) and there are no official guidelines outlining appropriate visitor behavior. In 2012, the community of Pond Inlet created a code of conduct for visitors to the community. The Government of Nunavut is now adapting the Pond Inlet code of conduct for visitors and has further developed other similar guidance documents including; a community code of conduct, an operator code of conduct, a visitor code of conduct and "do's and don'ts" of guided tours. There are federal level wildlife viewing guidelines and some behaviour restrictions at National Wildlife Areas, for example; however, at the territorial level, guidelines that reflect the local expectations and culture desires are largely absent. Cruise operators tend to reinforce appropriate behaviour among their clients and several long-term operators voluntarily hire local guides on all voyages to assist in developing an understanding of culture, though there are no requirements to do so.

Given the interest by cruise operators in the "Lindblad approach," many have taken on the idea of using education and interpretation, alongside staff observation and guidance of visitor behaviour. The Association of Arctic Expedition Cruise Operators (AECO) has industry guidelines that are now being used by some operators in Canada, and the guidelines of the Arctic Council's Protection of the Arctic Marine Environment (PAME) working group developed through a multi-party approach could be used. Cruise visitors might be well-controlled through these means (see [21,22]), however, there is much concern about the activities of pleasure craft travellers and whether they pay attention to best practices, community desires regarding tourist behaviour, territorial and federal laws and common sense [15].

4. Progress in Territorial Marine Tourism Management

Management of both cruise ship and pleasure craft tourism in Nunavut is now taking place within the context of a territorial Tourism Strategy and a marine tourism plan. In 2013, the Nunavut Department of Economic Development and Transportation (EDT) released *Tunngasaiji: A Tourism Strategy for Nunavummiut*. The Tourism Strategy is intended to develop tourism in Nunavut for the benefit of the territory and its communities, while ensuring that the people of Nunavut, the wildlife, and the environment are respected and protected [20]. Though it covers all tourism development in the territory, it does contain specific references to marine tourism and includes the objective of developing and implementing a cruise ship and yacht management plan to help communities and businesses to participate in this emerging market. The resulting management plan itself "reflects the guiding objectives and desired outcomes of *Tunngasaiji* and is based on further consultations with key stakeholders, input from legal advisors and other experts, and the programmatic knowledge of tourism staff within EDT" [60]. It was accepted by the territorial government and along with the Tourism Strategy now underpins support and control of marine tourism [18,59].

Tunngasaiji identifies the success indicators/outcomes of the Cruise Ship and Yacht Management Plan as follows: increased income to communities through provision of services, sale of arts and crafts; improved relationships with communities from more effective management of cruise ships and yachts; greater awareness of cruise and yacht owners and operators of regulations and licensing requirements [20]. The creation of the marine tourism management plan represents an important foundational step toward providing support for communities and businesses to pursue their interests in the sector, while providing a stronger framework for the territory to address its service and control gaps. However, as climate change and other global factors influence additional growth in the marine tourism sector in Nunavut it is important that innovative and contextually specific strategic management approaches continue to be prioritized.

5. Strengths and Weaknesses of the Management Regime

The effectiveness of management framework for marine tourism in Arctic regions can directly influence economic opportunities, safety and security, local culture, and environmental sustainability. The multi-level framework that exists in Nunavut has areas of strength but requires substantial improvement to ensure opportunities are realized and risks mitigated. Achieving management outcomes such as ensuring compliance with regulation, protecting the environment and encouraging economic development is very challenging in Nunavut given the size of the territory, the lack of monitoring infrastructure and resources, and the variety of institutions and agency stakeholders involved in managing the industry.

Current areas of strength in Nunavut include: a strong set of regulations aimed at safeguarding the natural environment, wildlife, protected lands and cultural heritage; an increasing demand for cruising opportunities, especially through the Northwest Passage; an industry with several passenger ship operators with over two decades of experience safely navigating in Nunavut waters; a robust system for environmental assessment and protection including the Nunavut Impact Review Board, territorial and federal processes; and, the potential for a comprehensive approach to planning through the Nunavut Planning Commission. Further, the establishment of the Tourism Strategy and the marine tourism management plan provide the territory with the tools to support communities and groups that wish to pursue marine tourism in their economic development planning. An associated review of legislation and licensing practices has enabled the Department of Economic Development and Transportation of the Government of Nunavut to clarify its approach to regulation as it takes firmer control of this sector of tourism.

Significant weaknesses include: inappropriate territorial licensing system for cruise vessels and a complex system of inter-jurisdictional regulation; lack of enforcement capabilities in the region (and neighbouring regions); lack of tourism data needed for decision-making and industry support; a complicated permitting system; the lack of a single point of contact in the territory or communities; an absence of site guidelines for heavily used and/or significant locations; and, limited availability of codes of conduct for visitor behaviour.

The large number of government departments and agencies with a role to play in management demands a more coordinated approach than is currently in place and possibly the creation of a single point of authority in the region. Currently in Canada, each level of government, and the various departments and agencies within, is focused on its specific area of mandate (e.g., culture, environment, or transportation.), but not enough attention is given to the importance of integrating management efforts across scales and across mandated responsibilities. This has led to management gaps, oversights, and communication difficulties. Other polar regions are not immune to these issues, but in some cases a streamlined approach with a clear communication protocol has been successfully employed.

6. Discussion—Strategic Management Options

For Nunavut to take advantage of the increase in marine tourism through a strategic development agenda, it will need to address weaknesses in the current passenger vessel and pleasure craft governance regime. It is perhaps disheartening that many of the weaknesses apparent today were identified by Marquez and Eagles [23] a decade ago, but it is noteworthy that challenges in marine tourism development of the type and scale being experienced in Nunavut are similar to challenges experienced in other regions such as the Kimberley Coast in Australia [61], New Zealand's Fjordland [62,63] and the Russian Arctic [9]. The territorial Tourism Strategy, changes in legislation and the marine tourism management plan go a long way in resolving some of the identified problems. Yet several management approaches need to be pursued more aggressively to ensure that marine tourism does not harm Nunavut's environment, culture, heritage and the daily life of residents, and to make best use of the competitive advantage now held by Nunavut because of its geographic and political position in the Canadian Arctic. Several strategic approaches are discussed below: streamlining the provision of information and the industry permitting system; improving tracking of all tourism vessels and enhancing data collection; and, developing guidelines for highly visited and/or significant sites and for tourist behaviour.

6.1. Streamlining the Regulatory Framework

Cruise operators and pleasure craft travelers would greatly benefit from the consolidation of regulatory, management, and voluntary and interpretative information into one online location that serves to educate operators about the region, but also facilitates the mandatory regulation and permitting requirements. Nunavut (and Arctic Canada) is known for its highly complex permitting process, which is currently curtailing the full potential of cruise tourism development in the region. Developing a two-way information exchange portal whereby operators can request permits, obtain interpretative and pertinent information from the region, and where the Government of Nunavut, its neighbouring jurisdictions, and the Inuit and Inuvialuit agencies can issue permits, provide updates, and gather industry data is a win-win situation for both operators and regulators/stewards of the region.

The complexity that exists within the passenger vessel regulatory system is currently limiting cruise tourism activity and local economic opportunities in Nunavut. Passenger vessel operators are required to obtain between 20 and 35 permits to operate in Nunavut, including permits required from federal agencies. This complexity is in direct contrast to the more streamlined systems that are in place in Antarctica and Svalbard that have a one-window approach to permitting based on the requirement for environmental review. The process will inevitably be more complex in Nunavut than in Antarctica or Svalbard where there are no or few human settlements; however, the one-window approach has the potential to improve the efficiency and effectiveness of management and help Nunavut meets its desired management outcomes [18].

The quickly growing pleasure craft sector requires a special management focus. As part of this effort, a first step should be a comprehensive information package available online that identifies requirements for safe operation, compliance with the rules, regulations and expectations of the territory, information on support systems, and other preparatory material about the Arctic environment also in a one-window approach. This portal can function as a marketing tool with links to relevant sources of information. Finally, partnering with existing cruise tourism organizations will further provide a resourcing benefit to Nunavut. This may be as simple as website linkages, but could also involve joint information campaigns and efforts to develop Nunavut-specific material. Given the limited resources available to support tourism development, it makes sense to use the networking capacity of AECO, its existing web presence, and its reach to European operators [64].

6.2. Improving Marine Tourism Data Collection and Analysis for Decision-Making

Given the high adaptability of tourism operators, who can easily change tour locations, timing, and activities based on rapid changes in global demand or social trends, it is vital that Nunavut has access to and fully utilizes accurate and reliable tourism data. Increased data availability is necessary in order to more fully understand tourism trends as well as economic impact and potential so that evidence-based decisions can be made. Extensive and longitudinal tourism data have been collected in Svalbard and Antarctica, becoming a foundation for management and investment decision-making. The dearth of data in Nunavut makes decision-making difficult—especially for an industry that is already extremely variable. Visitor exit surveys conducted by the territory in the past have established some understanding of the tourism market, but have been plagued by a limited sample size, geographical bias in the sampling methodology, and inconsistent and sometimes invalid survey instruments.

Limited effort has been made to understand the pleasure craft market in the region and very little is understood about the motivations, desires, satisfaction levels, and intentions of this growing market segment. In line with the Tourism Strategy, Nunavut should conduct specific, detailed surveys of each of these two market categories of tourists (cruise and pleasure craft) on a regular basis. Data obtained through exit surveys, specific market category surveys and licensing will provide valuable planning, decision-making and monitoring information to help with management through regulation and support. Furthermore, Nunavut could pursue efforts to have AIS (automatic information system) responders as mandatory equipment on all tourist vessels in its waters. Currently larger tourism vessels such as cruise ships are required to use AIS responders, but smaller vessels are not. Benefits of having these on all vessels (commercial and non-commercial, large and small) are related to safety and security, and an improvement to monitoring capability, but they would also provide an excellent source of data for understanding the changing temporal and spatial patterns of cruise and pleasure craft tourists. This would require collaboration with federal agencies as requiring AIS Responders on vessels is within Transport Canada's jurisdiction.

6.3. Developing Site Guidelines and Behaviour Guidelines

There is need to improve site management in Nunavut. In Antarctica and Svalbard, site guidelines have been established and site vulnerability assessments are conducted at highly visited sites to monitor the environmental and cultural impacts of tourism and to provide interpretive and educational information to visitors [65,66]. This approach to both controlling and supporting marine tourism in Polar Regions has been very effective in remote Arctic areas where in-person monitoring capabilities are limited and expensive and should now be considered best practice. Further, site-specific guidelines provide an evidence-based approach to management that is an improvement upon relying on the precautionary principle [67]. Site guidelines typically include suggestions on how to conduct visits to locations; they provide pertinent and site-specific navigational details, as well as cultural, historic and environmental interpretive information and, further, they direct traffic to areas deemed suitable for visitation and, by default, steer visitors away from more sensitive areas.

Highly visited and/or significant sites across Nunavut should be identified and a series of site guidelines developed. The guidelines should include both interpretative/educational information as well as instructions for behavior and use and be integrated with any existing guidelines, for example, at protected sites. Existing guidelines from Antarctica and Svalbard can be used as a template and adapted for Nunavut. Although the vast majority of cruise and pleasure craft tourism is occurring in Nunavut it is recommended that there be consultation with Northwest Territories, Yukon Territory, Quebec and Newfoundland/Labrador to ensure that site guidelines are consistent across the Canadian north. It is further recommended that basic vulnerability assessments of each site be conducting including a benchmarking exercise so that impacts can be monitored over time. This should include an analysis of flora fauna, natural or cultural heritage, as well as aerial photographs. Monitoring and subsequent vulnerability assessment exercises should be conducted periodically (5 or 10 year intervals) in order to track impacts. A booklet of site guidelines should be available electronically through a variety of sources (e.g., Nunavut Tourism, Government of Nunavut, and AECO websites) with hard copies available for purchase.

To complement the site-specific guidelines, the code of conduct for visiting Pond Inlet should be adapted to a territorial scale and distributed as needed for use in Nunavut communities and on cruise vessels and pleasure craft. The development and/or adaptation of other codes of conduct should also be considered. For example, the AECO code of visitor conduct for Arctic regions or the World Wildlife Fund (WWF) codes of conduct for tourists and operators could be adapted for use in Nunavut. If it is not possible to legally require operators to have paid Inuit guides/interprets on board vessels operating in Nunavut, then this should be included in a code of conduct and highly encouraged as a voluntary measure. It is also recommended that a series of wildlife viewing guidelines be established for the specific context of Nunavut and its regions.

7. Conclusions

Marine tourism across the global Arctic has been increasing in popularity over the past decade and growth in the sector is expected to continue. In Arctic Canada, the territory of Nunavut has experienced significant increases in cruise and pleasure craft traffic since 2005 when the region became more reliably accessible due to diminishing sea ice and increased access to the Northwest Passage. The increased opportunities for marine operations in Nunavut have led to a fleet of expedition cruise vessels and luxury yachts that return to the region regularly. Over the past five years Nunavut has also attracted larger cruise ships, atypical vessels such as the *World*, and an increasing number of smaller private motor yachts and sail boats.

Compared to other Arctic regions, Nunavut still attracts fewer vessels due to geography, remoteness from populated centres, and also because of a limiting management regime that has acted as a deterrent to some polar operators. The purpose of this paper was to examine the management regime for marine tourism in Nunavut and to describe a set of strategic management suggestions that may enable the sector to develop in a way that balances regional imperatives related to the economy, society, and the environment. After reviewing the context and strengths and weaknesses of the existing cruise and yacht governance regime in Nunavut and Canada, recommendations for improving upon an already robust management system include; (1) streamlining the regulatory framework; (2) improving marine tourism data collection, and analysis for decision-making; and (3) developing site guidelines and behaviour guidelines.

The need to streamline the cruise tourism regulatory framework has been well-established by research within the academic and government. However, further work is needed to examine options for coordinating the multi-jurisdictional and multi-stakeholder mandates and interests, including how to ensure appropriate management of tourism activities alongside the broad environmental assessment and planning bodies in Nunavut. The urgent need to improve marine tourism data collection is required to bring the region up to date with other Arctic tourism regions that already collect key tourism statistics and to facilitate better decision-making in the region which is currently plagued by a lack of evidence-based information. Implementation of new cruise tourism data collection measures will not be difficult and could be facilitated through the current permitting system. However, enhancing data collection of pleasure craft visitors to Nunavut, who are not required to obtain permits, will continue to be challenging. Research needs to be undertaken to understand the actual activities and impacts on environment and wildlife of both cruise and pleasure craft tourists. Regarding the development of site and behavioural guidelines, a number of research needs exist. A comprehensive temporal and spatial analysis of tourism vessel trends in Nunavut is necessary to more fully understand where and when vessels visit communities and significant shore locations throughout the region. It will also be important to identify the locations where site guidelines should be developed because once guidelines are developed this will lead to focused visitation in these areas and, consequently, less visitation in other areas. It will also be important to work with all stakeholders to develop a cultural/environmental sensitivity index for the region so that appropriate sites can be chosen.

Acknowledgments: Funding was received from the Department of Economic Development and Transportation, Government of Nunavut for work on a previous project which led the authors to conceptualize this manuscript.

Author Contributions: Margaret E. Johnston conceptualized and designed the paper. All three authors contributed to the background research upon which it is based. Margaret E. Johnston and Jackie Dawson wrote most of the paper, with Patrick T. Maher contributing to the writing and completing the formatting. Jackie Dawson prepared the table and the figure.

Conflicts of Interest: The authors declare no conflict of interest.

References

1. Orams, M. Polar yacht cruising. In *Cruise Tourism in Polar Regions: Promoting Environmental and Social Sustainability?* Lück, M., Maher, P.T., Stewart, E.J., Eds.; Earthscan: London, UK, 2010; pp. 11–22.
2. Stonehouse, B.; Snyder, J.M. *Polar Tourism: An Environmental Perspective*; Channel View Publications: Bristol, UK, 2010.
3. Pashkevich, A.; Stjernström, O. Making Russian Arctic accessible for tourists: Analysis of the institutional barriers. *Polar Geogr.* **2014**, *37*, 137–156. [CrossRef]
4. Tommasini, D. Tourism Experiences in the Peripheral North: Case Studies from Greenland. *Inussuk Arctic Res. J.* **2011**, *2*, 1–298.
5. Statistisk Årbog 2016—Turisme, Transport og Kommunikation. Available online: www.stat.gl/publ/da/SA/201608/pdf/2016%20statistisk%20%C3%A5rbog.pdf (accessed on 29 May 2017).
6. Visit Greenland. Greenland: Be a Pioneer. Greenland's Official Tourism Website. Available online: www.greenland.com/en/ (accessed on 29 May 2017).
7. Karlsdóttir, A. *Cruise Tourists in Iceland: Survey on the Economic Significance of Cruise Tourism*; University of Iceland Tourism University: Reykjavik, Iceland, 2004.

8. O'Brien, M.A. Sustainable Cruise Ship Tourism: A Carrying Capacity Study for Ísafjörður, Iceland. Master's Thesis, University Centre of the Westfjords, University of Akureyri, Isafjörður, Iceland, 2014.
9. Pashkevich, A.; Dawson, J.; Stewart, E.J. Governance of expedition cruise ship tourism in the Arctic: A comparison of the Canadian and Russian Arctic. *Tour. Mar. Environ.* **2015**, *10*, 225–240. [CrossRef]
10. Gavrilo, M. Developing tourism in National Park Russian Arctic. In Proceedings of the Personal Communication via a presentation to the AECO—10 Conference, Oslo, Norway, 15 October 2013.
11. Haas, C.; Howell, S.E.L. Ice thickness in the Northwest Passage. *Geophys. Res. Lett.* **2015**, *42*, 7673–7680. [CrossRef]
12. Howell, S.E.L.; Duguay, C.R.; Markus, T. Sea ice conditions and melt season duration variability within the Canadian Arctic Archipelago: 1979–2008. *Geophys. Res. Lett.* **2009**, *36*. [CrossRef]
13. Howell, S.E.L.; Wohlleben, T.; Dabboor, M.; Derksen, C.; Komarov, A.; Pizzolato, L. Recent changes in the exchange of sea ice between the Arctic Ocean and the Canadian Arctic Archipelago. *J. Geophys. Res. Oceans* **2013**, *118*, 3595–3607. [CrossRef]
14. Arctic Council. Arctic Marine Shipping Assessment 2009 Report. Available online: http://www.pame.is/index.php/projects/arctic-marine-shipping/amsa (accessed on 22 June 2011).
15. Johnston, M.; Dawson, J.; de Souza, E.; Stewart, E.J. Management challenges for the fastest growing marine shipping sector in Arctic Canada: Pleasure crafts. *Polar Rec.* **2017**, *53*, 67–78. [CrossRef]
16. Pizzolato, L.; Howell, S.E.L.; Derkson, C.; Dawson, J.; Copland, L. Changing sea ice conditions and marine transportation activity in Canadian Arctic waters between 1990 and 2012. *Clim. Chang.* **2014**, *123*, 161–173. [CrossRef]
17. Pizzolato, L.; Howell, S.; Dawson, J.; Laliberte, F.; Copland, L. The influence of declining sea ice on shipping activity in the Canadian Arctic. *Geophys. Res. Lett.* **2016**, *43*, 146–154. [CrossRef]
18. Dawson, J.; Johnston, M.E.; Stewart, E.J. The Unintended Consequences of Regulatory Complexity: The case of cruise tourism in Arctic Canada. *Mar. Policy* **2017**, *76*, 71–78. [CrossRef]
19. Stewart, E.J.; Draper, D.; Dawson, J. Monitoring Patterns of Cruise Tourism across Arctic Canada. In *Cruise Tourism in Polar Regions: Promoting Environmental and Social Sustainability?* Lück, M., Maher, P.T., Stewart, E.J., Eds.; Earthscan: London, UK, 2010; pp. 133–146.
20. Tunngasaiji: A Tourism Strategy for Nunavummiut. Available online: http://gov.nu.ca/edt/documents/tunngasaiji-tourism-strategy-nunavummiut (accessed on 29 May 2017).
21. Maher, P.T. Cruise tourist experiences and management implications for Auyuittuq, Sirmilik and Quttinirpaaq National Parks, Nunavut, Canada. In *Tourism and Change in Polar Regions: Climate, Environments and Experiences*; Hall, C.M., Saarinen, J., Eds.; Routledge: London, UK, 2010; pp. 119–134.
22. Maher, P.T. Expedition cruise visits to protected areas in the Canadian Arctic: Issues of sustainability and change for an emerging market. *Tourism* **2012**, *60*, 55–70.
23. Marquez, J.; Eagles, P. Working towards policy creation for cruise ship tourism in parks and protected areas of Nunavut. *Tour. Mar. Environ.* **2007**, *4*, 1–12. [CrossRef]
24. Snyder, J.M. The polar markets. In *Prospects for Polar Tourism*; Snyder, J.M., Stonehouse, B., Eds.; CABI: Wallingford, UK, 2007; pp. 51–70.
25. Klein, R.A. Cruises and Bruises: Safety, Security and Social Issues on Polar Cruises. In *Cruise Tourism in Polar Regions: Promoting Environmental and Social Sustainability?* Lück, M., Maher, P.T., Stewart, E.J., Eds.; Earthscan: London, UK, 2010; pp. 57–74.
26. Sheppard, V. Exploring the ethical standards of Alaska cruise ship tourists and the role they inadvertently play in the unsustainable practices of the cruise ship industry. In *Cruise Tourism in Polar Regions: Promoting Environmental and Social Sustainability?* Lück, M., Maher, P.T., Stewart, E.J., Eds.; Earthscan: London, UK, 2010; pp. 75–92.
27. Lück, M. Environmental impacts of polar cruises. In *Cruise Tourism in Polar Regions: Promoting Environmental and Social Sustainability?* Lück, M., Maher, P.T., Stewart, E.J., Eds.; Earthscan: London, UK, 2010; pp. 109–132.
28. Teeple, N. A brief history of intrusions into the Canadian Arctic. *Can. Army J.* **2010**, *12*, 45–68.
29. Stewart, E.J.; Dawson, J.P. A matter of good fortune? The grounding of the Clipper Adventurer in the Northwest Passage, Arctic Canada. *Arctic* **2011**, *64*, 263–267. [CrossRef]
30. Dawson, J.; Johnston, M.E.; Stewart, E.J. Governance of Arctic Expedition Cruise Ships in Time of Rapid Environmental and Economic Change. *Ocean Coast. Manag.* **2014**, *89*, 88–99. [CrossRef]

31. Council of Canadian Academies. *Commercial Marine Shipping Accidents: Understanding the Risks in Canada*; Council of Canadian Academies: Ottawa, ON, Canada, 2016.
32. Dawson, J.; Stewart, E.J.; Johnston, M.E.; Lemieux, C.J. Identifying and evaluating adaptation strategies for cruise tourism in Arctic Canada. *J. Sustain. Tour.* **2016**, *24*, 1425–1441. [CrossRef]
33. Robbins, M. Development of tourism in Arctic Canada. In *Prospects for Polar Tourism*; Snyder, J.M., Stonehouse, B., Eds.; CABI: Wallingford, UK, 2007; pp. 84–101.
34. Insignia Research. *Nunavut Visitor Exit Survey 2015: Final Report*; Nunavut Tourism: Iqaluit, NU, Canada, 2016.
35. Nunavut Tourism. *Nunavut Visitor Exit Survey—2011*; Nunavut Tourism & CanNor: Iqaluit, NU, Canada, 2012.
36. Crosbie, K.; Splettstoesser, J. Antarctic tourism introduction. In *Polar Tourism: Human, Environmental and Governance Dimensions*; Maher, P.T., Stewart, E., Lück, M., Eds.; Cognizant Communication: Elmsford, NY, USA, 2011; pp. 105–120.
37. Ellis, C.; Kriwoken, L.K. Off the Beaten Track: A case study of Expedition Cruise Ships in South-west Tasmania, Australia. In *Cruise Ship Tourism*; Dowling, R.K., Ed.; CABI: Wallingford, UK, 2006; pp. 251–258.
38. Walker, K.; Moscardo, G. The Impact of Interpretation on Passengers of Expedition Cruises. In *Cruise Ship Tourism*; Dowling, R.K., Ed.; CABI: Wallingford, UK, 2006; pp. 105–114.
39. Thomson, C.; Sproull Thomson, J. Arctic cruise ship island tourism. In *Extreme Tourism: Lessons from the World's Cold Water Islands*; Baldacchino, G., Ed.; Elsevier: Oxford, UK, 2006; pp. 169–178.
40. Jones, C.S. Arctic ship tourism: An industry in adolescence. *North. Raven* **1999**, *13*, 28–31.
41. Grenier, A.A. *The Nature of Nature Tourism*; University of Lapland, Faculty of Social Sciences: Rovaniemi, Finland, 2004.
42. Crystal Cruises. Northwest Passage Explorer. Available online: https://www.crystalcruises.com/voyage/details/northwest-passage-explorer-7320?reload=1 (accessed on 26 May 2017).
43. A Luxury Cruise Liner Is about to Sail the Arctic's Northwest Passage. Available online: http://news.nationalgeographic.com/2016/08/crystal-serenity-luxury-cruise-arctic-northwest-passage/ (accessed on 26 May 2017).
44. The World Gets Green Light to Transit Northwest Passage. Available online: http://www.nunatsiaqonline.ca/stories/article/65674the_world_gets_the_green_light_to_transit_the_northwest_passage/ (accessed on 26 May 2017).
45. Nunavut's Tourism Operators Roll out the Red Carpet for the Super-Rich. Available online: http://www.nunatsiaqonline.ca/stories/article/65674nunavuts_tourism_operators_look_for_luxury/ (accessed on 26 May 2017).
46. Dawson, J.; Stewart, E.J.; Maher, P.T.; Slocombe, D.S. Climate change, complexity and cruising in Canada's Arctic: A Nunavut case study. In *Natural Resources and Aboriginal People in Canada*, 2nd ed.; Anderson, R., Bone, R.M., Eds.; Captus Press: Concord, ON, Canada, 2009; pp. 414–439.
47. Johnston, A.; Johnston, M.E.; Stewart, E.J.; Dawson, J.; Lemelin, R.H. Perspectives of decision makers and regulators on climate change and adaptation in expedition cruise ship tourism in Nunavut. *North. Rev.* **2012**, *35*, 69–85.
48. Stewart, E.J.; Dawson, J.; Howell, S.E.L.; Johnston, M.E.; Pearce, T.; Lemelin, H. Local-level responses to sea ice changes and cruise tourism in Arctic Canada's Northwest Passage. *Polar Geogr.* **2013**, *36*, 142–162. [CrossRef]
49. Têtu, P.L.; Lassere, F. The expansion of cruise tourism in the Canadian Arctic: Analysis of potential and actual activities of cruise ship operators. In *From Talk to Action: How Tourism Is Changing the Polar Regions*; Lemelin, R.H., Maher, P.T., Liggett, D., Eds.; Lakehead University Centre for Northern Studies Press—Northern and Regional Studies Series #23: Thunder Bay, ON, Canada, 2013; pp. 78–92.
50. Lasserre, F.; Têtu, P.L. The cruise tourism industry in the Canadian Arctic: Analysis of activities and perceptions of cruise ship operators. *Polar Rec.* **2015**, *51*, 24–38. [CrossRef]
51. Stewart, E.; Dawson, J.; Johnston, M. Risks and opportunities associated with change in the cruise tourism sector: Community perspectives from Arctic Canada. *Polar J.* **2015**, *5*, 403–427. [CrossRef]
52. Guidelines for the Operation of Passenger Vessels in Canadian Arctic Waters. Available online: https://www.tc.gc.ca/media/documents/marinesafety/tp13670e.pdf (accessed on 29 May 2017).

53. Nunavut Travel and Tourism Act Consultation Report. Available online: http://www.gov.nu.ca/edt/documents/travel-and-tourism-act-consultation-report (accessed on 29 May 2017).
54. Nunavut Visitor Exit Survey: 2008 Final Report. Available online: http://gov.nu.ca/economic-development-and-transportation/documents/tourism-exit-survey (accessed on 29 May 2017).
55. Haase, D.; Lamers, M.; Amelung, B. Heading into uncharted territory? Exploring the institutional robustness of self-regulation in the Antarctic tourism sector. *J. Sustain. Tour.* **2009**, *17*, 411–430. [CrossRef]
56. De la Barre, S.; Maher, P.T.; Dawson, J.; Hillmer-Pegram, K.; Huijbens, E.; Lamers, M.; Liggett, D.; Müller, D.; Pashkevich, A.; Stewart, E.J. Tourism and Arctic observation systems: Exploring the relationships. *Polar Res.* **2016**, *35*. [CrossRef]
57. Maher, P.T. Tourism Futures in the Arctic. In *The Interconnected Arctic*; Latola, K., Savela, H., Eds.; Springer: Amsterdam, The Netherlands, 2017; pp. 213–220.
58. Pre/Post-Trip Marine Tourism Economic Benefits Reporting Form. Available online: http://gov.nu.ca/edt/documents/prepost-trip-marine-tourism-economic-benefits-reporting-form (accessed on 29 May 2017).
59. Johnston, M.E.; De Souza, E.; Lemelin, R.H. Experiences of marine adventurers in the Canadian Arctic. In *Arctic Tourism Experience: Production, Consumption and Sustainability*; Lee, Y.-S., Weaver, D., Prebensen, N., Eds.; CABI: Wallingford, UK, 2017; pp. 159–168.
60. Nunavut Marine Tourism Management Plan. Available online: http://www.gov.nu.ca/edt/documents/nunavut-marine-tourism-management-plan (accessed on 29 May 2017).
61. Kimberley Coast Cruise Management Strategy. Available online: http://www.tourism.wa.gov.au/Publications%20Library/Research%20and%20reports/Kimberley_Coast_Cruise_Management_Strategy.pdf (accessed on 24 February 2017).
62. James, S.J.; Rennie, H.G. Right of way: Cruise tourism in Fiordland, New Zealand. In *International Tourism Students Conference Proceedings*; Croy, W.G., Ed.; Waiariki Institute of Technology: Rotorua, New Zealand, 2002; pp. 1–6.
63. Southland Cruise Ship Visits at a Glance. Available online: http://www.es.govt.nz/Document%20Library/Other%20resources/Cruise%20ships/cruise-ships-factsheet.pdf (accessed on 24 February 2017).
64. Association of Arctic Expedition Cruise Operators (AECO). Available online: http://www.aeco.no/ (accessed on 29 May 2017).
65. Association of Arctic Expedition Cruise Operators (AECO). Site Guidelines. Available online: https://www.aeco.no/guidelines/site-guidelines/ (accessed on 29 May 2017).
66. Secretariat of the Antarctic Treaty. Site Guidelines for Visitors. Available online: http://www.ats.aq/e/ats_other_siteguidelines.htm (accessed on 29 May 2017).
67. Hagen, D.; Vistad, O.I.; Eide, N.E.; Flyen, A.C.; Fangel, K. Managing visitor sites in Svalbard: From a precautionary approach towards knowledge-based management. *Polar Res.* **2012**, *31*. [CrossRef]

resources

MDPI

Case Reprot

The Ortelius Incident in the Hinlopen Strait—A Case Study on How Satellite-Based AIS Can Support Search and Rescue Operations in Remote Waters

Johnny Grøneng Aase [1,2]

[1]   Institute for Marine and Antarctic Studies, University of Tasmania, Private Bag 129,
      Hobart, TAS 7001, Australia; johnny.aase@utas.edu.au
[2]   Department of Research and Development, Norwegian Defence Cyber Academy, P.O. Box 800,
      Postmottak, NO-2617 Lillehammer, Norway; jaase@mil.no; Tel.: +47-9285-2550

Received: 26 April 2017; Accepted: 24 July 2017; Published: 27 July 2017

Abstract: In this paper, Automatic Identification System (AIS) data collected from space is used to demonstrate how the data can support search and rescue (SAR) operations in remote waters. The data was recorded by the Norwegian polar orbiting satellite AISSat-1. This is a case study discussing the *Ortelius* incident in Svalbard in early June 2016. The tourist vessel flying the flag of Cyprus experienced engine failure in a remote part of the Arctic Archipelago. The passengers and crew were not harmed. There were no Norwegian Coast Guard vessels in the vicinity. The Governor of Svalbard had to deploy her vessel *Polarsyssel* to assist the *Ortelius*. The paper shows that satellite-based AIS enables SAR coordination centers to swiftly determine the identity and precise location of vessels in the vicinity of the troubled ship. This knowledge makes it easier to coordinate SAR operations.

Keywords: tourism; polar; search and rescue; SAR; Arctic; Svalbard; AISSat-1; Ortelius

1. Introduction

On Friday 3 June 2016 at 12:30 am local time, the tourist vessel *Ortelius* reported engine trouble in the vicinity of the Vaigatt Islands in the Hinlopen Strait. This strait separates the main islands of Spitsbergen and Nordaustlandet in Norway's Svalbard archipelago [1–3]. There were 146 persons on board, out of which 105 were passengers. The Governor's vessel, the *Polarsyssel*, was sent to the region to tow the *Ortelius* back to Longyearbyen where it arrived in the evening of Sunday 5 June. Neither the *Ortelius* nor her passengers were reported to be in any danger during the incident.

In this paper, the *Ortelius* incident is used as a case study to show how satellite-based Automatic Identification System (AIS) can help establish situational awareness and support search and rescue operations in remote waters like the Arctic and Antarctica.

The purpose of the Automatic Identification System (AIS) is to increase safety at sea [4]. It transmits information about the ship and voyage. All ships of 300 gross tonnage and upwards that are engaged on international voyages, cargo ships of 500 gross tonnage and upwards not engaged on international voyages, and all passenger ships, irrespective of size, must have and use AIS. The requirement became effective for all ships by 31 December 2004. Ships equipped with an AIS transponder must keep it in operation at all times, except when international agreements, rules or standards provide for the protection of navigational information. Military vessels do not have an obligation to shine an AIS transponder, but may choose to do so. These regulations are implemented through the International Maritime Organization (IMO).

The transmissions take place in the VHF band. As a rule of thumb, the distance to the radio horizon of VHF transmissions can be calculated by taking the square root of the height of the antenna measured in meters and multiplying this number by 4124. Mountains, islands and other obstacles will reduce the effective range. It turns out that the AIS signals can also be received by satellites in low Earth orbit. Norway has therefore pursued satellite-based AIS to increase situation awareness in the North Atlantic and Arctic Ocean, which are that nation's main area of interest.

Satellites in polar orbits have global coverage. This is an advantage over satellites in geostationary orbit, which only see approximately one third of the Earth's surface. A geostationary satellite is located 36,000 km over the equator, approximately 1/10 the distance to the Moon. Such satellites are much more complicated and expensive to maintain and launch than small satellites in low Earth orbit. The advent of relatively simple and inexpensive micro-, nano- and pico-satellites gives small countries access to services that used to be available for superpowers only.

Ice melting from man-made climate change has opened the Arctic as a high-end tourist destination. Areas that used to be blocked by ice contain beautiful landscapes and natural resources like oil, natural gas and minerals that are of great interest to private and state actors. The increased traffic in the High North led to the Arctic Council adopting the "Agreement on Cooperation on Aeronautical and Maritime Search and Rescue in the Arctic" in 2011 [5]. The Arctic nations have divided the Arctic into national areas of responsibility, where "Each party shall promote the establishment, operation and maintenance of an adequate and effective search and rescue capability within its area (of national responsibility)".

Article 7.3b of the Agreement states that "if a search and rescue agency and/or (Rescue Coordination Center) (RCC) of a Party receives information that any person is, or appears to be, in distress, that party shall take urgent steps to ensure that the necessary assistance is provided". This paper shows that satellite-based AIS enables the Rescue Coordination Center to quickly get an overview of ships in the vicinity of a disabled vessel. This knowledge enables the RCC to plan the SAR operation in a very effective way.

The author is aware of only one paper that quantifies tourist traffic in the European Arctic. Aase and Jabour (2015) [6] studies three areas in the European Arctic using AIS satellite data obtained between 2010–2014. One of these regions is the waters north of 80° N in the Norwegian SAR area of responsibility between 0 and 35° E. This region is located just north of Spitsbergen.

The number of tourist vessels north of Svalbard increased from 15 in 2010 to 22 in 2013. It then dropped to 20 in 2014. This is most likely an organic fluctuation in the tourism industry, with more or less ships each season highly dependent on market demand. The first tourist vessel was seen north of 80° N on 1 June in 2012, on 4 June in 2011 and 2013, and on 9 June in 2014. AISSat-1 was launched after the start of the 2010 tourist season, so there is no first date for 2010. There is no obvious pattern to determine when the season ends. The last tourist vessel was seen north of 80° N on 22 September 2010, while the tourist season lasted until 7 October in 2011. Tourist vessels were seen north of 82° N in both 2011 and 2012. A vessel is out of reach from geostationary communication satellites at this latitude. Lack of broadband communications complicates SAR operations.

2. Materials and Methods

The Technology

The Norwegian satellite AISSat-1 was launched on 12 July 2010 [7] as secondary payload on an Indian rocket. As of 24 April 2017, the satellite flies in an orbit where the altitude changes between 610 and 626 km [8]. It is inclined with the equator by 98.0°. The satellite will hence pass over different areas in the Arctic and Antarctica for each orbit. This can explain why the numbers in Table 1 change. When a ship is outside the field of view of the satellite, the AIS transmissions will not be recorded. On the next pass, the path of the satellite has changed, and the vessel may be seen. The satellite records the time when a transmission is received by assigning a time stamp in J2000.0 format. J2000.0 equals the number of seconds passed since noon GMT on 1 January 2000.

Data is downloaded from AISSat-1 when the satellite passes over the town Vardø in Norway's northernmost county, Finnmark. Some AISSat-1 passes in the Arctic take place below the horizon seen from Vardø, and there are hence some gaps in the data flow.

Table 1. Table showing the number of Type A and B transponders seen in the 200 km area of interest surrounding the Ortelius in passes on 3 June 2016.

Ground Time (J2000-Format)	Ground Time (UTC)	Number of Class A Transponders	Number of Class B Transponders
518210407	07:19:03	17	0
518216384	08:58:40	19	0
518222190	10:35:26	17	0
518227993	12:12:11	15	0
518233702	13:47:20	14	3
518239380	15:21:57	15	0
518245043	16:56:19	15	2
518250739	18:31:15	15	0
518256482	20:06:58	10	0
518262252	21:43:08	16	0
518268049	23:19:45	15	1
518273856	00:56:32	13	0

The technical characteristics behind the AIS system are published in Recommendation ITU-R M.1371-5 [9]. In [10], Clazzer et al. analytically model the AIS Self-Organized Time Division Multiple Access (SOTDMA) traffic pattern at the satellite and investigate the realistic behavior of SOTDMA via simulations. Shelmerdine [11] demonstrates a procedure for the processing, analysing, and visualisation of AIS data with example outputs and their potential uses. Over 730,000 data points of AIS information for 2013 from around Shetland were processed, analysed, and mapped. Tools used included density mapping, vessel tracks, interpolations of vessel dimensions, and ship type analysis. The dataset was broken down by sector into meaningful and usable data packets which could also be analysed over time. Density mapping, derived from both point and vessel track data, proved highly informative but was unable to address all aspects of the data. Vessel tracks showed variation in vessel routes, especially around island groups. Additional uses of AIS data were addressed and included risk mapping for invasive non-native species, fisheries, and general statistics. Temporal variation of vessel activity was also discussed.

AIS equipment Class A is ship-borne mobile equipment intended to meet all performance standards and carriage requirements adopted by the IMO [12]. Class A stations report their position autonomously every 2 to 10 s depending on the vessel's speed and/or course changes. Position messages are transmitted every three minutes or less when the vessel is at anchor or moored. The static and voyage related messages are transmitted every six minutes. Class A stations are capable of text messaging safety-related information and AIS Application Specific Messages, such as meteorological and hydrological data, electronic broadcast Notice to Mariners, and other marine safety information.

For Class A equipment, AIS position reports are transmitted as Messages types 1, 2 and 3 [13]. The messages contain the vessel's Maritime Mobile Service Indicator (MMSI) number. This is a unique nine-digit number that identifies the vessel that transmits the message. These messages also inform about the vessel's navigational status, like "under way using engine", "at anchor", "restricted manoeuvrability", "moored" or "aground". In these messages, one can also find information about the rate of turn, speed over ground, position accuracy, longitude, latitude, course over ground and true heading. A time stamp indicating the time of download in J2000.0-format is added to the data files by the satellite software.

Class A ship static and voyage-related data are transmitted in AIS Messages type 5. These messages contain the ship's MMSI number, and also the IMO number, call sign and ship name. They also inform about the type of ship and cargo type, overall dimension, type of electronic position fixing device, estimated time of arrival (ETA), maximum present static draught, and destination.

AIS equipment Class B is ship-borne mobile equipment that is interoperable with all other AIS stations, but does not meet all the performance standards adopted by the IMO. Like Class A stations, they report every three minutes or less when moored or at anchor, but their position is reported less frequently or at less power than for Class A equipment. The vessel's static data is reported every six minutes. Class B equipment does not send any voyage-related information. It can, however, receive safety related text and application specific messages. Class B transponders use a different communications protocol than Class A transponders.

Class B position reports are transmitted as AIS messages types 18 and 19. They include the vessel's MMSI number, speed over ground, position accuracy, longitude, latitude, course over ground, true heading and some technical information. Messages type 19 also include the ship's name and information about the type of ship and cargo.

Messages type 24 are Class B static data reports. They consist of two parts, A and B. Part A includes the MMSI number and the vessel's name. Part B also includes the MMSI number, in addition to the type of ship and cargo type, vendor ID, call sign, dimension of ship and type of electronic position fixing device.

All these AIS messages contain the transmitting vessel's MMSI number. This information is used in this work to identify the vessel. AIS messages types 1 and 18 contain a time stamp and the position of the vessel in latitude and longitude. AIS messages types 5 and 24 contain the vessel's name, call sign, IMO number and destination. From AIS messages types 1 and 18 the time stamp, MMSI number and position are extracted to text files in .txt format, which are readable in MatLAB and can be used to plot positions in Google Maps.

The Norwegian Coastal Administration (NCA) (Name in Norwegian: *Kystverket*) owns the AISSat data sets. The NCA determines if an applicant shall get access to the data. The global data base is administered by *Forsvarets Forskningsinstitutt* (FFI). The FFI provides the data sets for free as password-protected zip files when access has been granted. The data sets shall not be used for commercial purposes.

By using the map published in the first online news articles [3], the position of the *Ortelius* was estimated to be 79.4° N 19° E. FFI generously provided a data set with AISSat-1 readings of positions within a radius of 200 km from this position obtained on 3 June. The first batch of data was downloaded at 07:19 UTC on 3 June, the last at 00:56 UTC on the 4th of June. The data set contains downloads from 12 passes over Vardø (Table 1).

AIS messages types 1, 5, 18 and 24 are used in this study. The unzipped text files are read into an Excel spreadsheet. For messages type 1, the J2000.0 time stamp, MMSI number and position (longitude and latitude) are used. The data set was divided into 12 subsets, where each subset was the data downloaded from each pass. The NDRE generously converted the J2000.0 time stamp into UTC time. In each of these subsets, only the first position sent from a vessel is used.

3. Results

Table 1 describes 12 satellite passes over Svalbard on the 3rd and 4th of June 2016. Table 1 shows the times when the data download began in both J2000-format and time given in UTC. Norwegian, i.e., Central European, summer time is two hours ahead of UTC time. The two last columns show the number of Class A and Class B transponders found in the downloaded batches of data. A data set was downloaded five minutes (UTC 10:35:26) after the *Ortelius* reported her engine problems (UTC 10:30). 17 Class A and 0 Class B transponders were found in that batch of data. The data set contains information from the two passes before Ortelius reported her accident, downloaded at 07:19 and 8:58 UTC. In the download received at UTC 08:58, 19 Class A transponders were seen. The maximum number of Class B transporters was seen in the 13:47 pass. Three transponders were seen. This day the satellite saw four unique Class B transponders (Figure 4).

Tables 2 and 3 show information about the vessels seen in the downloads starting at 08:58:40 and 10:35:26. Only data from the first Type 1 message received from each ship is used. Column 1 shows the time in J2000.0 format when AISSat-1 received the first message from the vessel. Column 2, Groundtime, tells when the first message was received by the radio receiver in Vardø. Columns 3 and 4 provides the vessel's unique MMSI number and name. Columns 5 and 6 give the first position recorded from the vessel in each pass. The positions are plotted in Google maps in Figures 1 and 2.

Table 2. Vessels seen in the 8:58 UTC download from AISSat-1 on 3 June 2016. The positions are plotted in Figure 1.

J2000 Time	Ground Time	MMSI	Ship Name	Latitude (° N)	Longitude (° E)
518197774	518216384	257716000	Norvarg	78.194901667	14.518225
518197769	518216384	257785000	Norbjorn	78.2271	15.626295
518197743	518216384	258499000	Polargirl	78.228463333	15.607216667
518197769	518216384	259383000	Kvalstein	78.415078333	15.091848333
518197716	518216384	308198000	Sea Endurance	79.755633333	14.0061
518197797	518216385	209778000	Ortelius	79.857116667	17.901213333
518197874	518216385	228016600	Polaris I	79.000926667	12.226958333
518197813	518216385	231219000	Billefjord	78.228133333	15.609723333
518197966	518216385	257564000	Polarsyssel	78.243046667	15.542806667
518197919	518216385	257958900	Elling Carlsen	78.228358333	15.607108333
518197813	518216385	258301500	Longyear 2	78.229455	15.595758333
518197808	518216385	265339000	Origo	78.675666667	14.424033333
518197969	518216385	265472000	Stockholm	79.694685	12.072846667
518197840	518216385	265511830	Malmo	78.228395	15.63347
518197817	518216385	309336000	NG Explorer	78.349136667	19.403083333
518203825	518216386	230359000	Letto	78.66142	26.515886667
518203679	518216386	246337000	Antigua	78.229641667	15.599933333
518203756	518216386	259560000	Aurora Explorer	78.228448333	15.606318333
518215390	518216388	982575641	Munin	78.243265	15.545936667

Figure 1. The location of the vessels seen in the 8:58 UTC download plotted in Google Maps. This was the most recent dataset available when the *Ortelius* reported engine problems.

Table 3. Vessels seen in the 10:35 UTC download from AISSat-1 on 3 June 2016. The positions are plotted in Figure 2.

J2000 Time	Ground Time	MMSI	Ship Name	Latitude (° N)	Longitude (° E)
518215514	518222190	231219000	Billefjord	78.40383	16.231346667
518215513	518222190	257716000	Norvarg	78.234521667	15.58116
518215513	518222190	258301500	Longyear 2	78.229436667	15.595971667
518215515	518222190	259383000	Kvalstein	78.238475	15.600005
518215514	518222190	265339000	Origo	78.6755	14.423383333
518215514	518222190	309336000	NG Explorer	78.312518333	19.353716667
518215520	518222190	982575641	Munin	78.24277	15.543858333
518221167	518222192	209778000	Ortelius	79.195583333	19.60105
518221271	518222192	230359000	Letto	78.661575	26.517788333
518221264	518222192	231219000	Billefjord	78.621325	16.639601667
518221318	518222192	246337000	Antigua	78.229663333	15.600031667
518221376	518222192	257958900	Elling Carlsen	78.228355	15.60712
518221283	518222192	258499000	Polargirl	78.228463333	15.607218333
518221340	518222192	265511830	Malmo	78.228398333	15.633618333

Figure 2. The vessels seen in the 10:35 UTC download. This was the first received data set after the *Ortelius* reported engine problems. The *Ortelius* has moved significantly from the position in Figure 1.

In Figure 2, the vessels observed during AISSat-1s first pass over Svalbard after the *Ortelius* notified the authorities about her engine problems are plotted in Google Maps. Neither the *Stockholm* nor the *Sea Endurance* are seen in this data set. There are several possible explanations for this. Both vessels may have been sailing close to land, and hence entered radio shadows behind mountains which have prevented the radio signals to reach the satellite. The ship antennas may have been mounted in unfavourable places on the vessels. Co-channel interference or atmospheric/ionospheric interference are also possible explanations. The satellite may also have flown at more eastern longitude, and hence not seen the vessels.

The AIS data show that there were 24 vessels with Class A AIS transponders in the region of interest. Their positions are illustrated in Figure 1. Figure 1 shows that there were four vessels that could reach the *Ortelius* in reasonable time if it had stated an emergency. The *Stockholm* and the *Sea Endurance* were sailing in the fjords of north-western Spitsbergen. The *National Geographic Explorer* was sailing along the eastern coast of Spitsbergen. The *Letto* was sailing near Svenskøya Island.

The other vessels were located on the western coast of Spitsbergen, near the settlements Ny-Ålesund, Longyearbyen, and Barentsburg. It would take time for these ships to sail to the rescue of the *Ortelius*.

Figures 2 and 3 show the ships seen in the 10:35 and 12:12 UTC downloads. It should be noted that the vessels *Stockholm* and *Sea Endurance* are not seen in the 10:35 download, while the *National Geographic Explorer* and the *Sea Endurance* are not seen in the 12:12 UTC data (Table 4).

Four unique vessels were shining Class B transponders and transmitting AIS messages types 18 and 24. Figure 4 shows that all were located in the Isfjorden region on the west coast of Spitsbergen, and would probably not be able to support the *Ortelius* in a SAR operation.

Table 4. Vessels seen in the 12:12 UTC download from AISSat-1 on 3 June 2016. The positions are plotted in Figure 3.

J2000 Time	Ground Time	MMSI	Ship Name	Latitude (° N)	Longitude (° E)
518221298	518227993	265339000	Origo	78.675481667	14.423423333
518226957	518227995	209778000	Ortelius	79.195453333	19.60193
518227003	518227995	230359000	Letto	78.59905	26.655235
518227003	518227995	231219000	Billefjord	78.64916	16.435135
518227078	518227995	246337000	Antigua	78.229676667	15.599943333
518227021	518227995	257564000	Polarsyssel	78.257716667	15.496866667
518227078	518227995	257785000	Norbjorn	78.227035	15.626483333
518227136	518227995	257958900	Elling Carlsen	78.228366667	15.607118333
518227103	518227995	258301500	Longyear 2	78.229458333	15.59592
518227122	518227995	258499000	Polargirl	78.228461667	15.607258333
518226988	518227995	259383000	Kvalstein	78.290006667	14.942508333
518227008	518227995	259560000	Aurora Explorer	78.327628333	15.561741667
518226971	518227995	265472000	Stockholm	79.824723333	11.941258333
518227261	518227995	265509140	Freya	78.243206667	13.846441667
518227120	518227995	265511830	Malmo	78.228373333	15.633635

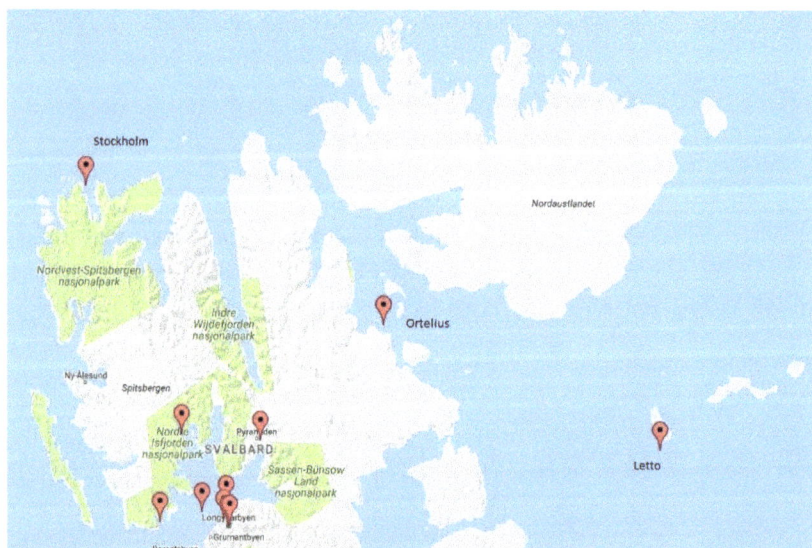

Figure 3. The vessels seen in the 12:12 UTC download. Note that neither the *Sea Endurance* nor the *National Geographic Explorer* are seen in this data set.

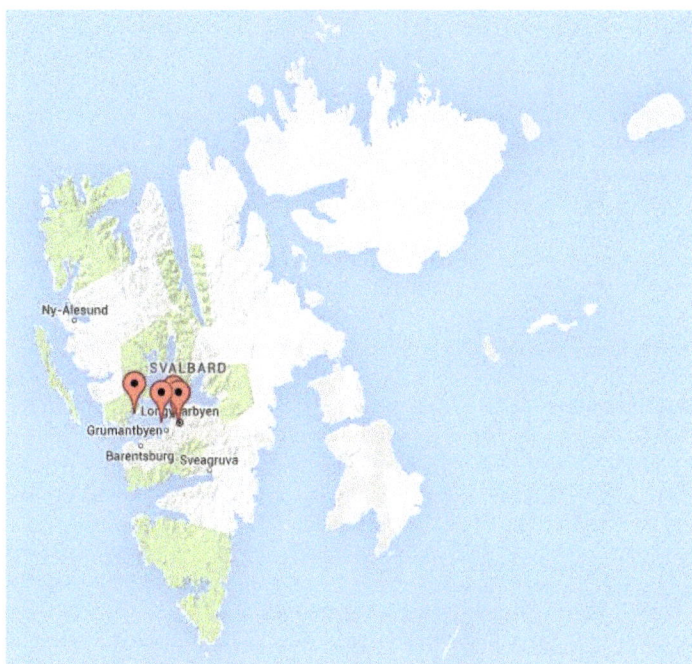

Figure 4. Location of vessels with Class B AIS transponders

4. Discussion

This case study shows that satellite-based AIS is a powerful tool in SAR operations in remote waters. The AISSat-1 satellite provided Norwegian authorities with data on the identity and position of vessels close to the ship that had run into problems. Fresh data were available just a few minutes after the *Ortelius* had reported the engine problems. The data sets show that there were four vessels in the vicinity that could assist in an emergency. The satellite orbits the Earth in approximately 100 min. The more satellites in orbit, the more frequent the updates. After the successful dual launch of NorSat-1 and -2 in July 2017, Norway has four polar orbiting satellites with AIS detectors.

It also shows that data from more than one pass should be studied to provide situational awareness. A ship is in the satellite's shadow when it is sailing behind an island, mountain or in a fjord and its transmissions will not be recorded. It may also be outside the footprint of the satellite, and its transmissions are hence not heard. The risk of losing vessels this way will decrease with the number of satellites carrying AIS receivers.

Not all ships may be suited to participate in a SAR operation. The International Code for Ships operating in Polar Waters (Polar Code) will enter force on 1 January 2017 [14]. The Code defines three categories of ships to operate in Polar waters:

Category A ship means a ship designed for operation in polar waters in at least medium first-year ice, which may include old ice inclusions.

Category B ship means a ship not included in category A, designed for operation in polar waters in at least thin first-year ice, which may include old ice inclusions.

Category C ship means a ship designed to operate in open water or in ice conditions less severe than those included in categories A and B.

It also defines ice conditions:

First-year ice means sea ice of not more than one winter growth developing from young ice with thickness from 0.3 to 2.0 m.

Medium first-year ice means first-year ice of 70 cm to 120 cm thickness.

Old ice means sea ice which has survived at least one summer's melt; typical thickness up to 3 m or more. It is subdivided into residual first-year ice, second-year ice and multi-year ice.

Thin first-year ice means first-year ice 30 cm to 70 cm thick.

The ice conditions in the waters surrounding the troubled vessel can be known by analysing satellite images [15], observations from Maritime Patrol Aircraft or from the vessel itself. Norwegian authorities receive data from the European Sentinel Earth Observation satellites and Canadian Radarsat satellites. The Sentinel satellites are equipped with optical and radar sensors. In case of a real emergency, one can safely assume that the Norwegian Air Force would task at least one of its P-3 Orion (soon P-8 Poseidon) Maritime Patrol Aircraft to the area to monitor the situation.

The ice and weather conditions in the SAR area may be so harsh that the RCC, for safety reasons, decide not to send any of the vessels in the vicinity of the ship in trouble to support it if they do not have a sufficient ice class. The identity of a vessel can be determined from its MMSI number, which is available in all AIS transmissions. The Regional Coordination Centres should have access to a data base where both the MMSI numbers and ice category are listed. This is a simple and efficient way to prevent Category C ships being tasked in SAR operations that require Category A or B vessels.

Not all waters along the coasts of Svalbard have been properly mapped [16]. Some waters along the south-eastern coast of Spitsbergen and the fjords of Nordaustlandet should be mapped better. A RCC should not send a vessel towards such dangerous areas.

In a real scenario, the *Letto* would probably be the first vessel to reach the *Ortelius* at the Vaigatt Islands. The distance is approximately 150 km, or 80 nautical miles. If sailing with a speed of 12 knots, it should reach the *Ortelius* in 7 h. The position in Figure 1 of the *Sea Endurance* is approximately 200 km (110 nm) from the *Ortelius*. The closest vessel is the *NG Explorer*, located near Dunérbukta on the east coast of Spitsbergen. To reach the *Ortelius*, the *NG Explorer* would have to go through the narrow Heley Sound between Spitsbergen and Barents Island, through the Freeman Sound between the Barents Island and the Edge Island, or sail the long journey south of the Edge Island.

5. Conclusions

This paper shows that satellite-based AIS is a powerful tool for coordinating SAR operations, especially in remote areas like the Arctic and Antarctica where land-based AIS is rare or non-existent. In this case, fresh position data were received just a few minutes after the Ortelius declared her emergency. This provided a good situational awareness. The analysis shows that not all ships appear in the data sets. It is hence recommended for RCC staff in future similar situations to go through recent data sets to verify that all vessels in the region of interest are known.

By using ice data from, e.g., radar satellites, an RCC can also determine if conditions make it unsafe for a vessel to participate in a SAR operation.

Acknowledgments: The author wishes to thank Øystein Helleren at Forsvarets Forskningsinstitutt for providing the data sets, and Befalets Fellesorganisasjon for a generous financial grant.

Conflicts of Interest: The author declares no conflict of interest.

References

1. Ylvisåker, L.N. Slept til byen. 2016. Available online: http://svalbardposten.no/nyheter/slept-til-byen/19. 7240 (accessed on 1 July 2017).
2. The Governor of Svalbard. Ekspedisjonsskip Slept til Longyearbyen av Polarsyssel (Press Release). Available online: http://www.sysselmannen.no/Nyheter/Ekspedisjonsskip-slept-til-Longyearbyen-av-Polarsyssel-/ (accessed on 1 July 2017).

3. Engås, C. Passasjerskip har motorhavari i Hinlopenstretet. *Svalbardposten* (Internet). 2016. Available online: http://svalbardposten.no/nyheter/passasjerskip-har-motorhavari-i-hinlopenstretet/19.7238 (accessed on 1 July 2017).
4. International Maritime Organization. AIS transponders. Available online: http://www.imo.org/en/OurWork/Safety/Navigation/Pages/AIS.aspx (accessed on 1 July 2017).
5. Arctic Council. Agreement on cooperation on aeronautical and maritime search and rescue in the Arctic. In Proceedings of the Ministerial Meeting, Nuuk, Greenland, 12 May 2011.
6. Aase, J.G.; Jabour, J. Can monitoring maritime activities in the European High Arctic by satellite-based Automatic Identification System enhance polar search and rescue? *Polar J.* **2015**, *5*, 1–17. [CrossRef]
7. Norwegian Space Centre. Norway's Satellites. Available online: http://www.romsenter.no/eng/Norway-in-Space/Norway-s-Satellites (accessed on 24 April 2017).
8. AISSat-1 Satellite Details. Available online: http://www.n2yo.com/satellite/?s=36797 (accessed on 24 April 2017).
9. ITU. *Technical Characteristics for an Automatic Identification System Using Time Division Multiple Access in the VHF Maritime Mobile Frequency Band*; ITU: Geneva, Switzerland, 2014.
10. Clazzer, A.M.; Berioli, M.; Lazaro Blasco, F. On the Characterization of AIS Traffic at the Satellite 2014:(1 p.). Available online: https://login.ezproxy.utas.edu.au/login?url=http://search.ebscohost.com/login.aspx?direct=true&db=edseee&AN=edseee.6964425&site=eds-live (accessed on 2 July 2017).
11. Shelmerdine, R.L. Teasing out the detail: How our understanding of marine AIS data can better inform industries, developments, and planning. *Mar Policy* **2015**, *54*, 17–25. [CrossRef]
12. Security NC-USDoH. Types of AIS Updated 10/21/2015. Available online: http://www.navcen.uscg.gov/?pageName=typesAIS (accessed on 1 July 2017).
13. Security NC-USDoH. Class A AIS Position Reports (Messages 1, 2 and 3) Updated 09/12/2014. Available online: http://www.navcen.uscg.gov/?pageName=AISMessagesA (accessed on 1 July 2017).
14. International Maritime Organization. *International Code for Ships Operating in Polar Waters (Polar Code)*; International Maritime Organization: London, UK, 2014.
15. English, J.; Hewitt, R.; Power, D.; Tunaley, J. (Eds.) ICE-SAIS—Space-based AIS and SAR for improved Ship and Iceberg Monitoring. In Proceedings of the 2013 IEEE Radar Conference (RadarCon13), Ottawa, ON, Canada, 29 April–3 May 2013.
16. SINTEF. *Analysis of Maritime Safety Management in the High North (MARSAFE)*; SINTEF: Trondheim, Norway, 2010.

MDPI

St. Alban-Anlage 66

4052 Basel

Switzerland

Tel. +41 61 683 77 34

Fax +41 61 302 89 18

www.mdpi.com

Resources Editorial Office

E-mail: resources@mdpi.com

www.mdpi.com/journal/resources

www.ingramcontent.com/pod-product-compliance
Lightning Source LLC
Chambersburg PA
CBHW051316020426
42333CB00028B/3363